Veizer Vizer Wiezer Wieser

VeizerVizerWiezerWieser

A MEMOIR AND A SEARCH: GRANITE CITY TO KOMPOLT

Keith Veizer

ISBN: 1507637780
ISBN 13: 9781507637784

Dedication

To my father, whose interest in and knowledge of all things Hungarian became a part of me. His stories, experiences, and memories inspired not only this book but many of my short stories. And also to my father's six brothers and sisters, who were, unlike my father, unfailingly patient with me but like my father, lively and entertaining and joyful.

George, Mary, John, Joseph, and Betty, circa 1920>

Preface

I STARTED DOING RESEARCH ON Kompolt and Hungary and Lincoln Place long before I was prodded into writing this book by one of my Veizer cousins in 2012. When Barbara, after listening to several of my Veizer stories over breakfast, suggested that I write a book about our family, I offered no resistance since I could think of no good excuse not to. I was retired; I had my journals plus notes from relevant books and articles; and I could, arguably, call myself a writer. Immediately it became clear to me that writing a book was what I had been planning all along. I offer this narrative to all my cousins--Veizers, Vizers, Wiezers and otherwisers, Gieses and Gieslers and Zieglers and Becks and Hacklers--and to my growing number of nieces and nephews, many of whom have little knowledge of Lincoln Place and Granite City and even less of Kompolt and Heves and Hungary. I began with the hope that I could learn how four branches of the family in Granite City are related or connected. This book is a search into the histories of the places and cultures mentioned above and of the history of Vizer families in all these places intertwined with a memoir of my father.

Added after the main narrative is a group of short stories inspired by my father or Lincoln Place or Granite City. These are fictions and should not be taken literally. Like all fiction, however, they aim for a truth beyond the literal.

Spelling of family names may seem inconsistent, but these spellings changed over the years for many reasons. For example, "Pech", "Bech," and "Beck" are variations of the same name. Even brothers sometimes used different spellings. I use Hungarian names (with their proper diacritical marks) when their use seems appropriate to the context: János for John, Jakab for Jacob, Erzsébet for Elizabeth, and so on.

Shirley Veizer Goin's wedding, 1957; My family: Juanita, Janice, Shirley, John, Keith

CHAPTER 1

Two Teams of
Happy Warriors

ON THE FIRST DAY OF my junior year P.E. class at Granite City High School in the fall of 1959, Coach Andy Sullivan was calling roll. "Keith," he said and paused in mock confusion. Then he pronounced, I suspect, the longest word he had ever uttered— "VeezerVizerWeezerWiser," (which I present here phonetically). I could have shared with him my dad's story of how this brain-withering multiformity came about, but I just said, "You were right the first time, Coach." Mr. Sullivan, also the varsity basketball coach of the Happy Warriors, had not, I could tell, paid much attention to my fading basketball career. And why should he have? Every year that I was in high school, white flight from the high school in Madison, right next to Granite City, was delivering remarkable athletic talents to Granite High, so I went from starting guard in the 8th grade at Coolidge Junior High to benchwarmer as a sophomore to not bothering to offer my talents as a junior. Later that school year, in February and March of 1960, the Happy Warriors, led by Madison natives and soon-to-be All-Staters Rich Williams and Bob Price, would notch upset victories in the state basketball tournament over Collinsville at the Kahoks' gym in the regional final and over Pinckneyville in the sectional final. Both these opponents were ranked #1 in Illinois when they were beaten by the Granite City

Happy Warriors, two of whom--silky-smooth Frank Knight and hard-nosed Max Prusak--had been my teammates and best friends at Nameoki Elementary School and Coolidge Junior High. Needless to say, excitement over the Granite City team's progress in the spring of 1960 was tremendous, and it was snowballing with every victory.

With its win over Pinckneyville the 1960 team advanced to the Sweet Sixteen, farther than any GCHS basketball team had since the 1940 squad. That team won Granite City's, not to mention Southwestern Illinois', first Illinois State Basketball Championship. Since seven players on the 1940 team--and all the starters--had been in Troop 9, the Lincoln Place Boy Scout troop led by my father John Veizer, a considerable part of my childhood was spent listening to stories about his Scouts' unparalleled success in Scouting competitions and the unequaled glory of the 1940 season. The 1940 Happy Warriors had triumphed in that One-Big-State-Tournament era over more than 700 other Illinois high school teams. My father then had the distinction of serving as master of ceremonies at the Magyarház banquet honoring the team. I learned about my father's role in this celebration seventy years after the fact in a microfilmed edition of the Granite City *Press-Record*. It's funny what my dad could be reticent about.

The players from Lincoln Place on this historic team who were in my dad's Boy Scout troop were Danny Eftimoff, Evon Parsaghian, Andy Hagopian, John Markarian, George Gages, Sam Mouradian and its star, Andy Philip ("Fülöp" in Hungarian). Andy Philip, after four years at the University of Illinois as the leader of the famed Whiz Kids and a thirteen-year career in professional basketball that ended with the Boston Celtics, was enshrined in the National Basketball Hall of Fame in Springfield, Massachusetts, in 1961. He played on five NBA All-Star teams and was the first NBA player with more than 500 assists in a season. In between his stints at the U of I, Marine First Lieutenant Andy Philip served as a forward observer at Iwo Jima. He was always a good man to have at the point.

Andy and the other boys had learned basketball, along with many other important lessons for life, at the Lincoln Place Community Center. The "Clubhouse," as it was and is commonly kno wn, had been constructed in 1922, about the time these boys were born. The residents of Lincoln Place supplied most of the labor with materials provided by the Commonwealth Steel Company, a large foundry which employed my grandfather, my father, and hundreds of others from Hungary Hollow, the original name of the Lincoln Place neighborhood. By 1940 the rigid boundaries of Lincoln Place were long-established: factory fences to the south; marshy land that would become the Army Depot to the west; West 20th Street, the border with West Granite, to the north; and railroad tracks to the east.

During the grim years of the Great Depression, these boys had earned their first pairs of basketball shoes by accumulating credits given for good behavior and for completing small jobs around the clubhouse or its grounds. These credits were kept track of and the precious basketball shoes were purchased by the legendary Miss Sophie Prather, supervisor of the Community Center, affectionately known as the "Little Mother of Lincoln Place." She was kind and generous and firm: the rubber-soled basketball shoes could **only** be worn on the Clubhouse basketball floor.

Miss Prather was a former teacher at Washington School, the public elementary school that served Lincoln Place and part of West Granite. She resigned her teaching job to run the Community Center and did so from its opening in 1923 until she died in 1936. My father, his siblings, and hundreds of others under her influence and care throughout those years adored this dedicated and indefatigable little woman. During a time when the foreigners in Lincoln Place were looked down upon by much of the rest of Granite City as alien and crude, Miss Prather spent twelve hours a day teaching them useful skills, good citizenship, and a love of reading and literature while their fathers and many of their mothers toiled in the mills.

According to a 1915 book about new industrial centers, *Satellite Cities: A Study of Industrial Suburbs* by Graham Romeyn Taylor, Hungary Hollow was "a forlorn neighborhood beyond the western bulwark of industries and railroads." Later, he refers to Hungary Hollow as "an isolated mass of immigrants.... No group in the community is more neglected, unless it be the negroes." On the same page, an anonymous factory official is quoted: "It is true that the district is an eyesore to Granite City, yet Hungary Hollow is necessary to the success of the large plants and the conditions are no different from those surrounding foreign communities in other cities. The large plants require common labor and Americans will not accept these positions." In other words, "Americans" could not be found to do dirty, arduous, low-paying jobs in dangerous factories. And then he added as if to reassure his readers about the respectability of Granite City proper: "Granite City is practically isolated from its foreigners and Americans do not mingle with them either socially or in a business way."

A more appealing image of the immigrant neighborhood is presented by Mr. Taylor later in this same chapter. "Visit Hungary Hollow in the latter part of May and you find every doorway and window framed in green brought in from the nearest woodland. On all sides you will hear singing and the music of the concertina, while every saloon and coffee house overflows with all sorts of festivity." A generation after Taylor's study was completed, the year the Lincoln Place-dominated basketball team won the state championship, relations between Granite City and Hungary Hollow had changed for the better, but not dramatically. No doubt the particular severity of the Depression in the Granite City area, which suffered the second-highest unemployment rate in the United States, had retarded social progress on both sides of the tracks as it had stifled Lincoln Place's interaction with the city proper. Nevertheless, Miss Prather's many years of teaching willing parents like Erzsébet Veizer the skills and knowledge that they needed to become American citizens, plus her efforts to educate and Americanize their children, had provided the long-term solution to integrating Hungary Hollow into the larger community.

The seven basketball players I mentioned and their contemporaries had grown up during the toughest years of the Great Depression. Few fathers or mothers were regularly employed during those years, and extreme poverty was the rule. In 1931, the mayor of Granite City formed a committee to help those in need. *The History of Granite City, Part III*, which I found online, follows that statement of purpose with this terse and gloomy statement: "Unfortunately, the committee could not function due to a lack of funds." As evidenced by my reading of microfilm copies of the Granite City *Press-Record*, incidents of suicide and madness increased significantly during the Depression. One Hungarian man walked in front of a fast early morning train and was killed. The article notes that he was being forced by financial difficulties to close his place of business the next day, but the writer does not speculate on the possible connection between these two facts. A Macedonian man went to the cemetery where his wife was buried and drank a bottle of poison while lying on her grave. He died the next day.

Younger men like my father tended to be more resilient. Laid off from the Commonwealth for more than four years during which he completed a stint in the Civil Conservation Corps, he found employment in 1935 in the state mental hospital in Manteno, Illinois, 250 miles north of Granite City. After working there for about a year and a half, General Steel Castings called him back to his job in the foundry. He returned to Granite City and Lincoln Place with a young wife--my mother--and a great deal of ambition and energy.

That emblematic and momentous 1940 Illinois State Basketball Championship was achieved as the nation and the St. Louis area were emerging from the Great Depression. It was an affirmation, a triumph, for the whole of Granite City, but especially for Hungary Hollow, which had seen and felt the worst of the 1930s.

This dramatic victory clearly led to real and symbolic changes in the relationship between Granite City and its immigrant neighborhood. Pacific Avenue, the main street of Lincoln Place, which was actually an extension of Niedringhaus Avenue on the west, or "wrong" side of the railroad tracks, was re-named Niedringaus Avenue. "Lincoln Place," which had been the official name of the neighborhood since 1916, was used more frequently and with more respect by residents and non-residents alike. A year after the state championship, school buses were provided to transport Lincoln Place students to the high school almost three miles away. It had been a long walk: up the hill across the railroad tracks and past the entrances to General Steel, American Steel and NESCO, then left down Adams Street past the Nestle plant for many blocks, and finally the last stretch along the entire length of Wilson Park.

Oh, and what about my 1960 Granite City Happy Warriors? More than a decade of post-World War Two prosperity in Granite City had in 1957 produced an expanded high school and a spacious new physical education and indoor sports center containing two gyms: one for the girls and a larger one with bleachers that would seat over two thousand fans for boys' varsity sports. This airy and well-lit facility replaced the dark and ancient auditorium-stage-basketball court in the main building, where action on the roundball court had for thirty years been flanked by gathered curtains, backdrops and props for upcoming dramas plus equipment for physical education classes. In spite of the long-overdue investment in a first-class sports venue, the 1960 Happy Warriors, after their two remarkable upsets over #1-ranked teams, were upset themselves by the West Frankfort Redbirds, a shabby looking team in black shoes from a depressed coal mining area in Southern Illinois which had already lost nine games that season, more than any other team remaining in the tournament. That 1960 Sweet Sixteen matchup was played at the East St. Louis High School gym. I, along with many other Veizers, Vizers, Wiezers, and Wiesers, watched from the bleachers in painful disbelief as our boys were out-muscled in double overtime by West Frankfort and its husky star Dave Pike, who would go on to play fullback for the University of Illinois football team. My father, however, was not surprised at the Happy Warriors' loss. And I don't think he was very disappointed either. **His** Happy Warriors of 1940 team still stood alone at the top--its legend unfaded and unchallenged. And as of 2015, it still does.

No doubt the legend of this team will be enhanced even further by *The Boys of Lincoln Place*, a Hollywood movie based on the book *Men of Granite* by Dan Manoyan, a sports reporter for the Milwaukee *Journal Sentinel*. Filming is supposed to begin in Lincoln Place in January 2015. Byron Bozarth, the coach of the state champs, will be played by William Hurt and the legendary Miss Prather by Shirley MacLaine. The script is being written by Armand Kachigian, whose roots in Lincoln Place are deep.

CHAPTER 2
The Name

ACCORDING TO MY FATHER'S STORY, four József Vizers including my grandfather (plus several other Vizers) came to Granite City in the first decade of the 20th century. He told me that all of them had emigrated from Kompolt, which is a village in northeastern Hungary near the historical city of Eger. All four of those József Vizers also worked at the Commonwealth, a steel foundry that at that time was a short walk from their homes "down the Hollow" (as he usually referred to Lincoln Place). Every workday four József Vizers walked up the modest rise that creates the Hollow and then turned to the right along the railroad tracks that led to the foundry's main gate. My father said that because of the multitude of Joe Vizers there was confusion every day that mail was delivered and, of course, every day that pay envelopes were handed out at the foundry. Was there a meeting at one of the taverns after work one day to resolve the problem? Or did each of the Joe Vizers solve the problem in his own way? My dad didn't have an answer to this question, and at this date it's probably unknowable. But he did say that there was no such problem when they all lived in Kompolt because the Joes were known by their nicknames. According to my father, our József's Hungarian nickname was "*Begro*," which Dad said meant "Lefty." According to my cousin George, Jr., Grandpa's nickname was "*Kisbegro*," which meant "Little Jug." I can't find either word in my Hungarian dictionary, but I did notice recently in one of my Hungarian lessons that "*balra*"

means "to the left." Given the impreciseness inherent in pronunciation, hearing, and memory, I suspect that *"balra"* was at the root of the nickname, for our József was left-handed like my father and *"kis,"* (small or short) and sturdy as a jug. He also liked the jug, but I haven't come across a Hungarian word for that yet.

Not every Vizer male who came from Kompolt and wound up in Granite City early in the 20th century was a József. According to Ellis Island records from the early 20th century, there were indeed four Józsefs from Kompolt who arrived there, also an András, a Lajos (Louis), a Peter, a Ferenc (Frank), a Jakab (Jacob), and a János (John). I haven't checked the 1920 census forms to see how many of these men were living in the Hollow then, but I suspect that most were.

John Veizer and his mother, Piedmont, West Virginia, 1909

CHAPTER 3

Why did They Come?

TRYING TO DETERMINE WHY so many people from Kompolt came to the United States just before and during the first decade of the 20th century, I consulted Juliana Puskas's thorough account of the history of Hungarian immigration to the United States: *Ties That Bind, Ties That Divide*. Ms. Puskas begins her sub-section on "Population Growth and Economic Change" with this statement: "In the four decades between 1870 and 1910 the population of Hungary grew from 13.6 million to 18.3 million." In just one decade, from 1890 to 1900, the 15-19 age group grew 26.4 per cent! This rapid growth was exacerbated by the Hungarian custom of dividing land and other property equally among one's sons. The lands of the peasants "were broken into increasingly small parcels and the large masses of the landless grew." In Hungarian communities like Kompolt where German traditions were upheld, the oldest son sometimes inherited all the land. This kept a significant amount of farmland intact, but it meant that the rapidly increasing number of younger sons in peasant families like the Vizers would have to find work in trades like blacksmithing or carpentry, or hire themselves out for low wages as agricultural laborers. By the 1890s, it was more and more difficult for younger men in Hungary to find employment of any kind.

After the Civil War in the United States industrial production and internal development, especially of infrastructure, were poised to grow rapidly. Labor was, however, in short supply because 625,000 men had died during the War, twice as many of disease as of battlefield wounds. Many thousands of survivors were disabled, a good number of them amputees. By the 1870s the infrastructure and technology for an industrial boom were in place: hundreds upon hundreds of railroad tracks and canals and channelized rivers provided the transportation; mines producing coal, iron, copper, and other ores provided the raw material and the power; Bessemer converters dramatically increased the pace of steelmaking, and new bridge, railroad and shipbuilding technology provided markets. Even if so many American men had not died or been disabled in the Civil War, labor would have been in short supply. The United States was still an agricultural society and agriculture was still labor-intensive. Most Americans held close to their hearts an agrarian and rural ideal and spurned the idea of living in crowded and, to them, unwholesome and unsanitary urban environments. Therefore, factory owners and other entrepreneurs in the United States tried to solve the labor shortage by sending recruiters to Central and Eastern Europe to find workers. Aiding their efforts was the fact that economic, political, and social problems were motivating ordinary people in these parts of Europe to trade the Old World for the New.

Twenty years after the failed Hungarian revolt against Austrian (Habsburg) authority in 1848-9, which ended with the execution of twelve Hungarian generals (and which included a crucial battle in Kapolna, just south of Kompolt), Hungary gained a significant measure of autonomy through the Austro-Hungarian Compromise and the Nationalization Act of 1867. These agreements restored the 1848 Hungarian Constitution, which had established a liberal constitutional monarchy. Hungary was granted self-government in internal affairs, though foreign affairs, defense, and finance would be conducted in concert with the Austrians.

However, little was altered for the peasants in Kompolt and other villages. According to Ms. Puskas, "the new political, economic and social conditions did not bring an immediate change in the structure that had developed under feudalism." In other words, "feudal lords" became "sole owners" while "serfs" became "sharecropper tenants." Seventy per cent of the these tenants had too little land to scratch out even a subsistence living.

My grandfather József Vizer was born in 1867, the year of the Compromise and one year before the Austro-Hungarian government mandated four years of elementary schooling for all children. In practice, basic literacy education spread slowly, depending a good deal on the nationality and language prevailing in the village, for only 51% of the people in the Hungary of that time were Magyars. (Its boundaries then encompassed three times more land than present-day Hungary, which was created after World War I by the Treaty of Trianon in 1920.) People with German roots, like the Vizers, were the largest minority group in the old Hungary--and also in the post-1920 Hungary--comprising about 15% of its residents in both, but there were also significant numbers of Slovaks, Croatians, Serbs, Romanians, and Roma (*cigány*, or gypsies). It's not clear to me yet what educational opportunities were actually available to József and the other future immigrants from Kompolt in the 1870s and 1880s when they would have been children, but Grandma Veizer, born in 1880, probably had more opportunities than her future husband.

In fact Kató Hámán, a woman born in Kompolt in 1884 and a descendant of of one of the original German families that migrated there in 1754, must have been rather well educated. She was a nationally known socialist, labor leader, and promoter of Esperanto, a synthetic language devised in the late 19th century as a way to promote international peace and understanding. Kató Hámán stridently opposed Admiral Horthy's right-wing government as a member of the Communist Party's central committee after Béla Kun's short-lived socialist government failed in 1919. She spent much of the rest of her life as a political prisoner. During the Soviet era, the main street in Kompolt was given her name. To further honor her, stamps were issued and statues were crafted, one at the entrance of the Western Railway Station in Budapest. After the Soviet departure in 1989, the street's name was changed to Deák Ferenc. According to *Wikipedia*, all that seems to remain of Kató's legacy is a marble plaque located in Memento Park in Budapest.

I'm not sure literacy or even some education beyond that would have helped the peasant population's economic plight very much. Industry was slow to develop in Hungary, and as Ms. Puskas points out in *Ties that Bind, Ties that Divide*, "agricultural wages were so low in the 1880s and the cost of living so high, that in the less productive regions a poor harvest meant actual starvation for the populace." There were other factors that spurred out-migration, like compulsory military service in the Austro-Hungarian army; but the lack of economic prospects in northwest Hungary was, without doubt, the primary factor. News of "agrarian uprisings" in this area in the 1890s even reached the pages of the New York *Times*, where it is noted in the March 27, 1898, edition that 5,000 landowners control 40% of the land in Hungary with the State and the Church controlling nearly as much. Very little was left for peasants, or "small holders" as they were called.

It should not be surprising that the recruiting efforts by American industry were well received. The news spread rapidly: America was the Land of Opportunity! Ultimately, the most effective recruiters and motivators were probably the earliest immigrants who wrote back to relatives and friends in eastern Hungary and Bulgaria and Macedonia and told them of good-paying jobs and the availability of cheap land in America. I'm not sure who was the first person from the Kompolt area to settle in Granite City, but he or she must have been someone of prodigious influence. My casual research, based on asking every Granite City Hungarian I encounter what village or county their ancestors came from, indicates that well over half of the Hungarians in Granite City have roots in or near Kompolt: the Sigites (or Szigeközis--three of whom visited Kompolt in April 2014), the Meszaroses, the Suesses, the Yuhászes, the Fülöps (Andy Philip's family), the Krisztiáns, the Vivods, the Barkós, the Basariches, the Bódis, the Kovácses, the Jaegers, the Jakkels, the Sobols, the Dorogházis, the VeizerVizerWiezerWiesers, and no doubt, many others.

My grandfather left for the United States in January of 1905 and was processed at Ellis Island on February 1. Departing Hungary without his family, probably accompanied by some other men from Kompolt, Kal, and Kapolna (a smaller, rural version of the Tri-Cities--Granite City, Madison, and Venice), he sailed from the (Adriatic port of Fiume, Austria-Hungary (now called "Rijeka," the third largest city in Croatia). József booked passage on the *Slavonia*, a passenger ship which would later carry his wife and other members of his family to America. Ellis Island records show that József was 37 years old when he arrived at Ellis Island; and that his hometown, county and native country were Kompolt, Hevesmegye, and Hungary. When his application for admission was processed at Ellis Island, József would have been given a health exam and then asked twenty-nine questions: to discover his immediate destination, to see if he was mentally competent, to determine if he was affluent enough not to become a burden to the government ($25 was the minimum requirement), and finally to assure the authorities that he was not an anarchist or a communist or a common criminal. After passing the interrogation, he was declared a legal immigrant and given a document affirming this. Then he was given transportation to the train station in New Jersey and directed to the train that would carry him to his destination.

Unlike many other immigrants, József Vizer started off in his new country with his old name intact. My parents' first neighbors and friends in Lincoln Place, the Andrias, were not so fortunate. Clem Andria's father, a Macedonian, had sailed from Europe as

Andria Gestakoff. Confusion in filling out papers at Ellis Island transformed his last name to "Andria," and so he remained...to the confusion of the rest of the Macedonians and Bulgarians in Lincoln Place, who all had "-off" or "-eff" at the end of their names. Nevertheless, Mary Andria, Clem's mother, became the first president of the Macedonian-Bulgarian Ladies Aid Society in Lincoln Place.

Many other new immigrants crossed the Atlantic but never reached Ellis Island. American doctors boarded ships carrying immigrants as they entered New York harbor and conducted quick examinations. Those who were diagnosed as having communicable diseases or who were deemed too sick or disabled to enter the United States were put in quarantine at the Hospitals for Contagious Diseases on Hoffman and Swinburne Islands while healthy members of their families were housed on Ellis Island. Those on the hospital islands who were declared unfit were sent back to Europe. Others, including many children, never left those islands alive. An internet article was sent to me by Alyce Sigite, whose father-in-law came from Kompolt with the name "Szigetközi," or island dweller. Entitled "The Forgotten of Ellis Island, Deaths in Quarantine, 1909-1911," it documents hundreds of deaths on these islands during those two years. Two of these unfortunates were Vizer children from Kompolt. Julianna Vizer, 6 years old, and her sister Erzsébet, 4 years old, were traveling with their mother Anna Vizer from Fiume on the Saxonia. The documents state that they were heading for Granite City to "meet up with their father András." On January 29, 1910, three days after their arrival, they died in quarantine on Hoffman Island and were buried in Woodland Cemetery, Staten Island.

Joseph Veizer, my grandfather, circa 1915

CHAPTER 4

Piedmont, West Virginia

I HAD ALWAYS THOUGHT THAT Piedmont, West Virginia, a small coal mining town with a population of about 2,000, was my grandfather's first residence in the United States because that was where my father was born in December 1908, a year and a half after his brother George was born there. However, I recently learned that on the day of my Aunt Anna's wedding to Ferenc Krisztián in Kompolt--June 9, 1906--she reported on an official form that her father--my grandfather--was residing in Luckey, Ohio. He was there, I recently learned, because the brother of his deceased wife Paulina Krisztián was working in Luckey as were a number of other men from Kompolt.

My grandfather's first wife Paulina Krisztian had died of tuberculosis in 1900 leaving him with two daughters, Anna and Katalin. I also learned that my grandfather's Krisztián brother-in-law returned to Kompolt from Luckey, Ohio, in about 1920 because of ill health. (His great-granddaughter Emöke Abasári, who contacted me in late 2013, has been the source of much of my information about the Vizer genealogy and the history of Kompolt.) A year after arriving in the United States, Jozsef had saved enough money working in Luckey to send for his second wife, twenty-six-year-old Erzsébet Bech and the second child born to them, two-year-old Mary. They arrived at Ellis Island on July 3, 1906, a month after Anna's wedding in Kompolt. He met them, and they proceeded to Piedmont, West Virginia.

I'm not sure why József chose Piedmont. Perhaps he had had some experience as a miner in Hungary, for there were and are mines in the Mátra mountains in Heves not too far north of Kompolt. It is very likely that men from Kompolt were already working in Piedmont. In any case, József worked as a coal miner, an even more dangerous job then than it is today. Accidental fatalities in the American workplace were at their historic peak in the first decade of the 20th century. There were 45,000 such deaths in 1905; two years later there were 3,000 fatalities just in America's mines, the most deaths in a single year in the history of U.S. coal mining. Ms. Puskas asserts that "These disasters illustrate the low esteem in which American society held the immigrant workers. Indeed, fourteen Hungarians who [later] died in another industrial accident had complained about unsafe conditions, only to be told, 'Never mind! There are many more Hungarians that will replace you!' In all these accidents, neither the employers nor the states provided any compensation to the injured or to the orphans and widows of the deceased breadwinners."

On December 6, 1907, the year József after began working underground in the United States, an explosion in a mine near Monongah, West Virginia, a few miles west of Piedmont, killed 361 men. This disaster prompted President Teddy Roosevelt to call for the creation of the U.S. Bureau of Mines. This agency has regulated mining, inspected mines and set safety standards ever since. Perhaps the Monongah disaster prompted József to start looking for another type of work in another place. Recently, I discovered in my grandfather's application for U.S. citizenship in 1917 that he had a "crippled left hand." This detail does not appear in his 1905 immigration application, so it is possible that an injury in a mining accident prompted the family's move from Piedmont to Granite City.

Two years after Anna Vizer's marriage in 1906, she and Frank Christian also departed for America on the *Slavonia* heading for Granite City, where some immigrants from Kompolt had already settled. Anna, born in 1891, was respectfully called "Nonnie," short for "nagynéni" or "aunt" in Hungarian) by her younger half-brothers and -sisters. I suspect this was because she was almost a generation older than they were and seemed more like an aunt than a sister. Anna's sister Katalin, or Katie, was six years younger than her. She did not arrive at Ellis Island until February 10, 1914, on the *Prinz Friedrich Wilhelm* out of Bremen, Germany. She joined her immediate family, all of whom were now in Granite City. If she had waited a few months longer, World War One would likely have made her departure impossible.

Anna Veizer Christian and Katalin Veizer Geisler,
Aunts Nonnie and Katie, circa 1920

Anna Veizer Christian with daughters Pauline and Ann, circa 1920

The year after Erzsébet arrived in Piedmont, Mary had a baby brother, my Uncle George ("György" in Hungarian). A year after that, in the waning days of 1908, my father John ("János" in Hungarian) was born. Dad always claimed that he was baptized in a Catholic church in Frederick, Maryland, which I discovered early in my research is a long way from Piedmont. Recently, I came across a copy of his baptismal certificate in my mother's papers which stated that John Vizer was born on November 26, 1908, and baptized on December 27, 1908, at St. Peter in Chains Catholic Church in

Westernport, Maryland. This town of 3,000 inhabitants is the westernmost port on the Potomac River and is connected by a bridge to Piedmont, West Virginia.

For some reason, my father maintained to his children he was born on December 1, except when we wanted to celebrate his birthday. Then he would claim that the first day of December was actually the day he was baptized and that he was really born on November 27, so it was too late to celebrate. Then the next year, when we wanted to celebrate on November 27, he claimed he didn't know exactly when he was born. We couldn't win. No birthday parties for Dad. No special cake, no ice cream for the kids. He was always a bit strange about holidays. But then, my dad could make any day special with surprises and stories and enchantment. He was not regulated by the calendar but by his feelings and fancies.

According to a Granite City *Press-Record* interview with my Aunt Mary on the occasion of her 50th wedding anniversary in 1972, József and Erzsébet moved with their three children to Hungary Hollow in 1912, joining the dozens, perhaps hundreds, of people from Kompolt and its sister villages who had settled there before them. In its early years Granite City, founded in 1896 on the flood plains of the Mississippi River, was called "The Industrial Magnet of the Midwest" and "The Little Pittsburgh of the Plains." After a brief but severe recession that began in 1907 (during which the immigrant neighborhood became known as "HUNGRY Hollow"), Granite City's factories were booming again by late 1910. József was hired at the Commonwealth Foundry soon after he arrived. Our Vizer family, soon to be the Veizer family, settled in The Hollow.

In the sixteen years before Jozef's family of five arrived in Granite City, industry and the need for labor had expanded dramatically. As David DeChenne explains in his 1990 article, "Hungry Hollow: Bulgarian Immigrant Life in Granite City, Illinois, 1904-1921," it was soon clear that traditional labor sources, even augmented by the importation of recent immigrants living in St. Louis, could not keep up with the demand. He writes, "Not until 1904, when the Macedonian-Bulgarians began 'swarming to the community,' did the labor supply rise to meet the demand." These immigrant workers, who came from Macedonia (a part of Greece) but considered themselves Bulgarians culturally, were escaping from an unsuccessful revolt "against their Turkish overlords." For Granite City employers and for the Macedonian-Bulgarians, the timing was perfect. By 1904, nearly eight thousand of them--almost all were men--had come to Hungary Hollow. Soon Granite City contained the largest number of Bulgarians of any municipality in the United States. There was even a Bulgarian newspaper (*Narodon Glas*), the only one in the United States; in addition, the first Bulgarian Orthodox Church in the United States was built in Hungary Hollow on Maple Street.

These Bulgarian and other eastern European men jammed themselves into "immigrant mercantile houses" where they lived six or eight to a room, often sharing a bed with a man on another shift and cooking for themselves. They lived as cheaply as they could--on as little as one dollar a month, saving money to send back or to take back to eastern Europe, where $1200 would make them men of wealth. Mr. DeChenne points out: "Evidence suggests that most of these Bulgarian men returned home [to Bulgaria] after working only a few years in Granite City industries." There was an ebb and flow of Bulgarians to and from Granite City during the early years of the 20th century. By mid-1909, near the end of the economic downturn, only a few hundred remained in Hungary Hollow. But by 1910, the local and national economies had rebounded and the neighborhood "was essentially repopulated with Bulgarians again."

Although some Hungarian men--and most of one Vizer family--returned to Hungary with the wages they had saved, Hungarian men like József Vizer were much more likely to bring their families to the United States in those early years than Bulgarian men, who moved in and out of Lincoln Place with the ups and downs of the economy. Mr. DeChenne says that many of the Bulgarians also returned to their homeland to fight in the Balkan Wars against the Ottoman Empire. Those who did not return to fight raised considerable sums of money through dances and benefits to send back to the freedom fighters.

József and Erzsébet Veizer's family continued to grow in Granite City. My Uncle Joe was born in 1914 and my Aunt Elizabeth, their last child, in 1916. Two other children, though, had been born to the József and Erzébet. My father told me that their first son József died shortly after his birth in Kompolt. In September of 2013, I discovered a record of that child's birth in the church records of Kompolt. He was born February 28, 1902, and baptized March 2. I did not have time that day to find the date of his death, but I know that he did not survive long enough to come to America with his mother and sister Mary. And then there was a sister who died tragically in Granite City.

One day when my father and I were visiting his older sister Mary on Hodges Avenue, he walked me to a field behind the Kirkpatrick Homes about two blocks from Aunt Mary's home in East Granite. In the overgrown field was a cemetery which I had never noticed before. At that time this plot of land--St. Mark's Cemetery, once owned by a priest in Venice, Illinois--was neglected, all but forgotten. It looked more like a large vacant lot than a sacred place. Nevertheless, my dad had no trouble finding a small stone with "Veizer" carved into it. I can't recall the first name or the exact dates on that stone, but I do remember receiving the impression that this sister was younger than my father but older than the youngest two children in the family, about thirteen years old when she died. He told me that a diphtheria epidemic had swept through Granite City, and that she suffocated while the family waited for a doctor to arrive. A simple tracheotomy would have allowed her to breathe and probably would have saved her life.

I looked for that cemetery in the fall of 2008, but all I found were a couple of tall monuments and a few flat stones obscured by a layer of soil and weeds. A man who lived across the street from the field told me that the land had been cleared to allow for a future expansion of the Kirkpatrick Homes, the first and still the only housing project in Granite City. I asked the cemetery's long-time neighbor what had happened to the remains of those who had been buried there, and he told me that they had been disinterred and transported a few years before to either the St. John's Cemetery on Nameoki Road or to the Catholic cemetery on Sunset Hill, depending on the wishes of the closest living relatives. He said these relatives had been consulted and their wishes duly carried out and recorded. I am not sure who was consulted in the Veizer family about her re-burial, but I learned that my father's sister is now buried in nearby St. John's Cemetery.

Helen and Mary Veizer, circa 1920

CHAPTER 5

Work and Play in
The Hollow

IN THE YEAR 2000, MORE than thirty current and former residents of
Lincoln Place were interviewed by students who were participating
in an oral history class at Southern Illinois University-Edwardsville.
They were asked what it had been like to grow up in Lincoln Place.
The oldest of these interviewees were born in the mid-1920s; the
youngest in the 1950s. In October of 2011, when I was visiting Granite
City for my 50th high school reunion, I spent a week of afternoons
in the city's main library, now called the Six Mile Regional Library.
In about forty hours over the space of five days, I read through a box
full of these interviews, writing notes and summaries and copying
direct quotes. As I did this, I experienced the re-creation of a unique
neighborhood. In the first few pages of this narrative I have already
used some of this information, and in subsequent pages I hope to
combine anecdotes and details from these interviews with memories
of my father's stories and my own memories to gain a better understanding of the early history of Lincoln Place, the Veizer family's
first real home in the United States.

At the beginning of the 1900s, Hungary Hollow was at its most
densely populated. Almost all activity there was geared toward making a quick profit--or saving money: to bring families from Europe,
to buy land in the Old Country, or to start a business here or there.

For these first factory workers there was little time or money for culture or recreation. In the early 1900s they toiled twelve hours a day and six days a week. By Illinois law, women could be required to work *only* sixty hours a week.

In Granite City, however, working hours in many of the factories, including Commonwealth Foundries and NESCO, were shortened not long after the Veizer family arrived. According to Graham Taylor in *Satellite Cities*, both factory officials and workers saw advantages in replacing two twelve-hour work shifts with three eight-hour shifts. Management was motivated by the prospects of greater efficiency and less waste by workers who were less physically tired and mentally fatigued. Factory managers determined that they would actually save money in spite of having to employ more workers at a twenty-percent greater cost. Workers would earn twenty percent less by working four fewer hours a day, but they appreciated the idea of increased leisure time. The highly unionized workers voted unanimously to adopt the new work hours. "We want the time to be with our families and do odd jobs around the house," some of the open-hearth workers said in Mr. Taylor's study. Some people in industrial management had contended that the workers would "dissipate themselves" with extra leisure time and be less fit for work, but they were soon proved wrong. Mr. Niedringhaus himself, who brought the first heavy industry to Granite City, is quoted as saying, "Steel work is so strenuous that any man who took to dissipation would be unable to keep up his efficiency even through the eight-hour shift. The fact that we have not had to discharge any of them shows in itself that the time is not badly spent."

By the time József, Erzsébet and their family arrived in Granite City in 1912, the Hollow was starting to settle down, to become more of a family place. There were more women in the population and more families that had come to stay than there were just ten years before. There were still some large "mercantile houses," but they weren't as crowded. In these years, a growing number of single men also roomed and/or boarded with families who had saved enough money to buy or build a house in the Hollow. The parts of the 1920 Census that I have looked at indicate that these boarders were often relatives or family friends from the same village in the Old Country. This made hard work for the wives, who cooked for their roomers and boarders and cleaned their rooms, but it was work that kept some of them out of the unwholesome and dangerous factories and near their growing families.

One of my father's most vivid childhood memories of Hungary Hollow was the annual winter pig killing (disznóölés in Hungarian). It was quite a party, and everyone in the family had work to do. The men strung up the pig from a tree branch and "stuck" it (cut its throat) capturing the blood for sausage, then burned off its hair, finally butchering the best cuts of the pig into bacon and the prime cuts. Margaret Elek Nonn says in her interview: "I don't know if you want to hear this, but my job was stirring the blood...my mother would fry the meat and then she would put it in this crock pot and then put lard all over it and keep it for winter." Women ground up the rest of the pig and added spices to make sausage (kolbász and hurka, or blood sausage). Theresa Vivod Petras in her interview recalled that the pig was slaughtered in the early morning, and then that the pig's hair was burned off with straw. She adds, "They used to cut the ear off. That was the best tasting."

The little boys' job (my dad's) at the pig-killing was to submit to a thorough foot washing before being lowered into a big pot to stomp and dance on the salted and shredded cabbage, helping it become sauerkraut. As I recently learned from a sauerkraut connoisseur, the purpose of all this youthful stomping and dancing was to make sure that the cabbage was flattened and on the bottom of the pot, completely covered by the liquid. Otherwise, the fermentation would be imperfect and the sauerkraut would spoil. Dad must have enjoyed the exercise, and even more the attention, because he so often talked about the joy of making sauerkraut.

A more frequent food ritual was the stewing of halászlé, or fisherman's soup, a fragrant paprika-red and fish-oil-yellow fish soup. It was prepared in a large pot surrounded by the cooks, usually beer-drinking men. József was one of the fish cleaners, and when he forced the scales off the fish with the edge of a spoon, he told the children that he was "taking their money," perhaps in the hope that they would pick up the scales. My father also talked about the pleasure of standing under a bag of milk hung on the clothesline which was on its way to becoming smearcase (cottage cheese). He loved to tilt his head back and catch the faintly sweet and milky whey in his mouth as it dripped from the bag. Mr. Naumoff, the coal and ice man, was also generous with treats. He would chip off pieces of ice for the children that would run to his truck in the summertime. That tradition lasted into my childhood, even though almost everyone had electric refrigerators by then. In those days the milkman was the reliable source for a thick sliver of hard, pure, mouth-numbing--not to mention absolutely free--refreshment.

Of course, in Lincoln Place there were desserts more elaborate than ice or whey dripping from a bag. Several of the Hungarians interviewed mention *palacsinta*, thin pancakes rolled up and filled with jelly or cream cheese. A more elaborate dessert was *"dobos"* or what Mrs. Petras calls the "three-layer cake." She says, "You made a layer of dough. You put a layer of jelly, and then you put another layer of dough." About seventy-five years ago, a Hungarian woman named Beulah Ledner opened a bakery in New Orleans and introduced her version of *dobos torta* to the Crescent City, the cake having been introduced to Budapest by a baker named József Dobos in the 1880s. The original cake had buttercream filling between the layers with a caramel glaze added to the outside to give it a brittle surface. The side of the cake was covered with crushed nuts. Ms. Ledner replaced the buttercream filling with custard and covered the whole with a buttercream icing. Today it is considered one of the elite New Orleans desserts and a cake that would satisfy 12-15 people can be bought online for $94.50. New Orleans pronunciation--and the tendency to "Frenchify" words to make them familiar--dictates that now Ms. Ledner's cake is called "doberge." In Lincoln Place there were also special desserts for holidays like *kolacs* (a word I cannot find in my Hungarian dictionary), also called "Christmas bread" or "Easter bread." Mrs. Petras describes it as a round bread made with yellow dough; honey covered the outside.

Life in Lincoln Place was not short of everyday pleasures. As a boy, my father made a daily trip to one of the many taverns in the Hollow to fill his father's beer bucket. In those days--just after World War One--and in that culture, fetching a foaming bucket of beer for one's father after work was as routine as bringing Dad the newspaper from the front yard was in my 1950s childhood. My father said that he always made a great show of strutting along Pacific Avenue, the main street of Lincoln Place, and swinging the shiny, beer-filled tin bucket by its handle in great circles, testing the laws of physics and filial piety--until the day the handle broke and the bucket flew. That day he went home with no liquid but the tears in his eyes. This bought him no sympathy from Papa.

Other Hungarian families had other rituals concerning the father's return from work. In her interview, Anna Kovacs remembers that before her father arrived home every afternoon, her mother would give her four older sisters a bath and dress them up in little white dresses. They had to sit together on a bench by the side of their house and wait for their dad to come home from his shift at the foundry. No doubt this display of sweetness and light had as kindly and positive an influence on this work-weary father as a foam-crowned tin pail of cold beer.

A note on Granite City saloons from Mr. Taylor's book seems appropriate here: "Restriction of saloons was prominent in the minds of the elder Niedringhauses when the town [of Granite City] was established, and their regulations still [in 1915] hold that the consent of the owners representing two-thirds of the lot-owners on a block must be secured before a saloon may be established on that block. This operated to keep the number of saloons down to about thirty-two. There was practically no increase for a period of five years prior to 1913. But the number then increased rapidly so that by the summer of 1914 there were fifty-two." As the population of Granite City at this time was around 12,000, that means there was one tavern for every 230 residents--man, woman and child. Of course, this was long before home entertainment centers, play stations, the internet, and the Wine-of-the-Month Club. Houses then did have parlors, which by definition were places for talk, as well as front porches with swings, but the talk must have been more interesting and the relaxation more swinging in the ubiquitous saloons of Granite City and Lincoln Place.

Several of the Lincoln Place residents who were interviewed for the oral history class speak of Old Country festivals and games and activities that made the transition to America and the Hollow. Richard Depigian describes the "jailhouse" game, which seems to have been based on some historical re-enactment. It was used to raise money for charity. The men would build a jailhouse. Then they would "steal" women in the community and put them in the jail. Then, he says, "you would have to pay so much to get them out of there." Mr. Depigian's wife Susan talked about the grape leaves used in making *tolma*. "The best ones," she says, "were in Sunset Hill Cemetery and the best time was the last week of May....After the priests blessed the graves, the women went with their shopping bags to pick the tender leaves." Nazareth Donjoian recalls the egg breaking game. On Easter, children would tap their hard-boiled eggs against their friends' eggs. "If you broke someone's egg, you got to keep the egg," he says.

The main Hungarian festival in Lincoln Place was the grape festival in May. Sandor Toth says the May Queen would be picked by how many tickets were sold in her name. The girls dressed up in Hungarian costumes, dresses that were pleated all the way around.

"They wore a red velvet vest with gold braiding and gold buttons," he says. "The men wore pants that were pleated so tightly that they looked like skirts." Anna Kovach remembered that festival, too. She says, "They hung up all these packaged fruit, all different kinds that were hung from the ceiling....If you caught one of the guys pulling a fruit off the wire, then you got to grab him and he had to pay for it." Anna also fondly recalls the festivities on the day after Easter: "The boys would have bottles filled with perfumed water. They would go around to the girls' homes and sprinkle them, and if they caught them, they were supposed to get a kiss from that girl...Tuesday was supposed to be a girls' day, but they didn't do it because you had to go back to school." It was left to my first Hungarian language tutor (Miriam Sipos from Sopron, Hungary) to explain this all to me after *Húsvét*, or Easter, 2013. She gave me a vocabulary list for all the key words involved in the *locsolás*, or "sprinkling." The girls, she told me, are flowers. And the boys are watering them. I guess the girls in Hungary run faster these days because she says the boys now use seltzer bottles to spray them and buckets to drench them. Or perhaps the boys are just slower or shyer. The boys do offer poems (*vers*) to their flowers, though, after they have soaked them. There must be a lot more to it now because in that language lesson I also learned the words for ham (*sonka*), lamb (*bárány*), crepes (*palacsinta*), and plum brandy (*pálinka szilva*).

The Fourth of July was always an important holiday for every nationality in Lincoln Place. No matter how good or bad the economy, almost everyone was happy to celebrate the birthday of their new country. Over the years on the Fourth of July there were pageants, picnics, ball games, and, no doubt, too much drinking. On July 4, 1943, I was seven days old. It was a hot day on Poplar Street, and my crib was set next to the window. My mother left the room for a minute and when she came back and looked in the crib, there was a bullet lying next to my head. My father knew who the culprit was and rushed into the street. One of our neighbors, short of fireworks I suppose, had been firing a pistol into the air. My father grabbed him by the shirt and shook him. He dropped the gun and his wobbly legs folded up under him. My mother pulled my dad into the house and saved the drunk from a thrashing. I always liked that story. I was at the center of it, and I was totally blameless, a seldom repeated coincidence in later life.

The author on Poplar Street in Lincoln Place, 1947

CHAPTER 6

Yonchy

My father loved to talk about his childhood adventures. Before the Granite City Army Depot was built in the 1940s, it was an easy walk from the Hollow to the Mississippi River and its murky backwaters. Wading in Chouteau Slough, little Yonchy and his friends caught catfish in washtubs when the water was low or falling. They swam in the dangerous Mississippi, sometimes all the way to Gabaret Island and Mosenthein Island, both of which were then used for grazing cattle. One day, swimming back from one of the islands, he ran out of energy or got a cramp and thought he was going to drown. Finally he gave up trying to swim. Miraculously, his feet settled on a sandbar. When he recovered his strength, he splashed his way to the bank, or I would not be writing this.

In her interview Margaret Elek Nonn remembers that her family kept five cows on the land between Lincoln Place and the Mississippi River where the extensive Army Engineer Depot was built in 1942. She says, "My mother would milk every morning and night. And then, my sister and I, we had to take the milk from house to house. No bottles. My mother had buckets. And then we would take the cows out to...where the Depot is now....And a man would watch them....And the gypsies would try to steal them from us."

Anne Kovach recounts lovely memories of walking in the levee area in her interview. "There were no homes out there. And it was just beautiful on both sides of this road that was just lined with trees," she says. But this levee was not a strong one. The Hollow flooded several times before the late 1940s when the eight-and-a-half-mile-long Chain of Rocks Canal was constructed to allow barges and boats to bypass a dangerous section of the Mississippi River. Although not built for the purpose of flood control, the new levees required for this huge Army Engineer project put a stop to the regular flooding of Lincoln Place.

My mother used to tell a story of her early years living in Lincoln Place during the late 1930s. One spring night flooding was predicted, and my father was preparing to do what he had, no doubt, done several times before: join hundreds of other men from the Hollow and Granite City sandbagging the levee. Mother begged him not to go. She was afraid he would be swept away by the raging waters. Dad was not afraid of anything, so of course he went, but he was also capable of dramatizing a situation for a young wife and new mother in a strange new neighborhood. He came back safe and sound later that night, a bit of a hero. Later, he would become a hero to his only son, as all fathers should, at the least, aspire to be...not that they should make it apparent that they are trying hard to do so.

My father did not just boost himself, though. He was the biggest booster I ever heard for Lincoln Place, Granite City, and Madison County, and one of the best informed. "Lock #27 was built," he would say, "so boats and barges could go around the treacherous Chain of Rocks just north of St. Louis," a 17-mile stretch of the Mississippi that was filled with rock ledges, making it virtually un-navigable. (I assume this is why Lewis and Clark spent the first part of the winter of 1803 on Gabaret Island before moving just north of the Chain of Rocks to what is now Lewis and Clark State Park to prepare for their westward journey into the unmapped and largely unexplored expanse of the Louisiana Purchase.) Dad would then explain that Lock #27 was the southernmost lock on the River, the 29th between Minneapolis-St. Paul and St. Louis, and "one of the largest locks in the world." The lock system lifted--or lowered--a small boat, or a large tugboat and its string of barges, fifteen feet. A load three barges wide and five barges long could be accommodated with an impressive surge of swirling waters. It was a Big Show. Thus, Lock #27 became Attraction Number One for our visiting relatives and friends.

My father seemed to know everything that was unique and extraordinary about Granite City and Madison County: the length of its rolling mills, the tonnage of the largest castings made at his foundry, the best kind of soil for horseradish, the shoe size of the Alton Giant, why Union Starch smelled so bad, and how American Steel's foundry was different from General Steel's. His job as a foreman in the foundry and the consequent importance of that job to the war effort was, I imagine, what kept him from being drafted into the military in World War Two. He was proud of the tanks his company made for the war effort, the huge and silvery strip mining gears they made that gnawed at coal seams, and the wide-track steam locomotive underframes his company made for South Africa for years after the USA had switched to diesel power. He seemed just as proud that Granite City was the Horseradish Capital of the World and loved to point out to visitors the vast fields of horseradish--one of his favorite vegetables!--on West Pontoon Road and near Horseshoe Lake. There is now a local festival celebrating horseradish, but it's located a few miles away in Collinsville, not Granite City, which I believe would have disturbed him. Not surprisingly Collinsville has also appropriated "Horseradish Capital of the World," which would have perturbed him. Just up the road from Granite City, the tiny village of Poag, he told me, was the Muskmelon Capital of the World. My dad saw to it that his only son grew up in a special place, a place of wonders within wonders and of surpassing excellence...and gasp-worthy strangeness.

He told me about two Turkish brothers who lived in a house near the Veizer home when he was an unusually curious child. These brothers made the questionable decision to share a girlfriend, who often entertained them with her belly dancing. According to my father, the youthful observer of this show, one brother beat a drum and the other played a nose flute (yes, a flute with his nose). Inevitably, one night they exchanged their musical instruments for knives and went at each other. The drummer was killed or the nose-flutist was killed, or both were, depending on the audience for the story, or the whim of the storyteller. My father never told a lie, but he never met a story he did not feel he could improve upon.

CHAPTER 7

Armenian Neighbors

SOME STORIES MY FATHER DID not need to embellish. He often told me of an Armenian man and wife who walked slowly down Cedar Street to the Army Depot early every morning for the ceremonial raising of the American flag. After the Armenian genocide and the destruction of Armenian communities in Turkey and nearby parts of the Ottoman Empire in 1915, this Armenian man, with the help of the Red Cross, spent seven years searching for his wife and children. When he found his wife and brought her back to Hungary Hollow, where many other Armenian refugees had settled, her mind was blank, and she was hobbled by crushed bones in her feet. Those feet had been nailed to the floor by Turkish soldiers while her children were bayoneted in front of her. It is estimated that more than one million Armenians were killed in this first genocide of the 20th century. This man and his wife, who paid tribute to the United States every morning for providing them shelter, were two of the survivors.

As the Armenian Richard Depigian said in his interview, "You will find that few people of our generation had grandparents...And most of those people came without papers. By that I mean no birth records. Nothing." Andrew Hagopian, one of the players on the 1940 basketball champions, relates a brief history of the genocide in his interview: "Where my parents were born, they [the Turks] started this thing back in the 1890s. The original persecution of the Armenians started then. But the genocide occurred when the war [WWI] was on. Everybody else [the Allies and their foes] was occupied with their problems and so the Turks took advantage of that. And they drove the people off the land they had lived in for hundreds of years. Took all their property, put them outside into the desert....And many of them perished walking through the desert as the Turks harassed them....They (the Turks) destroyed any records of the Armenian community that was located in the eastern end of Turkey....Today all that area is a vast no-man's land. Some of the Kurdish people live there, but it's a downtrodden and empty area."

Mike Torosian, who used to go duck hunting with my dad and who was a good friend of my cousin Ronnie Veizer, in his interview encouraged people to read *The Forty Days of Musa Dagh*, written and published in 1933 by Franz Werfel, an Austrian writer who spent many years researching the Armenian genocide. I took Mike's advice. This lengthy novel is a dramatic account based on an actual incident near the end of World War One: two thousand Armenian villagers retreated from their village to a nearby mountain that bordered the Mediterranean shore. They dug up some guns that they had buried when the persecutions had begun and improvised strong lines of defense. The villagers, led by a well-educated Armenian who had served as an officer in the Turkish army during the Balkan Wars when Armenians were allowed to enlist and serve, held off three separate attacks, first by Turkish police forces and then by units of the Turkish army. Many villagers died in the defense of this mountain retreat, but most of them escaped down the steep path to the sea during the third attack and were saved by two French ships that had come to their rescue.

It disturbed Mr. Torosian in his SIU-E interview that an Arts and Entertainment Network documentary--*Secret History, Hidden Holocaust*--filmed and edited in the 1990s, has never been released, though Mike's continued queries to A&E moved them to send him a copy of this film. Nor has a movie version of *The Forty Days of Musa Dagh* ever been released, even though film rights have been purchased more than once. The producer Irving Thalberg, the "Boy Wonder of Hollywood" in the 1930s and the model for F. Scott Fitzgerald's *The Last Tycoon*, bought the movie rights and planned a production a year after the novel was published. Later, an Armenian-American millionaire, John Kurkjian, actually produced in 1982 a movie based on the novel, but it was not released to theaters. More recent attempts to produce a movie about *Musa Dagh* by Sylvester Stallone and Mel Gibson have been nipped in the bud. Pressure on the U.S. government by the Turkish government has suppressed or waylaid all these projects. Turkey continues to deny that a genocide happened in spite of extensive documentation that it did happen. However, the strategic importance of Turkey to the United States has strengthened their hand and delayed the day of reckoning.

Although never released to the general public, the two-and-a-half-hour "director's cut" of the Kurkjian's 1982 version of *The Forty Days of Musa Dagh* is available on YouTube. Out of necessity, this film dispenses with many of the interesting sub-plots and lesser characters of the novel, but the main characters are well-portrayed, and the core of the story, the resistance on Musa Dagh, is vividly dramatized. A documentary film entitled *Epic Denied: Depriving the Forty Days of Musa Dagh*, which focuses on the attempts over the past eighty years to film and release a movie based on the novel, is scheduled to be completed in mid-April 2015. It will be interesting to see if this documentary is approved for release, and it will be extremely ironic--given the title--if it is not.

But there was some consolation for the Armenians who found their way to Lincoln Place after the Holocaust. Mike Torosian's memories of Lincoln Place echo those of so many other interviewees of all nationalities: "My experience was that it was the most wonderful childhood anyone could really have." Charles Merzian, Granite City's first two-time Illinois State Wrestling champion, talks about "this guy who moved out of Lincoln Place when he was nine years old because he had to go to the orphanage. Yet he still talks about

Lincoln Place." Mrs. Dena Lovacheff suggests a reason for the health and happiness in the community: "Everyone was in the same boat and raised the same way, I guess." Venka Ambuehl, born in 1925, adds, "Whether it be food, funerals, they just worked together. Nationality didn't mean a thing."

The immigrants and their children were resourceful. They made the most of what they had and figured out how to manage in spite of the miseries they had escaped in the Old Country or the difficulties they met in their new one. Charles Merzian offers a wonderful example of that. "This one Armenian had a tavern down there [in Lincoln Place] and he didn't know how to read or write, but he could sketch very nicely and he would sketch your face and then, if you had a beer or whatever, he would write "5" or "10" under your face." Another kind of resourcefulness is illustrated by one of my favorite stories from the interviews. Nazareth Donjoian relates this family story: "My dad sent him [Tojos] money to come over here and Tojos had a girl he was going to marry, so my dad told him to bring another woman for him from Armenia....And my dad wasn't too happy with my [future] mother, so a lot of other bachelor Armenians that were in Lincoln Place, they said, 'Well, Kaspar, if you don't like her, we'll take her.' So he changed his mind. He thought if someone else wanted her, he better keep her."

CHAPTER 8

Mexican Neighbors

ACCORDING TO JOE YBARRA, THE first Mexican families who came to Lincoln Place arrived just before World War I due to the "dislocations caused by the Mexican Revolution of 1910." Subsequent political and religious turmoil in the 1920s and 1930s led to more migration. Joe's family came from Guadalajara in 1924. Other families came from the northern states of Sonora and Chihuahua as well as from Aguascalientes, Guanaguato, Michoacan and Durango. Without a doubt the labor shortage during World War I drew some of those early Mexican immigrants to Lincoln Place, where the majority of the men worked at American Steel. Most of the businesses in Lincoln Place during its heyday were owned by Macedonians or Armenians, but Joe Valencia owned a tavern on Niedringhaus next to Spiroff's Tavern. The original Mexican Club was formed by a Mr. Santacruz, Guillermo Oropeza, and Joe's father Salvador Ybarra. According to Joe, Mr. Oropeza especially contributed "a great deal to the preservation of Mexican culture in the neighborhood." The thriving Mexican Honorary Commission grew out of the Mexican Club and since the early 1970s when the Hungarian population in Lincoln Place aged and waned, the MHC has occupied the old Magyarház on Spruce Street, where it holds festivals and celebrates major Mexican holidays. The MHC also organizes Mexican dance groups that perform in colorful and authentic costumes for these and other festivals in the St. Louis Area. Mary Castillo, a singer and amateur folklorist who later married Andy Philip, used to travel to Mexico to search for new songs to add to her repertoire. I fondly remember going to La Sala, a nightclub and Mexican restaurant in downtown St. Louis where she performed for several years. The Granite City Mexican community has grown dramatically over the years, but it has kept alive its roots in Lincoln Place and its Mexican traditions.

Today on the basement walls of the MHC hangs Bobby Galvan's photograph collection of Lincoln Place sports heroes. Andy Philip and the other players on the 1940 state basketball champions are there, as is soccer great Ruben Mendoza, who planted the seeds of Granite City's highly successful soccer program after playing on the the the 1952 and 1956 United States Olympic teams and the 1954 World Cup team. This program, which began at the Clubhouse in the early 1960s and spread rapidly to Collinsville and other East Side cities and towns, led directly to Granite City's twelve Illinois State High School Soccer Championships. Most prominent on the walls are photos of the Golden Gloves boxing champions developed by the LAC (the Lincoln Athletic Association) in the 1950s and 1960s: Paulie Bogosian, whose father Jack was the founder and head trainer of the LAC along with Gene McGovern, was a Golden Gloves champion in 1956 along with Mercie Mendoza; Joey Becerra was named "Outstanding Boxer" in the 1957 Golden Gloves in Kansas City after he knocked out five of six opponents; Joey's brother Augie was an All-Army champion in the late 1950s; cousins Joey and Connie Ybarra were crowned champions in St. Louis in 1961 and 1962. Bobby Galvan, one of the first soccer phenoms Ruben developed, is also represented on the wall. As a teenager he scored four goals in a 7-0 victory against a team that was considered the top junior team in the St. Louis area. For this feat, he was tagged "a young Pele" by a St. Louis newspaper writer. Bobby displays many of these sports photos and others at the Lincoln Place Heritage Festival in mid-September.

One of the most interesting and powerful stories contained in the SIU- Edwardsville interviews is Linda Hernandez Garcia's. Her mother was a widow with three daughters to raise by herself after her husband was shot at Chain of Rocks Park and her son, the oldest child, drowned in a canal when he was seventeen. Linda's mother suffered from epileptic seizures and seldom left the house. She supported her family by providing meals and laundry service for twenty-five Mexican men who worked at American Steel. "We [Linda's daughters] came home from school at lunchtime to take their lunch to them at American Steel," Linda recalls. "The Mexicans were all ladies' men. They were impressing the ladies so they wore white shirts all the time....And the starch had to be just so. It had to be Argo starch. You had to cook it and get it just right." Her mother made the girls' dresses out of flour sacks. "They used to have flowers and stuff on them. They were pretty nice, you know, and when you didn't know any different, they were pretty." And in their dresses they went to high mass at St. Joseph's Church. "We were excited... even if you see it every Sunday. It was the only thing we had."

Linda had another responsibility. She was the only one of her sisters who could sense when her mother was having a seizure. "I'd bolt out of school and I'd run all the way home. Sometimes I'd find her outside. Sometimes I'd find her on the stove where she was burnt. And the principal would follow me. And he'd say, 'Linda, I will bring you home when that happens....And then I went to junior high school and they had finally gotten some medication that eased them."

When Linda went to high school, she was allowed to leave school at noon. If she missed the bus, she walked more than two miles to work at Glik's Department Store in Madison from one o'clock to six. Then she would walk back up Madison Street a mile or so to St. Elizabeth's Hospital and wash dishes from 6:30 to 11:00. She was so short that she had to stand on soda boxes to do her job, which paid 25 cents an hour. When Linda completed high school, she continued to work at the hospital, putting in thirty years on the graveyard shift.

Linda lived in Lincoln Place all her life, and in her interview she continues to reflect on the experience. "It wasn't that everybody liked each other. No, that doesn't happen in real life. But if there was any need of any kind, there were always people you could go to, knock on their door, and say, 'I need help' and they would help you." In her later years, after Lincoln Place had changed and the first generations had passed on, Linda liked to walk down the streets and remember who lived in each house, bringing their former inhabitants back to life in her amusing way: "I wonder what they would think if they saw how somebody fixed their porch?"

Magyarház in Lincoln Place, built in the 1920s, which is now the Mexican Honorary Commission

CHAPTER 9

Boy Scout Camps

MIKE TOROSIAN AND OTHERS I have quoted were a generation or more younger than my father, and several of them were in Troop 9 when my father was the Scoutmaster. Dad's devotion to Scouting started early. As much as he enjoyed growing up in the Hollow, I think the most cherished moments of his childhood occurred during his summer weeks at the Cahokia Mounds Council's Camp Rankin. There was a Boy Scout troop in Lincoln Place by the early 1920s, and every summer Troop 9 would travel to this camp in the hardwood forests of Missouri's Ozark foothills near Ironton, Missouri, and Taum Sauk, the highest point in Missouri. My father always asserted to me that he packed only two things for camp: his swimming trunks and a toothbrush. ("And you probably only used one of them," I remember commenting.) At fabled Camp Rankin there was a stream and plenty of room for hiking, swimming, fishing, and canoeing, plus time to build things with axes and ropes, to use a compass to navigate in the forest or find your way back to camp, to learn to tie all manner of knots, and--most important--to set up a camp, rough or long term. He would have loved to achieve the distinction of being an Eagle Scout. However, he never was a strong enough swimmer to earn the Lifesaving merit badge, which was required for the Eagle rank. "They really made it hard on you," he often told me. "I had to pull a bigger guy in, and he would fight me until I had to give up." I was a little ashamed when I earned the Lifesaving badge one

45

summer at Camp Sunnen thirty years later because I knew I was not any stronger a swimmer than he was. I don't think I ever mentioned my achievement to him. It was a rare display of tact on my part. I'm not sure how many summers my father was able to go to Camp Rankin as a boy and as a Scout leader. "Not enough" is probably the best answer, for in addition to stream and woods, Camp Rankin, like all paradises, contained a fatal flaw: an aging wooden dam upstream from the camping area. One year Camp Rankin was declared "unsafe" by state authorities, and Camp Rankin was closed to Scouts forever. But all through my childhood, after my father would tell me tales about the wonders of Camp Rankin, he would inform me that the old dam was still standing all these years later, still holding back the waters.

I won't forget the first time my father transported me and some of my fellow Scouts from Nameoki School's Troop 46 to Camp Sunnen, the Cahokia Mounds Council's new camp in the Mark Twain National Forest near Potosi, Missouri. In 1954, years after Dad's beloved camp was closed, Camp Sunnen was opened. When we arrived that summer Sunday afternoon, he looked around and then walked around the grounds of the camp and the shore of the lake, shaking his head in disapproval. He was right to do so. I had to agree: this camp fell far short of the Camp Rankin my father had installed in my head. Nevertheless, our Troop 46, and especially its Beaver Patrol, had a great time that week and for several summers after that in the lesser, lower heaven of Camp Sunnen, which has expanded over the years to serve not only Cahokia Mounds Council but four others in southwestern Illinois.

I'm not sure why my father resigned as Scoutmaster of Troop 9. Once I heard him say that it was because he had opened the first tavern in the Hollow after Prohibition ended and that someone in the Scouting hierarchy objected to that connection. But Congress ended Prohibition in 1933, the year his mother died, the year he left for the Civil Conservation Corps. The timing does not sound quite right to me. He always said that he had a tavern for a while called Yonch's--the Hungarian nickname for John, but he was never clear about when it opened or for how long. (Another Hungarian Yonch, Yonch Siuramy, opened a Yonch's on Niedringhaus Avenue a few years later, which he operated into the 1960s.) Perhaps someone in the Scouting community did have a long memory or a grudge. Or perhaps my father just became too busy because of family, working in the foundry, and serving in political office.

I do know that he did not involve himself during my Scouting years except to drive me and my friends to Camp Sunnen every summer. He did make one spring camping trip with my troop from Nameoki School. It was a father-and-son outing to Greenville Lake. After dark and "lights out," the other fathers drank beer and played cards late into the night. My dad liked to do a little of the former and a good deal of the latter, but he turned up his nose at such behavior on a Boy Scout camping trip and slipped into his blankets early that night next to me and my sleeping bag. He was an idealist, and I recognized that quality in him more and more as I grew older. His mother, Miss Prather, Scouting and the books he loved had taught him that there was a right way to do things, and that there was a time to stand--or lie down--alone. All those good influences were reinforced by my mother, an even sounder model of decency and tolerance. Perhaps he had come to agree with those who thought it was inappropriate for someone who had owned a tavern to be a Scout leader.

CHAPTER 10

Motherly Influences

My father's mother Erzsébet was, I believe, the most important person to him in his formative years and for the rest of her life. He adored her. In pictures she looks as stern as her husband, but I think that pose just reflected the photo-fashion of the time. Life was serious then, a daily struggle much of the time, and it ill befit a serious person with serious responsibilities to belie that fact in one of those rare opportunities to pose before a camera. My father was proud that his mother, unlike his father, learned to speak and write English well enough to become a United States citizen. In fact, as Aunt Mary's granddaughter Mary Ann Schweppe recently told me, Grandma Veizer already knew a good deal of English before she came to America. I'm not sure how she learned it, but there were very likely a number of people from Kompolt who had already been to the United States and returned home by the time she was a young woman. Perhaps someone in her family, perhaps an older brother, was one of them.

I feel sure that Grandma Veizer did better on the final oral test question of the citizenship test than Charles Merzian's father, who, when asked by the immigration judge who would replace the President of the United States if he died, answered, "The second President!" According to Charles, the judge said, "OK, you pass." I suppose it was understood that the men of Lincoln Place had less time to study and less aptitude for history, for there are several similar stories in the interviews concerning men and citizenship hearings. Annette Vartanian Simpkins says in her interview that she caused her father to fail at the last stage of citizenship. The immigration judge asked her what language was spoken in the house. She answered: "'My father don't let me speak anything but Armenian.' Well, needless to say, my father didn't get his citizenship papers, and he chased me all the way home."

Like a majority of the men in Lincoln Place, József Veizer spent his time at work in the dust and fiery heat of the Commonwealth, and after work in one of the Hollow's many taverns with men who spoke Hungarian. My father said his Papa kept a bottle of whiskey under his bed to get him through the night, but he never missed a day of work. In her early years in Granite City, I believe that his wife Erzsébet had worked at NESCO, the "stamping works," when it was producing most of the enameled kitchenware used in the United States. (NESCO products, once the most popular cookware in the United States, are now collector's items.) Then and later she handled the money in the family, which according to Ms. Puskas's research, was standard practice in Hungarian families in the Old Country and the United States. Erzsébet was a good manager, a wonderful cook, and did everything she could to make all of her children happy and successful. My dad never quite said so, but I believe he felt that he, the middle child, was her favorite. Or perhaps Erzsébet was the sort of mother who could make all her children feel that way.

Another woman who figured large in my father's life and in the lives of many other children and adults in the Hollow was Miss Sophie Prather. When the Community Center was built in 1923, my father was fifteen. He was already working full-time at the Commonwealth, driving a tractor that pushed black sand cores into huge ovens that baked them until they were hard enough to hold liquified steel. Nevertheless, he still found time to involve himself in activities at the Clubhouse. Miss Prather was employed, along with an assistant or two, to initiate and manage the many programs at the new Community Center: woodworking and pattern making for boys, various types of needlework and crocheting for girls, citizenship and English language lessons for adults, plus games and vigorous activities for all. Annette Vartanian Simpkins says in her interview that instructors were even brought in to teach piano. The Community Center, with its large play areas on the west and south sides, was the vital center of Lincoln Place. The building (which is maintained and operated now by the Granite City Park District and is the site of the annual Lincoln Place Heritage Festival in mid-September) was open from nine in the morning to nine at night with Miss Prather presiding for twelve hours a day six days a week. At nine o'clock every night, the Commonwealth factory obligingly blasted its steam whistle, and children at the Clubhouse rushed to their homes.

After his shift at the Commonwealth, my father was involved in activities for older children at the Clubhouse. He always loved to read, but Miss Prather directed his reading, and there weren't many classics appealing to juvenile males that he had not read and re-read: *Tom Sawyer* and *Huckleberry Finn* by Twain, *The Call of the Wild* and *White Fang* by Jack London, *Treasure Island* and *Kidnapped* by Robert Louis Stevenson, *Kim* and *The Jungle Book* by Rudyard Kipling, and the book he mentioned most often, Harold Bell Wright's *The Shepherd of the Hills*, a dramatic tale of life in an Ozark Mountain community and how it is affected by a once prominent preacher and theologian who finds the peace and simplicity he has been searching for in this remote community. I recently read this novel, and it was not hard to see why my father was enchanted by its powerful appeal to the beauty and sublimity of nature, which he sought all his life and in every season on fishing and hunting excursions. The following quote from the novel parallels some of my father's melancholic reflections: "Before many years a railroad will find its way yonder. Then many will come, and the beautiful hills that have been my strength and peace will become the haunt of careless idlers and a place of revelry. I am glad I will not be here." It was no coincidence that in 1937 my parents spent their honeymoon on Lake Taneycomo in Missouri's Shepherd of the Hills Country. Fortunately they were able to enjoy the serenity there before the novelist's sad prophecy was fulfilled, and Branson, Missouri, became the site of more than fifty musical theaters.

At the clubhouse he also played basketball and baseball and jijos (bottle cap baseball, a game unique to Lincoln Place as far as I know). After he returned to Lincoln Place as a married man from his Depression-driven travels, he became the proud Scoutmaster of the Clubhouse Boy Scouts, Troop #9, sharing his love of the outdoors with teenage boys from Lincoln Place.

Few children from the Hollow went beyond 8th grade in the 1920s; my father finished his eight years of elementary education at St. Joseph's School in 1922, and I think they served him well. The nuns had taught him to be a good speller, encouraged his love of words and helped him become an effective writer, and gave him a sound understanding of basic math, which he used every day as a foreman in the foundry. They had also made him ambidextrous by smacking his left hand with a ruler when he used it to write. For the rest of his days he could write, pitch a ball, cast a lure, and do anything equally well with either hand.

After eighth grade, he wanted to go to a "commercial" school in St. Louis to learn bookkeeping and basic business practices. In fact, he did begin that course of study, traveling back and forth on the Illinois Terminal streetcar to his classes every weekday. After a month or so, his father could not or would not pay the tuition. Disappointed, my father began to work at the Commonwealth in 1923 when he was only fourteen years old. He lived at home and helped support the family for many years, saving his money to buy two houses in Granite City in the 1920s, one that he lived in with his family and one as a rental and an investment. Unfortunately, he lost both houses when he was laid off in the early years of the Great Depression. The Commonwealth all but shut down in 1931 for several years, and this crisis had a lifelong effect on him. Thereafter, he was very conservative with the money he had and not inclined to borrow any, paying for new cars and all major appliances with cash. When we moved from Lincoln Place to Grand Avenue in 1948, he made a large down payment on the new house. He did the same thing in 1952 when his down payment was more than half the cost of our new house on Pontoon Road. Here he lived for the rest of his life, avoiding debt and slowly accumulating adequate savings, ready as he could be for the next Great Depression.

Struggling through the Depression had extreme effects on the way its survivors handled their money. Many people were cautious like my father, always wary of another severe downturn in the economy; others were fatalistic and ran up maximum debt to live the high life while they could. One of the consequences of my father owing nothing to anyone was that I received an "Honorary" Illinois State Scholarship when I graduated from high school. Some of my classmates whose families possessed more and bigger cars parked in the driveways of bigger, fancier houses and had mothers who were gainfully employed received actual money as their Illinois State Scholarship. I was annoyed, even angry. However, I don't remember my father ever complaining about the label on my State Scholarship, not that he ever went so far as to tell me he was proud of it. (Or of me...though I discovered when I went to work at General Steel myself that he had found other audiences for that sort of thing. How else could those foremen and chippers and burners I met when I worked there have known that I earned straight A's almost every semester and was headed for the University of Illinois?) I did receive a $400 scholarship for my freshman year from Dad's employer, General Steel, but I don't recall him complimenting me on that scholarship either. In his mind, I think that was what mothers were for. I suspect that's how it worked with József and Erzsébet.

A far greater loss than the two houses he lost during the early years of the Depression was the death of his mother in 1933 at the age of fifty-three, probably from undiagnosed diabetes. Insulin had been discovered as an effective treatment in the 1920s, but it was not generally available because large quantities could not be produced in laboratories yet. I don't think my father ever got over the pain of losing his mother. Every year on the anniversary of her death, which was around Easter, he was somber and withdrawn, far from his usual self. My father married my mother Juanita Boyd in 1936, three years after his mother died. He was twenty-eight then, older than any of his brothers or sisters were when they married. My father's long residence with his mother and father and younger siblings was, I think, a measure of his devotion to Erzsébet.

My grandmother Erzsebet Veizer, circa 1930

CHAPTER 11

The Civil Conservation Corps

JUST WEEKS AFTER HIS MOTHER passed away, my father enlisted in the Civil Conservation Corps, one of the first programs Franklin Delano Roosevelt put in motion to counteract the effects of the Great Depression. I recently obtained five pages of his records from the National Personnel Records Center, which is located in St. Louis. From these documents I learned that when he signed up for the CCC, he had been laid off from the Commonwealth since December, 1930, two-and-a-half long and frustrating years, no doubt. According to those records, he had worked as an "electric welder" and "chauf," which I take to mean "chauffeur," a job description he must have gained when he operated a tractor that pulled racks of sand-formed cores in and out of large ovens. On his physical exam performed at Jefferson Barracks, Missouri, his height was listed as 64 inches on one line and 63 inches on another. The second measurement was the more accurate, I think, as it was closer to the height listed on his General Steel ID card years later. The twenty-four year old CCC recruit tipped the scales--rather, barely moved them--at 117 pounds. He passed the physical easily, the only comment being that his feet were a little flat, "second degree and non-symptomatic." A chart shows that he was already missing four teeth on the upper left side. I would like to know the story behind that gap.

The official government records beyond the physical exam are far more sketchy than I would have hoped. They do say he was appointed an "Assistant Leader" on July 1, 1933, confirming what he had always told me about being a "kind of corporal." A few extra dollars a month was his reward for the added responsibility. He was assigned to Camp Abernathy Mountain, near Ryderwood, Washington, called "The World's Largest Logging Camp" in the 1920s. Ryderwood is a few miles from the Pacific Ocean, a few miles south of Olympic National Park and west of Tacoma. It also appears in the records that he authorized $25 each month--most of his salary--to be sent back to his unemployed father at 1743 Maple Street in Lincoln Place, standard practice for most of the recruits. One of the primary purposes of the CCC was to employ young men so they could help support their families. There's nothing in these records, though, indicating that these months were the most wondrous and adventurous of my father's life and among the happiest.

The wonders began even before he arrived at Camp Abernathy Mountain. Waking up one morning on the train that carried him and many other recruits to "The Great Northwest" (as he always called it), he looked out the window and discovered that the train had stopped in Weiser, Idaho, the county seat of Washington County. Soon the train was crossing the Weiser River and entering Oregon: good omens both. He was, no doubt, feeling at home in these picturesque mountains and valleys, in his mind, I think, a sublime and more dramatic version of his beloved Camp Rankin in the Ozarks.

From my earliest years I remember my father telling me stories about lumberjacks working their way up trees more than a hundred feet tall--Sitka spruce and Douglas fir and red cedar--lopping off branches as they went. The lumberjack's finale was "topping the tree" when he could climb no farther, cutting through its swaying top section and sending its bushy crown crashing to the forest floor. All that secured the lumberjack to the slippery tree trunk were long spikes on his feet, a leather strap around his waist and superhuman balance and strength.

Dad also talked about sailing ships carrying timber and other products up and down the Pacific Coast, sailors high in the rigging. He talked about making friends with Native Americans he called "Hoshpikosh" Indians, "canoe Indians" whose chests were big, whose legs were bowed, and whose arms were long and strong. In my research I have never found a tribe with that name, but maybe it was a common expression the canoe Indians used meaning "Hello," or "What's up?" or "Do you have any beer left?" When I grew older, I had doubts about some of the stories my father told, but not those CCC stories because he brought back photos from the Great Northwest, small black-and-white images of daring lumberjacks, fully-rigged sailing ships, CCC buddies, campsites, and the forests and mountains he never grew tired of talking about. In the few photos in which my father appears, he sports a mustache. My favorite pair of photos: in one, he sits on the hood of a jeep with three buddies gravely gazing into the camera; in the other, he emerges into the sunlight from a stand of tall trees gripping a fly rod. "Mount Rainier," "Mount Hood," "the Cascades," "the Columbia River"--these were the magic names of his youth, and my childhood. At the time I wondered why he did not just load the family into our car when his two-week summer vacation came around and head west. I was certainly ready to go. But what did I know then about cherished memories? I was just starting to gather some.

According to an article in *Wikipedia*, during the nine years of its existence the Civil Conservation Corps enlisted three million volunteers. This army of young men "planted nearly three billion trees to help re-forest America, constructed more than 800 parks nationwide and upgraded most existing state parks, updated forest firefighting methods, and built a network of service buildings and public roadways in remote areas." By any measure it was one of the most popular and successful programs the federal government has ever developed.

John Veizer in the Civil Conservation Corps, 1933

CHAPTER 12

Grandma Veizer's Table

GRANDMA ERZSÉBET DIED TEN YEARS before I was born. However, I do possess the Veizer family's round-topped and very heavy kitchen table. It appeared in our house on Pontoon Road just after my father and a friend from the foundry built a small den in the basement in the mid-1950s. I'm not sure who in the family had been keeping the table--Uncle George, I think. Since my father intended it as a pinochle table, he immediately painted the table a jarringly bright green. My mother's sense of taste was jarred, too, but she said little at the time. In the early 1980s, when my widowed mother was leaving Granite City to live in Champaign near my sister Shirley, she encouraged me to remove the green paint from the table, refinish it, and cart it back to New Orleans in my van. She knew she would not have room for it in her one-bedroom flat in the Round Barn Apartments. Though I have never been interested in interior decoration, or even interior betterment (being similar to my father in this respect), I took on this project with enthusiasm. My enthusiasm grew when I discovered underneath that garish green surface a lovely dark-brown oak veneer. That beautiful surface was marred by one indelible black scorch in the shape of a flatiron. Had Erzsébet been distracted from the painstaking task of ironing her husband's shirt or Betty's dress or little Joe's pants by some emergency, laying the hot iron on the surface of the table instead of placing it in its metal holder? I'd love to know what it was that drew her attention from her ironing. But if

I did know, I'd be unable to imagine innumerable scenarios: a back-yard squabble, a distracting explosion at the mill, a crying child. Or perhaps little Betty was learning to iron on her own. The table sits in the middle of my New Orleans kitchen, still sturdy and useful, holding utensils, condiments, and memories.

CHAPTER 13

National Enameling and Stamping Company

As FAR AS I KNOW, Erzsébet's children attended St. Joseph School, and all of them except my father (including my father's older half-sisters) went to work at NESCO, "the stamping works," for varying lengths of time. According to *Wikipedia*, the National Enameling and Stamping Company, established in 1896 by the Niedringhaus brothers, was the first factory in Granite City and the reason for its incorporation within the farming community once known as Kinderhook. This mostly German settlement was located on the American Bottom, the fertile flood plain of the Mississippi, but the farmers of Kinderhook were in a short period of time vastly outnumbered by factory workers.

The crucial ingredient in NESCO's enameling process, the ground-up granite rock that gave texture to the finish of the pots and pans it produced, provided the fast-growing new city its name. This huge factory contained a phenomenal 1.25 million square feet of floor space, and by 1919 it produced most of the enamelware sold in the United States. At its peak NESCO employed over 4,000 men and women, producing a profit of $30 million per year (more than $350 million today). In 1927 NESCO separated itself from its steel production unit, which became Granite City Steel, and GCS soon became the biggest employer in town. This factory was for a long time one of the largest independent steel mills in the nation. With its towering blast furnace and lengthy rolling mill, it is now owned by U.S. steel and is still the biggest employer in Granite City. Yet the utilitarian blast furnace had a romantic side: innumerable young Granite City couples ventured their first kiss--and many after that-- within view of its spectacular nightly eruptions.

Like all the factories in Granite City, NESCO was a dangerous place for its workers. A slip or a moment of inattention could lead to smashed fingers and joints or even death. My father's older brother George lost fingers on both hands while working there, and his sister Mary lost the last joint on one of her fingers. Young Joseph, who became a foreman there, remained unscathed, and worked at NESCO until it closed down in 1956, years after aluminum, stainless steel, and tempered glassware had replaced graniteware. The last NESCO products I remember were small stainless steel electric appliances and colorful TV trays which we received as Christmas gifts from relatives who worked there. (Many NESCO products are now on display in the foyer of Granite City's main public library.)

My Uncle Joe and his wife, the statuesque and stylish Margaret Magyar, had four children when they left Granite City. Although they wanted to relocate to Florida, Joe's best job offer came from Jones and Laughlin steel mill in Toledo, Ohio. The always nattily dressed Joe and his family of four--Candy, twins Terry and Timmy, and Craig --settled there, later adding the surprise baby Joel fifteen years after Craig was born. Joe worked at "J and L" until he retired, when he was free to play golf every day the weather allowed, always thinking about the hole-in-one, which he finally achieved in his seventies. And he had a picture and trophy to prove it!

CHAPTER 14
Lincoln Place Businesses

FROM THE 1910S TO THE 1970s, Lincoln Place was the definitive American "melting pot." By 1917 Mexican families and a growing number of Armenians who had fled from the Ottoman Empire and the first ethnic cleansing of the 20th century had joined the Hungarians, Bulgarians, and Macedonians in the Hollow--and in the ever grow- ing number of factories in the Tri-City area. When they had saved enough money, some of these new residents joined more settled resi- dents in opening businesses in the Hollow: taverns (the Varadians, the Nighohossians, the Szuromis, and the Sendejases to name a few), a restaurant (the International,) a dry goods store (the Kakokis), two coffee houses for the Armenians and one for the Macedonian- Bulgarians, a dry cleaners (the Mooshegians), a shoe repair shop, two barber shops, a bakery, and grocery stores (the Vartans, the Meyers, the Mitseffs and Lovacheffs), a sweet shop (the Haroians), and Simone Bogosian's confectionary-pool hall (known as Sim's) that contained a table always available for card games, usually penny pinochle. Sim's also had a windowless brick side wall perfect as a backstop for jijos, bottle cap baseball. There was also Wiezer Tile, a flooring business run by Kenny and Joseph, Jr.'s father Joe Wiezer. Before my time there was even a movie theater, a hardware store, and several cafes. In the 1960s and 1970s when other businesses were fading away, Ruben Mendoza opened his first sporting goods store and Nellie Bogosian opened a dress shop in her father Simone's building.

All the grocery stores are gone now; Vartan's was the last to close, I think. They were the key businesses in the community, and not just as the providers of groceries and credit. Andreas Matoesian, who became a judge in Madison County, says in his interview: "I know from looking at the old naturalization records...they were at City Hall in Granite City. They've been moved to Edwardsville...I noticed that a lot of the names of witnesses, witnesses vouching for that person's credibility, were the grocery owners."

The recently released 1940 census, now available on the internet, shows no discernible ethnic housing patterns in the Hollow, which underlines the "melting pot" metaphor. On the 1600 block of Poplar Street, the location of my first residence on earth, there resided the Macedonian Dukleffs, who owned a soft-drink bottling company, the Romanian Roussoffs, the Bulgarian Margulins and the Eftimoffs, who operated a fruit and vegetable truck, the Armenian Tatosians, Hagopians and Shakinians, the Hungarian Wiezers, Veizers, Doroghazis, Kovácses, Maylaths, Barths, Kudelkas, Verases, and Takacses, the Yugoslavian Krauses, the Serbian Spaiches, and the Mexican Castillos and Ibarras. The other twenty-plus blocks of Lincoln Place show a similar diversity.

There are only a few businesses in Lincoln Place today. Ernie and Annie's is still popular with people from all over Granite City as it has been for over fifty years, especially on Fridays when a special team comes in to prepare their distinctive and delicious bean tacos. The Mexican Honorary Commission runs a bar for members and their guests four nights a week in the basement of the old Magyarház. The other taverns closed years ago, and many of the buildings they were in are no longer standing.

Two blocks on the south side of Neidringhaus were destroyed in the great fire of 1953. Early in the evening of September 21st, flames surged 150 feet into the air. Fanned by strong winds, this fire endangered the whole of Lincoln Place. Two people died, nine were injured including four firefighters, and nine buildings on both sides of Niedringhaus were destroyed, including two large rooming houses. Over one hundred people were left homeless. The firefighters were initially hampered by the lack of pressure in the hydrant lines because the lines "dead ended" in Lincoln Place. Therefore, it did not take long for the Granite City Fire Department pumping trucks to completely empty the pipes. It wasn't until a pumper from the GCFD was connected to a hydrant within the Army Depot that water sufficient to extinguish the fire was available. The Depot's resources finally subdued this wind-driven fire that had started in a small rubbish pile and saved the rest of Lincoln Place from going up in smoke.

I remember going with my father to Lincoln Place early the next morning when the ruins were still smoldering and listening to his fishing buddy Charlie Vartan talk about how he had climbed up on his roof with his garden hose to keep the fire from spreading to his home. By that time it had already jumped across Niedringhaus Avenue to ignite Duke's Bookstore and Slim's Pool Hall. We stood on the sidewalk across the street from the charred shells of the rooming houses and watched as wrecking crews prepared to bring them down. At a City Council meeting the following Monday, George Veizer and the other alderman representing Lincoln Place took the lead in demanding stricter fire hazard inspections and mentioned several other buildings that were as dangerous to live in as the two rooming houses that had been destroyed. The Fire Chief recommended that a circulating water system be installed which would eliminate the dead end in Lincoln Place. All this was done in time, but the population of Lincoln Place and the vitality of its business section had already begun to decline before the great fire, and it accelerated after that.

The one thriving new business establishment in Lincoln Place today is the Garden Gate Tea Room, a popular restaurant on Niedringhaus, which has earned the highest online rating of any in

Granite City. The tea room and the lovely gardens surrounding it were opened in 2000 by Ms. Brenda Whitaker, a woman who has put a great deal of effort into reviving Lincoln Place. On the Garden Gate's website, she writes, "After fifteen years as a steelworker in the same mill, I traded my hardhat and steel-toed boots for a wire whisk, and the adventure began. I hope you enjoy my eclectic tea room rich with history that combines two of my favorite things, gardening and cooking." Ms. Whitaker recently fulfilled another dream--creating a theatre--by transforming the First Baptist Church on Delmar Avenue. She established Alfresco Productions to produce its inaugural season of dramas and musicals in 2014. Alfresco has already staged everything from *Little Shop of Horrors* and *Arsenic and Old Lace* to *Alice in Wonderland*. It has also presented silent movies, choral concerts, and Elvis impersonators.

Lincoln Place is now a sedate and modest but well-maintained residential neighborhood. Vestiges of the old ethnic families remain, but there are newer residents who know little of the history of the neighborhood. Jobs are elsewhere now. What was left of the huge NESCO plant burned to the ground a few years ago. American Steel has expanded and seems to be thriving, but General Steel Castings (the old Commonwealth foundry) closed down for good in the 1970s. Most of the innards of the factory were, rather ironically, shipped to Mexico. If any other business place operates in Lincoln Place, I have not noticed it. The old Magyarház comes to life on Mexican holidays, when hundreds of people fill the old building and the streets outside. The Armenian community is active also, but its old church on Maple Street (which they purchased many years ago from the Bulgarian and Macedonian community when it was the St. Cyril and Methody Orthodox Church) became too small for the steadily growing congregation. The center of their community since 1997 is St. Gregory the Illuminator Armenian Apostolic Church, just off West Pontoon Road in north Granite City. Their Community Center, a popular place for high school reunions, wedding receptions, and other events sits on five acres near the church and opened in 1986. St. Cyril and Methody Eastern Orthodox church, the direct descendant of the oldest Bulgarian Orthodox Church in America, is now located on Maryville Road on the northern edge of old Nameoki.

CHAPTER 15
First Cousins

THE HUNGARIAN HOME, OR MAGYARHÁZ, built in 1925, was the largest space for public events in the Hollow. In the early years dramas were performed in Hungarian on the stage, and Mary Kovach says that a Hungarian immigrant new to Lincoln Place even established a Hungarian radio station there for a while. Like the contemporary St. Gregory Community Center, it was not used exclusively for celebrations and meetings of their own ethnic community. Other nationalities used it for their holidays and wedding receptions. I remember attending weddings there as a child, with lively music and energetic dancing on the second floor and endless supplies of fried chicken, potato salad, pigs in the blanket, sausage, beer and soda on the ground floor. It was hard for me to choose between the floors, so I remember hesitating on the the sidewalk trying to make up my mind whether to run down the basement steps for more food or climb the wide steps to the main entrance for more music and dancing.

George Veizer, Jr. and Mary Catherine

The first wedding at the Magyarház that I remember was George Veizer, Jr. and Mary Catherine Sudholt's when I was five years old. Three years before this event in January 1945, George, Jr. and many of his GCHS classmates had been encouraged to graduate a semester early in order to join a branch of the military. George, who was president of his senior class, led the way, joining the Navy and shipping out shortly after the January graduation ceremony. He was trained as a baker's assistant and learned from an ancient Navy vet some useful baking tricks on the ship to which he was assigned. When he returned to Granite City, he started working for Taystee Bread in St. Louis. And not long after that George married his high school sweetheart, Mary Catherine Sudholt. For me, the wedding reception was a real happening. Maybe my first. My mother and father even danced together, a rare treat and to me an unforgettable delight. Even though they didn't polka with the vigorous stomping and ear-splitting yips of some of the other dancers (none louder and more vigorous than George's brother Ronnie, who would soon be in the Navy himself after he graduated from GCHS in 1950), I could not take my eyes off them. It was so strange. They were not Mom and Dad anymore: they were a dazzling couple with their own feelings and concerns.

George, Jr.'s leadership skills were soon recognized, and in the mid-1950s, he was sent by Taystee Bread to the American Bakers' Institute management program at Northwestern University. After he graduated, he was promoted to superintendent of the St. Louis bakery.

When I graduated from high school in 1961, I did not have a job, which was a hot issue between me and my dad, who had already been working in the Commonwealth for four years when he was my age. About six weeks before the end of school I had quit a part-time job at the first fast-food outlet in Granite City, Chef Burger on Madison Avenue and 27th Street. Following a day of college prep classes, tennis practice, senior class play practice (I was assigned the role of the drunken choirmaster in *Our Town*), then hours of homework and/or real work at Burger Chef, I did not have much time for sleep. I was nodding off in class and was being unpleasant to a couple of my teachers, not to mention sending out bags of sandwiches with globs of condiments but no meat in them, so I quit. The tension between father and son increased after my graduation in June, so I "ran away" for a week, hitchhiking to Manteno, Illinois, to bask in post-graduation glory in the presence of Grandma Boyd and my mother's other relatives. In a few days, though, I was found out and sent home on a train. A summer job in the wrapping room at Taystee Bread--my first job which earned more than minimum wage--was waiting for me. George, Jr. had already advanced far enough at Taystee Bread to find a job for a deadbeat relative! What greater measure of success could there be? During the next few years George's career path would take him and his growing family to Detroit, Atlanta, Jacksonville, and finally to southern California where he managed large bakery chains until he retired. And his family kept growing. There are now more Veizers in and around Los Angeles than I can keep track of.

George's brother Ronnie entered the Navy after high school as well and worked as a journalist for *Stars and Stripes*, the newspaper of the U.S. Armed Forces, traveling widely and covering such events as the coronation of Queen Elizabeth II. Shortly after he returned from his Naval service, he was injured in a serious auto accident on Nameoki Road in his torpedo-like Nash sedan. (A few years before that I had held on to him for dear life while he was operating his Cushman motor scooter. Fortunately our closest call was a long skid on gravel on the levee road.) While he was recovering in Granite City's St. Elizabeth's Hospital, he had the good fortune to be tended by Wilma Siever, a lovely blonde nursing student from Calhoun County, fifty miles north of Granite City. Wedged between the Mississippi and Illinois rivers, Calhoun is the most isolated county in Illinois. It is the only county without railroad tracks, and, as my father knew from firsthand experience, it is one of the duck hunting capitals of the Midwest. Ronnie and Willie soon married. Ronnie became a full-time Granite City police officer, and shortly after that, Willie gave birth to the first of their seven children. Gail,--or "Bachtown Gail" as she was called because of her mom's hometown--became the resident princess of Bachtown every summer. In the mid-1960s, Ronnie became the Chief of Police in Granite City and served in that capacity for twenty years. He also served as the President of the Illinois Association of Chiefs of Police for a two-year term. After he retired as Chief, he went to work as chief deputy to the Madison County Sheriff for ten years.

Ronnie and Willie Veizer's family, circa 1975>

I recently learned from Aunt Anna's grandson Jim Giese that Joey Giesler, Aunt Katie's only grandson, also served in the Navy in World War Two. I had forgotten that. As soon as Jimmy mentioned it, I remembered a photo of handsome young Joey in his Navy blues. What I did not remember, and probably never knew, was that Joey had served in the Pacific on a PT (Patrol Torpedo) boat, the small (about eighty feet long) but fast (up to 45 mph) type of boat that the young John F. Kennedy commanded. The military effectiveness of these boats was dramatized in the movies *PT-109* (1963), which was about the exploits of Kennedy and his crew, and *They Were Expendable* (1945), a movie noted for its realistic depiction of military action. Joey was officially in charge of the ship's galley, but on a vulnerable boat with such a small crew (three officers and fourteen enlisted men), he, no doubt, had to be ready to perform any task in a crisis. According to the Wikipedia entry on PT boats, because of the shortage of refrigeration space on the PT boats, one of Joey's main tasks as galley man would have been to use his wits to supply fresh food for the crew: trading with bigger boats, scoring food in native seaside villages, and "fishing," dropping grenades off the side of the boat and waiting for stunned fish to float to the surface.

According to his cousin Jim Giese, Joey was involved in action in the decisive Battle of Leyte Gulf in 1944, the first time the Japanese used kamikaze fighters. After losing this battle, the Imperial Japanese Navy was crippled and its major fuel supply cut off. It was never again a major force in the War. According to Wikipedia, many PT boats took part in the Battle of Leyte Gulf and played a significant role in the victory using their four torpedoes, two .50 caliber machine guns, Oerlikon 20 mm cannon, and their speed and maneuverability to torment the enemy. The Japanese often referred to them as "devil boats." Their three 12-cylinder Packard engines used high octane aviation gasoline, making them even faster on the attack and a more difficult target.

After the war was over, Joey returned to Granite City and worked in St. Louis in the garment industry, cutting and assembling material.

I remember him as lithe and nimble, favoring my Uncle Joe in looks and style. He married Myrna Damotte, whose younger brother Skip was one of the best distance runners on the high school team when I was running cross country. Joey and Myrna made a lovely couple, not to mention four good-looking sons: David, Darren, Dana and Drew.

Joey and Mary Geisler, circa 1925

Mary Geisler Ziegler, circa 1940

CHAPTER 16

My Father's Music

My father loved music of all kinds. He often spoke of Sam Andria playing his saxophone on the porch. A few years later Sam was playing in the famed Stan Kenton band, one of America's most important and innovative big bands from the late 1940s to the early 1970s. That achievement and his long-lived popularity in the St. Louis area earned him a place in the St. Louis Jazz Hall of Fame. Sam was also an artist in the kitchen. In 1978, he and his wife established Andria's in O'Fallon, still one of the finest and most elegant restaurants on the East Side of the river. Another of Dad's favorite musicians from Granite City was Joe Schirmer, a guitar and banjo player, who appeared with Russ Daley and Davey "Nose" Bold in the early days of St. Louis television.

Dad's favorite instrument, though, was the Hungarian *cimbalom* (tsim-baw-lome), a grand version of the hammer dulcimer. He must have heard this instrument played at celebrations when he was a younger man, though, for I never had the pleasure of hearing one at the Hungarian Home. In fact, I never saw one being played until 2003, when I visited The Valley of Beautiful Women, a collection of wineries and restaurants in Eger, Hungary. Less than fifteen miles from Kompolt, the Valley comes to life in the early evening when Roma (gypsy) ensembles begin to play in many of the bars and restaurants. In the Valley you can hear all the *cimbaloms* you want and drink all the wine you want for a price of--in 2003--fifty cents a glass, no cover charge. I did both...more than once.

My father was also fascinated by drums. When we were visiting Erzsébet's brother, my father's Uncle Louie Beck, in Miami Beach in 1950, we attended an outdoor symphonic concert. For my father, the dynamic fellow on the kettle drums was the star of the show, and he talked about his performance for days. In 1971, during his only visit to New Orleans, he had the pleasure of listening to Louis Cottrell's jazz quintet at Dixieland Hall. I worked there at night the first year I lived in New Orleans, selling traditional jazz record albums, water-colored prints of New Orleans scenes, and framing pastel and char-coal portraits created in the patio by artists who were as entertaining and unrestrained as they were talented. A charcoal portrait of Mom and Dad by one of the artists I worked with, the brilliant draught-sman Francisco McBride, whose work was in the collections of Edward G. Robinson and Vincent Price among others, has become a treasured family possession. That night at Dixieland Hall my father loved listening to Louie Cottrell's clarinet, Alvin Alcorn's trum-pet, "Frog" Joseph's trombone, and Jeanette Kimball's piano, but it was the drummer who made the show so memorable for him. That drummer was the supremely talented Louis Barbarin, the brother of drummer Paul Barbarin, who wrote "Paul Barbarin's Second Line," "Bourbon Street Parade," and many other New Orleans traditional jazz classics. His younger brother Louis was a small yet powerful man, who tastefully and effortlessly embellished every song in the repertoire. I was proud to be able to introduce my father and mother to Louis after the show.

Most of the members of Louis Cottrell's group were, what are called in New Orleans, "Creoles of color." They trace their descen-dants to free blacks, who formed a significant part of the New Orleans' population in pre-Civil War days, the largest such popula-tion by far in the United States. Many of these free blacks in early New Orleans were prosperous emigrants from Haiti, and in 1811 fully one-half of the people in New Orleans were Haitian by birth. A few of these Creoles of color even brought slaves with them when they fled the Revolution there and settled on Mississippi River plantations north of New Orleans. Other free blacks were descended from liasons between wealthy young New Orleanians in the 19th century and their Creole concubines, selected at elegant "Quadroon balls." Children of these long-lasting relationships were often sent to Paris or the North to be educated. I mention all this because cultural history and complexity always interested my father. He was not a scholar in any sense of the word, but his curiosity and interest in such matters made him, I believe, a very tolerant person for a man of his time and place.

CHAPTER 17

Attitudes

I NEVER HEARD A RACIAL or ethnic slur from either of my parents. Dad admired Jackie Robinson and the first generation of African-American players for what they had to overcome to compete on a level field. He liked Satchel Paige's style and wit as much as I did. He liked Louis Armstrong as much as Mother liked Nat King Cole and Mahalia Jackson. I believe he saw that their struggle for respect and recognition paralleled that of the immigrants in Lincoln Place, and he realized that their struggle was much more difficult and fraught with a level of resistance and violence that European immigrants seldom faced. Most of the chippers, burners and grinders who worked for my father in #10 Building were African-Americans. I grew up hearing about the mighty Riggs, who handled a chipping hammer with ease, as if it were no more than an electric toothbrush. My father passed on stories to me about these men and the stories they told him with appreciation for their lives and their story-telling skill. A vivid memory from my childhood is my dad leaving the house on a week night all dressed up for the funeral of one of the men who had worked for him. Several times he stood in the pulpit of a little black church in Madison or Venice or East St. Louis and gave a eulogy, memorializing the personality and character of a man he had worked with for twenty years or more.

My favorite stories were about a man I thought was named Bukkaholli. This fellow had been working at General Steel longer than my father, but he still lived with his ancient mother and took

76

good care of this eccentric old woman. Her feisty behavior and Bukkaholli's efforts to make peace with her generated many stories. Because of the sound of his name, I always assumed Bukkaholli was some kind of Slav or Italian, related perhaps to the Hochulis or the Paolis. It was not until he told me one day with a laugh that Bukkaholli had bought some farmland in Missouri and a white man was farming it for him that I realized that Bukkaholli was African-American. I thought hard for a moment and asked my dad, "Is his name Booker Holly?" "Of course," he said, then slowly, "Booker... Holly. Nobody calls him just 'Book-er' though.'"

I would never say that my father was without racial prejudice. I sincerely doubt that any American, white or black or Hispanic or Asian, is up to that standard. My father sincerely liked the black men who worked for him and they liked him. He appreciated their humor and their style and their music. It did not bother him when a black man made a success of himself in any endeavor. He did not think any person should be discriminated against by law. In 1962, my first summer working at General Steel, I ran over to #10 Building on a break and found my dad. It was somewhat like patting the frame of your bed to make sure you are awake. I had imagined what working on the floor of General Steel would be like so many times, and now I was there, actually talking to my dad on the job. As I hustled back to #6 Building, two older black men stopped me with a gentle wave. "You must be Mr. Johnny's son." "Yes, I am," I said. "He told us all about you, son. All them awards and such." "He did?!" I said, surprised and shocked. "Your name's Keith?" one of them asked, and I nodded. "I tell all these young fellas when they come in here. If you can't work for Mr. Johnny, you can't work for nobody." "Thanks," I said, "thanks," and ran back to #6 with a lot to think about.

My first trip into Dixie when I was seven was, I think, my father's first also. We were driving to Florida to see my dad's Uncle Louie, who had retired from Johnson & Johnson in New Jersey and settled in Miami Beach with his wife Rose. The South started for us in

Paducah, Kentucky, the first place we stopped for a meal. Dad was as observant as usual. "All the waitresses, all the people out front are white. But see back in the kitchen. Everyone's a Negro." Of course, there weren't any Negro customers sitting in the restaurant either, but he didn't mention that. "I don't understand these Southerners," he said. "They keep these people down, don't pay them anything, but they let them cook their food and take care of their babies." Dad's position on race, like that of many immigrants and their children, was roughly the opposite at that time to the Southern position. For him black people as American citizens were entitled to respect, status, and prosperity, but at that time I don't think my father wanted his family to be in close physical contact with them. Over the years, he evolved on this. In the early 1950s his widowed mother-in-law moved to the grounds of the state hospital in Manteno and shared an apartment with a black woman who worked with her in the kitchen. Grandma was very fond of her roommate, and they shared that apartment peacefully until my grandmother retired. One of my most vivid memories of Grandma is of her and her roommate waving out the window of their apartment at us. "There's good and bad on all sides," was the mantra Grandma lived by. When my sister Janice was assigned a black roommate at SIU-Carbondale in the mid-1960s, they got along, and I never heard Dad complain.

As is well-documented in James Loewen's *Sundown Towns*, Granite City was completely white even in the 1960s; black people on foot were seldom seen anywhere in town except in factory parking lots, and they were certainly not welcome in town after dark. Those hundreds of black people who worked in the city's factories were expected to leave town as soon as their shifts were finished. There were a few black families who lived at the Army Depot, but their children were quietly bused to Madison's schools while the white children there were bused to Granite City's schools. Racist talk and attitudes were common in Granite City, and it was not surprising when George Wallace's campaign for the Presidency in 1968 gained traction in Granite City.

One day in the summer of that year, Dad and I were sitting in a bar with a member of the East Side Levee Board, a powerful political force, dominated at that time by the Democratic Party. A couple of loud characters entered the bar wearing straw hats with wide "Wallace for President" bands around them. They were parroting Wallace slogans while my dad and his friend looked at each other with wry smiles and shook their heads. My dad's friend asked him if that wasn't...and he mentioned a name. My dad nodded yes, and the Levee Board member stood up and walked over to the two, who obviously recognized him just before he said, "Doesn't your wife work for..." and he mentioned a county agency. "We was just cutting up," one of the men said, and they both took off their hats and left the bar immediately. At that point the East Side Levee Board bought a round for the house, and we all had a good laugh. Considering Granite City's racial climate at the time, my father was an enlightened man.

When I saw Dad's Civil Conservation Corps records for the first time, I noticed something that put one of his most powerful stories in a different context. Next to "My usual trade or occupation" he listed "Chauf + "Elec Weld" (Chauffeur and Electric Welder.) "Before electric welding, or arc welding, was invented," he had told me more than once, "welding was done with carbon sticks. It was the dirtiest job in the Commonwealth, and all the welders were black. Then electric arc came along and overnight it was a white man's job. And with better pay. All the black welders were laid off or put on other jobs. It didn't matter how good they were at welding." I was eleven or twelve years at the time, and this was about the worst injustice I had ever heard about. "That wasn't right, was it, Dad?" "No," he said. "No, it wasn't." But he never added that he had been an electric arc welder, even though he told me that story several times during the early years of the Civil Rights era. He always told me that he had been a burner, someone who used a cutting torch to remove risers (excess steel that rose above the casting). When steel filled the risers, one could be sure that the mold was filled completely with molten steel. Perhaps, he added "welder" to his CCC application to pad his resume. Or perhaps, he told me had been a burner because he felt some guilt for taking a good job from a black man. Both are possibilities. There was nothing simple about my old man.

The welding story became an important one for me. It opened my eyes to the rigged game that black people were forced to play if they desired any degree of success, the injustices and indignities they had to swallow. That story, I think, had something to do with my applying to teach in a summer program at Miles College in Birmingham, Alabama, which was the 1967 model for what became the Upward Bound program. During that violent summer an Illinois license plate was enough to get me stopped and questioned by the state police in Mississippi and Alabama and to get me tailed by a Birmingham police car more than once. Four little black girls had been blown up, murdered by a bomb, in their Sunday School class less than a year before in a church not far from the Miles College campus. Initially, some public officials in Alabama claimed that the bombing was planned and carried out by Martin Luther King and the NAACP to attract attention to their cause. These officials did not bother to note that this was the fiftieth bombing of a Black-owned business or church in Birmingham since World War I. No one had been arrested for this most recent bombing or any of the others, but the police were following me! Three years later I began my thirty-five years of teaching in the public high schools and colleges of New Orleans, a city with the richest and most complex African-American history and culture in the United States. Whether this was the intended or unintended consequence of my father's story, I will never know for sure. I do know that I have never been sorry that he repeated that story to me or that I listened to it carefully.

CHAPTER 18

The Great Depression

IN THE EARLY 1920S SEVERAL acts of the U.S. Congress slowed immigration from Middle and Eastern Europe to a trickle. New immigration quotas were established based on the national origins of citizens in the general population at the time. It was another rigged game. The quotas for immigrants from the British Isles, Germany, and France dwarfed the quotas for those immigrants who wanted to come to America from Central and Eastern European nations. The great American Industrial boom that had required so many new workers for so many years had started to slow down. At the same time, agricultural work in America was becoming more mechanized, requiring fewer workers. Small farmers like my mother's father were not doing well even in the Roaring 20s. Families from rural areas, who had started to move into cities during World War One, continued this migration, looking for jobs in factories that had seemed undesirable a generation before. Nativist groups like the Ku Klux Klan spread into northern states, especially Indiana where several members of the Klan were elected to federal and state office. Their new targets were immigrants and Catholics, and "America for Americans" was one of their popular rallying cries. It's a cry that still surges up in difficult economic times.

A feverish prosperity continued into the late 1920s, though weakness in the rural economy foreshadowed darker times. In 1929 the stock market crashed, and soon after that, the Great Depression began. The Tri-City area--Granite City, Madison, and Venice--was the second hardest hit area in the United States in terms of unemployment and the resultant poverty. General Steel Castings, the company that bought the Commonwealth in 1928, employed the largest number of Lincoln Place residents. It shut down "temporarily" in 1931, leaving hundreds from that community out of work. Other local plants followed suit or remained open with skeleton crews. As I mentioned earlier, my father was laid off in December of 1930. He had roughly eight years of seniority at the age of 22. His father was 62 at that time and had worked at the Commonwealth for almost twenty years. There was no unemployment compensation at the time and little government relief. In the Veizer family and most others in Lincoln Place, there were not many dollars in savings accounts, and just a few dollars were coming in from odd jobs, occasional work. Other than that, there was only charity and credit.

For the Veizer family the most important source of credit during the Depression, perhaps the only one, was Vartan's Market. Somehow the Vartans were able to supply the necessities of life to the Veizers and other families, hoping to be repaid fully when the Depression relented. My father and other young men from the Hollow were able to earn some money after the Commonwealth closed by finding their way to farms in the Midwest—"riding the rails like hobos," he said-- where they helped to harvest crops in Kansas, Nebraska, and other places. He had been "a wheat shocker and a corn husker," phrases he loved to use. A more dangerous adventure involved transporting bootleg whiskey in the trunk of a car. One nervous trip was more than enough for him though, and he never made another delivery.

Annette Vartanian Simpkins says in her interview that her father Aranos was a bootlegger in the 1930s. It's possible my father made that one bootlegging trip for him. To support his five daughters Aranos had worked the night shift at American Steel before the Depression and sold vegetables out of a truck in the daytime. Before Annette was born, he had opened, she says, the first movie theater in Granite

City right there in Lincoln Place. He also directed Armenian plays. He was an enterprising fellow indeed. It's not completely surprising that he became a bootlegger when opportunity arose. And it's not completely surprising that he was caught by Prohibition agents.

Even everyday survival sometimes involved taking risks. My cousin George remembered walking along the railroad tracks with his father collecting lumps of coal in a burlap bag. Railroad detectives, always called "railroad bulls" by my dad, carried guns and sometimes used them to discourage "riding the rails" and pilfering. George and George, Jr. were luckier than one of the Dorogházi boys, who was shot in the stomach by a "bull" while on a late night coal-gathering run. After he was shot, he ran home and crawled into bed, not telling anyone what had happened until his mother found him in his blood-soaked bedclothes in the morning. He survived.

CHAPTER 19

For Better or Worse

WHEN MY FATHER RETURNED FROM the Western mountains and his work for the CCC in the fall of 1933, General Steel was still not up and running. He applied for a job with the state of Illinois about a year after he returned and was hired. He was sent to the rapidly expanding state mental hospital in Manteno. The severity of the Depression was literally driving thousands of people crazy. In those days before thorazine and other powerful anti-depressants, patients were sometimes hard to control. My father described his job at the Manteno institution as "night guard." Patients were expected to follow a set routine. At night they were supposed to stay in their beds and not roam around looking for food or sex or trouble. Armed with a "soap jack," a bar of soap in a sock, my father enforced those rules in the dead of night against hulking madmen twice his size using his powers of persuasion more often than his soap jack.

During the day he slept, sharing a room and a bed with a man who worked the day shift at the asylum. His room was in a large white house in Manteno owned by Frank and Bertha Boyd, who also worked at the state hospital. Frank, who was forced to sell his farm when grain prices plunged in the early years of the Depression, was a licensed barber at the hospital and Bertha a "dietician," a sterile term for a woman who made the best chicken and dumplings in this wide world. The Boyds had bought their house in Manteno with the meagre proceeds from the sale of their southern Illinois farm near

Dongola. Their hundred acres, their farm implements and their animals brought in less than $2000 at auction, just enough to buy that house in Manteno, almost 300 miles to the north. The house was spacious enough to accommodate the Boyds, their two daughters and a few roomers. Their son Wayne was already married but would eventually move to Manteno.

My mother Juanita was the older of the Boyd daughters, nineteen when she met my father. Before long these brave children of the Depression fell in love, perhaps helped along by the melody of "Stardust," their song. Not long after that, they were secretly married in Manhattan, Illinois, not far from Manteno, but far enough away, I guess, for a "secret marriage" to stay secret for a while. I'm not sure what brought their secret to light. It might have been my father being notified that General Steel was stoking up one of its open hearth furnaces again and re-hiring many of its long-laid-off employees. In any case, the newly married couple traveled to Granite City in 1936 and settled in Lincoln Place, living in an apartment in the Szepesi house on the main street of Lincoln Place, still known as Pacific Avenue in 1937.

Hungary Hollow was quite a change for my mother-to-be. She had never heard anyone speak a foreign language, and now foreign words were what she usually heard, whether she was in the backyard hanging up wet clothes and sheets or shopping at Vartan's or walking in the neighborhood with her husband, who seemed to be able to communicate in all the languages. It must have been puzzling and frustrating for her at times, but her new relatives were friendly and kind to her, as were her neighbors on all sides. There was some earthy woman-talk my mother overheard that my father refused to translate for her, however. These loud and humorous exchanges usually had to do with the sexual prowess of their husbands, or the lack thereof. I do not remember my mother ever saying anything negative about living in the Hollow, her first eleven years in Granite City. Everything she told me reflected the almost idyllic community evoked by most of the participants in the SIU-E interviews. One of my earliest memories is of Mom and my older sister Shirley dressing me up like a girl for a Halloween costume contest at the Community House. To enhance my frilly dress they placed a ruffled bonnet on my head and told me to bat my eyelashes for the judge. I was only three years old so I complied and laughed along with them, hilariously. I won. Later that year I failed miserably at the Clubhouse. A big wooden boot with a thick lace was used to teach the fine art of shoe-tying. I tried to tie a bow until tears flowed. I was a candidate for Velcro long before it was invented.

John and Juanita's first child, my sister Shirley, was born in Granite City in July 1937. The young husband and father was full of energy after he returned to his home turf from his exile in Manteno. He immediately became the Scoutmaster of the troop sponsored by the Clubhouse. As I've mentioned before, his troop included most of the boys who would made up the 1940 Illinois State Championship basketball team. According to my dad, the boys in his troop were outstanding at all the Scouting skills and proved it over and over again in regional Scouting skills competitions. The Cahokia Mound Council's blue ribbons and gold medals in knot tying, fire building, lariat twirling, wood carving, and so on were usually won by members of Troop 9. For their consistent excellence the troop was awarded the Best Troop prize by the Cahokia Mounds Council: a teepee large enough to hold the entire troop on a camping trip. Winning this useful, towering symbol of high achievement and teamwork was one of the proudest achievements of my father's life. At camporees and other Council get-togethers, everyone knew where to find Troop 9 from Lincoln Place.

Juanita and John Veizer, 1936

CHAPTER 20

Dad's Fishing Buddy

ONE SCOUT FROM HIS TROOP, Charlie Vartan, became my father's best friend and fishing partner for years. Charlie was the best fly fisherman I ever saw. He also became my protector on long fishing trips with my dad. I loved to go on these trips, but at the time I did not have the patience or the concentration or even the knot-tying skills to be a good fisherman of any kind, much less a fly caster. Charlie always understood. He was one of a kind. Anyone who observed his easy slouch and relaxed manner would think he was strictly "country," not an Armenian from the city who worked in aviation electronics at McDonnell-Douglas.

Charlie had two speeds except when he was fly fishing: slow and slower. Dad and I once waited for what seemed like an hour in his driveway for Charlie to get ready for our long drive to Montauk State Park on Missouri's spring-fed Current River. He had probably fallen asleep two or three times while pulling on his socks. Dad was working the "afternoon" shift then: three p.m. to eleven p.m. On a Friday night after Dad finished his shift, the three of us would often make the four-hour drive in the dead of night along two-lane and even more treacherous three-lane highways into the Ozark foothills. We usually reached Montauk--or the equally distant Bennet Springs State Park on the Meremac River--an hour or so before dawn and ate breakfast in a cafe full of dedicated trout fishermen. When the air-raid siren went off at dawn bringing the trout fishing day to a rousing start, we were already standing at one of Dad's and Charlie's favorite spots, fly rods rigged and poised to flick a Wooly Booger or a Malibu. Those were wonderful trips, but to my dismay, I never caught even one rainbow trout. The highlight of the trip back to Granite City for me was Toki's Bar-be-cue in Rolla. I didn't stay awake for long after stuffing myself there. Somehow Dad always managed to drive us home safely, even though by the time we arrived back in Granite City he had been awake for almost thirty hours: working eight hours, driving four hours each way, and fishing the hours in between.

Every year Charlie and Dad and a couple of friends would drive to Montauk for Opening Day, usually the first day of spring. One year it was bitterly cold on that day, and one of Dad's friends slipped him a pint of whiskey, advising him to warm himself up. When he came back a few minutes later for his pint, Dad handed him a half-empty bottle. "I didn't know you drank that much!" he exclaimed. "I don't," Dad said. "But you know, alcohol is just the thing to keep your line guides from freezing over. You should try it."

Dad and Charlie: Mutt and Jeff: hare and turtle: yin and yang. My dad never had a better friend or a better fishing partner. During my junior year in high school, Charlie died of a massive heart attack while taking an after dinner nap in his easy chair. I don't think he was forty years old yet. He had three young children and a wonderful wife, Isabel, the sister of Evon Parsaghian, the second-highest scorer on Lincoln Place's state champions. Isabel never re-married; my dad never went trout fishing again.

About twenty-five years ago a friend in New Orleans introduced me to a cook she had worked with in the kitchen at Snug Harbor, the Crescent City's original Frenchman Street jazz club. "He's a real nice kid, and he's from St. Louis like you," she told me as she introduced us. I told him I didn't really know that much about St. Louis because I was from Granite City. "So am I!" he said. "My name's Kenny Vartan." I was in shock for a moment. "My name's Keith

Veizer," I said. "And I haven't seen you since you were five years old when your hair was curlier than Harpo Marx's." I shared as many memories of his dad and my dad and Kenny's older brother as I could in about half an hour. Then we arranged to meet the next day. "I travel all over," he told me then. "In Granite City, they call me 'The Greyhound Armenian.'" The next time I heard from him he was manning a weather station on a remote island in Alaska.

CHAPTER 21

Quirks

My father's approach to life was straightforward and righteous, but he wasn't self-righteous. I never knew him to backbite or chisel or yearn for things he could not have. He did love to play little tricks and practice deceptions, just for fun. And he was also someone who could appreciate this quality in others. One of my favorite stories--and Dad's--concerned a pair of shoes that he wore for years and years. One Saturday morning when he and my mother were shopping in St. Louis, my father came across an odd-colored pair of loafers--greenish-tan, I'd say--with an equally odd texture--faintly like animal skin, but not inspired by any particular animal I could identify. He asked the salesman how much they cost and was surprised how cheap they were. My mom's good taste, I'm sure, suggested to her why they were inexpensive, but she seldom imposed her taste on Dad except to tell him when his socks were inside out. My father continued to express his admiration at how well-made the shoes were and how much better they looked than higher-priced shoes on display. Then he began to wonder aloud that something must be wrong with them; perhaps that was why they were so cheap. At that, the salesman picked up one of the loafers, took a pen knife out of his pocket, and sliced a tiny piece off the inside corner of one of the heels. "You're right," he told my dad. "These shoes have a defect. They're damaged goods. I couldn't sell them at the regular price." My father was delighted--with the shoes and with the story.

And every time he retold it, he took off the shoe with the "defect" and showed it to his listener.

And then there were his own tricks. One afternoon he came home from work with a bandage on the back of his right hand and a little red box gripped by his other hand. He told me in a matter-of-fact way that he had lost a finger at work, a common enough story in local factories, not to mention in the Veizer family. Nevertheless, his disfigurement was very upsetting to me. I could not help thinking of Uncle George's thick stubs, which he loved to grind into my ribs. It was even more upsetting when Dad asked me if I wanted to see the finger. I did not want to, but I could not resist taking the lid off the box. And there it was! A thick hairy finger--undoubtedly my father's and no one else's--covered in blood and iodine. He let me gape at it a while before he wiggled it and pulled it out of a hole in the bottom of the box.

Dad had a superhuman tolerance for spicy foods. When he had the yen for raw horseradish, he would fork it out of a jar and into his mouth. Then he would offer me some. One of his favorite tricks at work was to open a jar of home grown, extra-hot Hungarian peppers and snack on them at lunch. Inevitably, one of the newer men on the job would say, "I love peppers. Are these ones hot?" "Oh, no," Dad would say, and chomp down on another one. "They're sweet as can be." The hook was set. The new guy would pull one out of the jar, take a manly bite, and all hell would break loose in his mouth. It was all in good fun, of course. Foundry workers played rough.

Taking on Goliath was a recurrent theme in my father's life, in politics and at foremen's meetings at General Steel Castings, which absorbed the locally-owned Commonwealth Steel Company in 1928. He was the foreman most often appointed by his fellows to "bell the cat" at their periodic meetings with the bosses. He was chosen to voice contrary opinions about productivity and safety and other matters that were held by most foremen, but which upper management did not want to hear about. He also refused to sit quietly when management annually announced to the foremen in Granite City that their bonuses were made possible by the greater efficiency of General Steel's two foundries in Pennsylvania. He never believed that yarn, but he did not have access to the company's books, of course. It was impossible to make his case until GSI was forced to close down one of those "profit-making" Pennsylvania foundries. The vindication he felt then was considerable, so much so that he did not, could not, keep from wondering aloud at the next foreman's meeting where the Granite City foremen's bonuses would come from now. He was less than pleased when General Steel transferred foremen and other management from Pennsylvania to Granite City and assigned them to supervisory positions. Once again he was assigned the task of "belling the cat," which he did with his usual panache.

My father usually rooted for the underdog in sports, too. I imagine this is the reason I grew up a devoted fan of the St. Louis Browns. His keenest baseball memory was his painful attempt to catch one of Jimmy Foxx's fabled line-drive home runs to the left-field bleachers at a Browns game in the 1920s. My father's hands took the sting out of the ball, which was then picked off by an undeserving fan behind him. His hands were swollen and sore for quite some time. In the 1920s, when the Browns were at their peak, competing for, but never quite making it to the World Series, he favored the Browns over the Cardinals. The Yankees--with Ruth, Gehrig, and a host of other immortals--were always better than the Browns in spite of the best efforts of Browns Hall of Famer George Sisler, slugger Ken Williams, and the 188-game-winner Urban Shocker. In the 1930s he was just as fond of the Cardinals' more successful and very entertaining Gas House Gang with Dizzy and Daffy Dean, Pepper Martin, Frankie Frisch, Rip Collins, and the mighty Hungarian slugger, Joe Medwick ("Medvig" he always reminded me, neglecting to tell me that "*medve*" is Hungarian for "bear"). "Ducky" Medwick was the last National League hitter to achieve the Triple Crown: leading the NL in batting average, home runs, and runs batted in in 1937. By the time of my childhood in the early 1950s, the Magyar aura had worn off the Cardinals and my father was once again following the increasingly futile Browns, the team of his childhood, so unenthusiastic about the Cardinals that he sometimes referred to the quintessential Cardinal hero Stan Musial as "Mr. Pop Up." Since I cannot remember another syllable of criticism of Stan the Man from any other source, I can only speculate that, in my father's mind, Stan was too nice, too bland, and too quiet to be a worthy successor to the mischievous and pesky personalities of the Gas House Gang. After the 1953 season the St. Louis Browns relocated to Baltimore, where--as the Orioles--they won the World Series in 1966, 1970, and 1983. The St. Louis Browns endure as a fading footnote in baseball history, but they remain a vivid and dramatic chapter in my memory.

I first gazed upon a photo of the 1932 Verhovay Insurance Company's baseball team six years ago at the Lincoln Place Heritage Festival. I had heard about this team from my father frequently during my baseball playing days. Marvin Moehle, a descendant of the Macedonian cousins who founded the Hollywood-Andrews Studio, Granite City's premier photographers for decades, put a large photo of this team on display along with many other pictures of Lincoln Place groups. My father always told me he had been a part of the team, not as a player, but deeply involved nevertheless. And there he was at 23, the year before he joined the CCCs, kneeling to the left of the team, several of whom I recognized. Marvin had failed to identify anyone in the photo, so I supplied names to the faces I recognized: "Vee" Vartan, "Skinny" Meszaros, Manuel Valencia, Mr. Hinterser the postman, and Bill Vivod, my uncle-to-be. In 1932 this team had played an exhibition game in Lincoln Place featuring George Sisler, Joe Medwick, and the pitcher Al Brazle. The next year, with a lineup strengthened by the addition of players from outside Lincoln Place-- like Lefty Barylske, long, tall pitcher Pete Cardner, and future St. Louis Browns catcher, Hungarian Sam Harshany--the Verhovay team won a National Championship amateur tournament played at the Chicago World's Fair.

In the early 1950s my father and I more often attended Browns games. I rejoiced in the twilight of Leroy "Satchel" Paige's career; in attending Ned Garver's magical twentieth win on the last day of the 1951 season, a season in which the Browns team won only fifty-two games total; and in cherishing the baseball cards of Clint Courtney, Duane Pillette, Dick Kokos, Bobby Young, Billy Hunter, Dick Sisler (George's son), the soon-to-be-immortal Don Larsen, another future Yankee ace "Bullet Bob" Turley, and even that paragon of mediocrity Hank "Bow Wow" Arft. And though I still have many baseball cards from the 1950s--including Ted Williams, Yogi Berra, Willie Mays, Whitey Ford, Bob Feller and a couple hundred others that my father did not give away to my younger cousins while I was away at college, my St. Louis Browns cards are still the only ones that narrow my attention and expand my heart, shortening my breath and making me remember what it was to be nine years old and--I don't know how else to say it--in love. Loving a team in spite of its almost daily failures and cherishing both small achievements and unbelievable moments was intoxicating: Bobo Holloman pitching a no-hitter in his first major league start, a feat never duplicated in the modern era, or Satchel Paige, forty-five years old at least, shutting out the original Washington Senators in Griffith Stadium for the last 5 2/3 innings of a seventeen-inning game on June 3,1952, hitting three singles and knocking in the winning run to bring his record to 5-1. I remember listening to both games on the little table radio which was sat on the bookshelf built into headboard of my bed. Loving the hapless Browns was not a bad preparation for the Real Thing: every once in a while, something wonderful happens. (By the way, if you want to relive great moments such as the above, box scores of all Major League games back to 1914 can be found at <Baseball-Reference.com>).

CHAPTER 22

Politics

IN THE BUSY YEAR AFTER my father married and returned to his job at General Steel Castings, he also entered the political arena and was elected a Granite City alderman in 1937. I'm not sure if he had been involved in politics before that beyond voting regularly. The only story he told concerning politics that might have come before then was about the time he and some of his buddies decided to play a practical joke. Since there were few, if any, Republicans in Hungary Hollow, there had never been a Republican precinct committeeman, even though the position regularly appeared on the ballot. After my dad noticed this vacancy, in the next election he and some fellow pranksters wrote in the name of one of their friends for Republican precinct committeeman. This fellow was duly elected Republican precinct committeeman--as was the Republican candidate for governor. Soon after their friend assumed his post, some of the pranksters and many others in the Hollow were beseeching him for a little work on the state or county road crews.

In the spring of 1937, soon to be a father for the first time, John Veizer ran for Alderman in Granite City's Fifth Ward, which included Lincoln Place and West Granite. According to my dad, there had never been anyone from his own predominantly ethnic neighborhood elected to this office. This was primarily because the voting population in West Granite, a blue-collar neighborhood of families with Southern roots, was notably larger than that of Hungary

Hollow, and this disparity was magnified by the fact that so many of the adults in the immigrant neighborhood, like his own father, had not yet become citizens and could not vote. However, between 1920 and 1930, according to Ms. Puskas, "the percentage of Hungarian immigrants in the United States who became naturalized virtually "doubled." No doubt that trend was reflected on Granite City's voting rolls as well.

The SIU-Edwardsville interviews provide differing opinions about the tensions between the people of West Granite, a neighborhood filled primarily with those who had migrated from the South, and the recent immigrants of Lincoln Place. West Granite was no more prosperous than Lincoln Place, and residents of both neighborhoods shared the ups and downs in the economy. Mary Asadorian emphasizes the hostility between the two neighborhoods: "All we had to do was cross 20th Street, and that's when it started, 'Hunkies ride on monkeys.'....Here's this street, [Washington] elementary school was here. This was Lincoln Place; this was West Granite. We didn't mingle, no shape or form. Why, I'll never know." My dad used to say the fights between Lincoln Place and West Granite boys were conducted with brickbats thrown from one side of 20th Street to the other. Nazareth Donjoian, born in the 1920s as Mrs. Asadorian was, admits there were fights, but after he returned from World War Two, he found that "whenever we went to East St. Louis and if any guys from Lincoln Place got in trouble, we'd always holler out 'West Granite' or 'Lincoln Place', and these guys we used to have fights with they'd come and help us, you know. That's one thing we did, we stuck together when we was out somewhere." Like Mr. Donjoian, my father had mixed feelings about West Granite. He fondly remembered the fights and the insults back and forth, but he had many friends at work from West Granite, and he must have counted on getting a few votes from the other side of 20th Street. He would need them to win.

My father often told me that the incumbent in the 5th Ward in 1937 was a well-liked heavy drinker from West Granite nicknamed

"Railroad Shorty." He had earned his nickname in the most painful way, losing both his legs to the wheels of a freight car. He was well-known, Dad said, for rolling his flat, four-wheeled stool up and down every bar in West Granite and Lincoln Place. In spite of Railroad Shorty's popularity, my father won the 1937 election and served two terms on the City Council. During these years he was also elected to a two-year term on the Madison County Board of Supervisors and also found time to serve on the YMCA's Board of Directors for several years.

Recently, researching my father's political career in microfilmed copies of the Granite City *Press-Record*, I uncovered some interesting details. I learned that in 1937 Granite City changed the way it elected aldermen. In the past, two aldermen had been elected from each of the city's wards every four years to four-year terms. In 1937 it was decided to offset the terms of the two aldermen in each ward so that every two years after that, one alderman would be elected to a four-year term. To accomplish this, the two alderman elected in 1937 would draw straws for the four-year term. My father finished second of six candidates in the balloting, winning one of the two seats available. Then he drew the short straw; so he received the two-year term. In 1939 he had to run for that office again, and this time won a four-year term, finishing first out of five candidates. Looking at the names of the candidates in 1937, I noticed a worrisome discrepancy in my father's story: there had been two incumbents, not one, when he ran in 1937. I began to wonder if the Railroad Shorty story was too colorful to be true, an outrageous embellishment: in other words, a product of my father's fertile imagination.

After I grew older and became acquainted with Nelson Algren's novels, I encountered a character in *Walk on the Wild Side* nicknamed Railroad Shorty. This Shorty was also a bar fly who had lost his legs to the wheels of a box car. I became a little skeptical of my father's tale, but I forgot to ask him about this coincidence. By 1975 it was too late to ask my father about Railroad Shorty or Camp Rankin or the CCCs or anything. I kept reading about Nelson Algren though. One day I learned in an Algren biography by Bettina Drew (*Nelson Algren: A Life on the Wild Side*) that this Chicago writer had spent a good deal of time in East Saint Louis gambling and hanging around with some small-time gangsters in the Buster Wortman network. Buster and his numerous henchmen were considered the Mafia of the St. Louis area when I was growing up. Then I learned that Algren had written *A Walk on the Wild Side*, one of his best known novels, while living above the Boundary Tavern, so named because it straddled the boundary line between Granite City, which closed its bars down at 1:00 a.m., and Madison, which paid no attention to such trifles as closing hours and was more open than Granite City to all sorts of late-night commerce. Suddenly it seemed much more likely that Nelson Algren had heard stories about Railroad Shorty at the Boundary and other Tri-City watering holes than that my father had read Nelson Algren's book or just made up the story.

Then in December 2012, I camped in the Granite City Library for two days researching my father's political life and the Depression years in the Tri-City area. As I mentioned earlier, in 1937 he ran against five other men: Roy Jarrett, Robert (Bob) Ingraham, the incumbent E.M. Herman, Ted Adams and the incumbent L.U. Logan. Mr. Logan received a few more votes than my father and then drew the the longer straw. None of these five are Lincoln Place names: no -offs, no -effs, no -ians, no terminal vowels. So Dad was right about that. He was the only candidate from the Hollow. When he ran two years later for a four-year term, only one of the previous candidates was in the field. To make sure voters knew just who he was, Mr. E.M. Herman was listed on the 1939 ballot as E.M. (Shorty) Herman. The added nickname did not garner him enough votes to defeat John Veizer, however. I am more inclined to believe my father's story about Railroad Shorty now than when I first heard it at ten years old.

Two factors seem to have persuaded my father to leave the political life. Number One was my mother. By the summer of 1943 when I was born and my father's four-year term was completed, she had two children to look after. She had managed to earn a driver's license; however, because of my father's time-consuming political duties, which were often followed by late night pinochle and gab sessions at Sim's Place, she was often left without a car and felt stranded on Poplar Street. This was especially true on Sunday mornings when she wanted to take herself and her children to Third Baptist Church, located near Wilson Park. Also I suppose there were many distracting calls and visits to the house from my father's constituents, an unavoidable part of a politician's life.

The other factor that led him away from local politics was disillusionment with political wheeling and dealing. Both his half-sisters, Anna and Katie, had spent time in the Madison County Tuberculosis Sanatorium in Edwardsville. Until the 1970s, every county in Illinois had a tuberculosis sanatorium or access to one in a nearby county, and such a hospital was especially needed in Madison County, where both crowded living conditions and poor air quality led to a high incidence of the disease. A doctor who performed most of the autopsies at Granite City's St. Elizabeth Hospital stated in a 1978 *Press-Record* article: "...in an adult Granite City resident who has been here for some length of time, I have yet to find a lung without some degree of emphysema." Tuberculosis was even more common in the river valley section of the county, where most of the county's factories were. There were no miracle drugs for TB until after WWII. The most effective treatment before those drugs were developed called for months or years of isolation in a colder than normal room, a hearty and balanced diet, and in more severe cases, pneumothorax. This simple surgery involved introducing air into the thorax, which caused the diseased lung to collapse. While the lung was dormant, the tuberculosis bacteria were starved of blood and nutrients and slowly died off. However, this process can take a long time. His sister Katie, my father told me, spent ten years in the sanatorium because each of her lungs had to be collapsed in turn. I'm not sure how long Anna was in the sanatorium; I don't believe her case was nearly so bad as Aunt Katie's.

While my father was serving on the Madison County Board of Commissioners some contracts involving the County Sanatorium came up for consideration. Though I don't know what the specific issues were, he felt that some commissioners were sacrificing the needs of the sanatorium and its patients for the gain of themselves and their friends. For good reason he took this issue personally. He fought against the majority and lost. Not too long after that, my mom got her wish. In 1943, the year I was born, after having served six years on Granite City's Board of Aldermen and two as an assistant Madison County supervisor, John Veizer was out of elective politics. He did not run for alderman in 1943, and he missed re-election as an assistant supervisor on the Madison County Board by thirty-one votes. He never ran for political office again, though he was often consulted by others who were interested in being elected, and sometimes he was asked by a group of concerned Lincoln Place citizens to write a letter about a neighborhood issue to the Granite City *Press-Record*.

I remember one letter. The tavern owners of Lincoln Place did not like a new ordinance which required them to remove the paint they applied to the bottom few feet of their front windows to make it hard for children, wives, employers--and policemen, I suppose--to peer in. I don't recall the arguments my father made, and I haven't found a copy of it yet, but the letter must have failed to achieve its goal because the paint barriers were soon scraped from the windows of all the bars in Lincoln Place. Not long after that the police sent the largest, most mature-looking eighteen-year-old boy they could find into several Lincoln Place bars to buy a drink. The drinking age in Illinois was then twenty-one for males and eighteen for females. (The drinking age for females was increased to twenty-one in the summer of 1961, just after I graduated from high school.) Then the city prosecuted the bars that had served him alcohol. I believe my father also wrote a letter criticizing this questionable tactic.

The Veizer family was, however, not out of elective politics for long. John's older brother George was elected 5th Ward alderman in 1945 and served eight years. He was also appointed a State License Commissioner. To create an office for himself Uncle George enclosed the front porch of his house on the 1700 block of Spruce, a rather chilly enclosure during the winter months, as I recall. It was furnished with a desk, a file cabinet, and multiple chairs (the biggest and most comfortable for my rotund uncle). On the wall behind the desk, there were photos of the Illinois governor and of other elected officials (all standing with Uncle George, of course).

Uncle George was always involved in some kind of law enforcement. In spite of being five-foot-four, he radiated authority. In his younger days he was the bouncer of choice at rowdy dances and road houses. He used a billy club deftly and enjoyed his handiwork, I was told by his son George, Jr. His last job was a long stint as a security guard at Granite City's A.O. Smith plant. One of my favorite Uncle George stories concerns his attempt to enlist in the Army shortly after Pearl Harbor. He was already thirty-five years old, but he was initially accepted, my father told me. On the troop train to Chicago, he was elected squad leader by the other recruits. Of course, at Fort Sheridan the medical staff discovered that half of his fingers were stubs, and he was sent home. Uncle George never lacked enthusiasm or serious purpose.

Uncle George's powers of observation must have been very useful in his law enforcement career. In the summer of 1961 he helped my father find a car for me to drive to work at the Taystee Bread bakery in St. Louis. My "Grey Ghost" was a 1940 Plymouth with 28,000 miles on the odometer. That car was so clean and ran so smoothly that the improbable mileage total must have been correct. The interior even smelled fresh and new. About a month after my dad bought it for less than $200, a late-model car ran a stop sign and plowed into my Grey Ghost. No one was injured, but the Plymouth's left front fender was bashed in beyond repair. Fortunately, Uncle

George remembered seeing a 1940 Plymouth in a junk yard in Alton not long before. He also remembered that its left front fender was unblemished and gray. Two days later I was rolling across McKinley Bridge in my perfectly restored 1940 Plymouth at 10 p.m. to package hot dog buns for a Cardinals double-header.

CHAPTER 23

Dad the Businessman

IN 1946 FREE OF POLITICS and war-required overtime, my father had a new venture underway. For most of the necessities of life, Lincoln Place was self-sufficient. It had the best and friendliest bakery in town, five grocery stores, some of which produced their own sausage and all of which contained butcher shops and ethnic grocery items available nowhere else in town, two confectionaries, three coffee houses, a pool hall, a large social hall, a community center, a cafe, two barber shops, a dry goods store, and at least nine taverns in three blocks of Niedringhaus Avenue. On the other side of the tracks in downtown Granite City were located doctors and dentists, department stores like Carp's and Leader's, clothing stores like Fleischman's and Schermer's and Helman's, and all the drug stores and jewelry stores and furniture stores. My father felt that the only glaring deficiency in post-World-War-Two Lincoln Place was its lack of a service station.

Before the Second World War, not too many people in Lincoln Place could afford an automobile, and only the restless young felt they needed one. Very few of them could afford one, though, during the Depression years. Then after February of 1942, two months following Pearl Harbor, automobiles were no longer manufactured for civilian use. American automobile factories were redesigned and retooled to produce tanks, trucks, jeeps, airplanes, landing craft, and other products needed for the war effort. Until the war was over, these former automobile factories produced nothing else. After victories in Europe and Japan dramatically reduced the need for war materiel, the pent-up demand for automobiles in the United States was addressed. The factories in Granite City had boomed during the War, and many workers had accumulated savings. Prospective automobile buyers around the nation gladly put down deposits with car dealers in order to be placed on waiting lists. My father must have done that, for I have a picture of him standing proudly beside a brand-new black 1946 Ford. (Was there any other color that year?)

To serve this flood of new automobiles and this era of unprecedented prosperity in Lincoln Place, my father, still working as a shop foreman at General Steel, had a Standard Oil station built out of concrete blocks for $2000 on the corner of Niedringhaus and Spruce, just across from the Community Center lot. Another facet of his plan--which served a national need and echoed a patriotic publicity campaign--was to create a job for a returning veteran. This was his plan: the young vet would operate the service station during the daytime and Dad would keep it open for a few hours after he returned from General Steel. A young Hungarian veteran from Lincoln Place, another one of Dad's former Boy Scouts I believe, took the job.

For a four-year-old boy a service station was the most fascinating of places. I especially remember the opaque white-and-red glass crowns on top of the two gas pumps. Watching the numbers on the gas meters of the pumps mounting slowly--as they did in those days--was mesmerizing. The numbers advanced so slowly that I think I might have learned to count by watching them. A two-thousand-dollar service station was not going to be equipped with a hydraulic lift, but it could have a grave-like service pit. Metal rails on each side of the pit guided a car's tires, keeping them from slipping over the edges. The pit itself was dark and dirty and oily, and I loved toddling around under a car and peering up into its hidden mysteries with Dad or his employee clanking around under the car.

The hanging light in its metal cage, the long funnel rising out of the big can used for catching used oil, the wheezing grease gun, the heat radiating from a cooling engine: these were wonders that my mother tried to shield me from, but my father understood.

That such a tempting attraction--and my dad--were just up the block and around the corner from our house near the beginning of Poplar Street must have often been on my mind. One day when I was almost four years old, I noticed that my minder, sister Shirley, was distracted, and I made a break. I ran straight to Niedringhaus Avenue, knowing I didn't need to cross it--and shouldn't--but I hesitated at the corner. Left or right? Directions were harder for me than counting--and still are--but sometimes I'm lucky. I turned right and another sprint took me to Dad's filling station. My minders (my mother had joined the chase) were not too far behind, but I had grabbed the golden ring and was standing at the edge of the pit. Mother was very upset, and Dad was, I could tell, very proud of me: a pattern that was to continue until my adolescence...and then, kind of reverse itself for a few years.

In a year or two it was clear that Dad's business plan was not working. The young vet proved unreliable, and then he found a better-paying job in St. Louis. An old friend who had promised to have the gas tanks of his delivery trucks filled at the station relocated his business to Alton so that bit of regular income was lost. Drive-in business by old friends, acquaintances and constituents was slow, even though--Dad was right!--there were a growing number of automobiles in Lincoln Place. Dad was probably not a very good business man. He was a strong leader with considerable insight into people and their feelings; he even had, I think, what is now called "charisma." However, he was something of a romantic (not that he would have ever used this term), and as such, "the bottom line," the cash nexus, did not obsess him. Intangibles were more important to him: friendship, loyalty, reliability, trustworthiness (this list begins to remind me of the twelve parts of the Scout Law, which he lived by). So he sold his little filling station and the lot it stood on, disappointed but not bitter. He had figured that anyone who lived in Lincoln Place would be proud to buy gas and have their cars serviced in their neighborhood if they could, just as they bought their groceries there. He was not all wrong. In 1948 he sold his independent Standard Oil station to the Ukrainian Fryntsko brothers, who did make a go of it, adding service bays--with hydraulic lifts--to the original building, eventually more than doubling the size of it. They kept that business thriving for over thirty years.

My father never went into business again. At forty years old, he started to slow down. Politics and business were now in the past, and the years of working in the gritty air of the foundry were starting to take a toll on his energy and his health. Of course, he persisted in his job as a foreman at General Steel Castings. He handed his paycheck to his wife every month, following Old Country custom. On the last Friday evening of every month, Mom would make little stacks of $20 bills to cover monthly expenses as they sat quietly at the kitchen table: no kids allowed. He took a small allowance for himself--for cigars, bowling, and fishing trips--and had a $25 U.S. Savings bonds deducted from his pay every month, just as he had since the beginning of World War Two. Sacrifices were made so that their savings account would grow: they paid cash for everything so that money would be available when their three children left Granite City for higher education.

CHAPTER 24

Education

EDUCATION WAS MY MOTHER'S QUIET passion. She was unable to attend school after the eighth grade because the family farm near Dongola in southern Illinois was many miles from a high school. After the farm was sold and the Boyds moved to Manteno in northern Illinois, Mom's younger sister was able to graduate from high school. Her sister then proceeded to Illinois State Normal and became a certified teacher. I'm sure Mom's disappointment at not being able to continue her schooling had something to do with a set of *World Book* encyclopedias that appeared in our house when I was six years old. A few years before that my mother's love of music had provided my sister Shirley with a piano. This must have been what prompted me to create a violin out of any two sticks within reach. I would saw with my bow energetically and hum a tune as loudly as I could. However, all this effort and "signifying" in the month or so before Christmas produced only a miniature plastic violin with a one-pitch harmonica in its base. I made do with the twenty-volumes of the encyclopedia. I would study those encyclopedias for hours on end sitting in dim light behind the sofa and near the hot air register, learning about dingo dogs, orangutans, Greenland, pygmies, and other far-flung exotica. When I was in first grade, I was called into the principal's office. I did not know enough to be terrified. It turned out to be the only benign summons I ever received to any such office: Miss Coulter just wanted to meet the boy who read encyclopedias.

My obsessive reading might have been what caused me to be in need of eyeglasses long before my defective vision was discovered when I was in fifth grade. It also might have been what drew me to New Orleans, a hot air register for most of the year. While I became a young man with too much information, Shirley, and then sister Janice, studied piano for many years with Ms. Olive Krohman in her studio above Fleischman's Men's Store. Both my sisters would become pianists at Third Baptist Church, and both would accompany the Advanced Mixed Chorus in high school. In fact Janice would receive a music scholarship to Southern Illinois University in Carbondale.

Dad was usually working the "afternoon shift" (3 p.m. to 11 p.m.) while I was in high school, so he was unable to go with Mother to my concerts, operettas, and class plays, performances she never missed. But when Janice was in high school, Dad had gone back to days and was able to attend one of her Christmas concerts. He was duly impressed by Janice's accompaniment of several of the GCHS choirs on the high school's beautiful grand piano. Finally it was time for the grand finale: all the choirs belting out the "Hallelujah Chorus" from Handel's *Messiah*. The grand piano was rolled off the stage, and an even more impressive instrument took its place, an organ with split double-ranked keyboards and two sets of pedals. My father wondered aloud to my mother who was going to play this magnificent organ, but my mother kept her counsel. When little Janice walked back on the stage and climbed onto the driver's seat of the organ, my father was shocked. No doubt he was still agape when her hands started playing two keyboards at a time and her feet began to dance around on two sets of pedals. I would have given anything to be there. Mom's rendition of the story gave a pleasure all its own, with the unstated moral clearly being: Dad never gives his kids enough credit. I felt there was something for all the Veizer kids in that moral--especially me, of course.

My mother sometimes pointed out to my father that most of the Macedonian and Armenian children from Lincoln Place families went on to college, but most of the Hungarian children did not. Mike Torosian confirms this in his interview: "I'm guessing that 75%-80% of the second generation [of Armenians] went to college." My father did not contradict her observation, though he certainly never waxed enthusiastic on the importance or prestige of a college education as the working class fathers of some of my friends did. While some of those friends were awarded money from their fathers even for the B's or C's on their report cards, let it be recorded for all time that I never received a nickel, even for an all-A's semester! To take the charitable view, I will assume that my father was putting those dollars--which I certainly could have and would have used to buy more beer and to have a more glamorous social life--into my college fund. Fortunately, on the subject of higher education as on many others, my father deferred to my mother's better instincts, and all three of us were sent away to school: Shirley to Jewish Hospital School of Nursing in St. Louis, Janice to SIU-Carbondale, and I to the University of Illinois in Champaign-Urbana.

CHAPTER 25
Chris's Bakery

ON THE FAR CORNER OF the lot dominated by Dad's service station was a small and inconspicuous brick building. There was no sign hanging above the door and no printing on the window announcing the name of the proprietor or the nature of his business. I do not believe that building even contained a front window. Yet this humble business place was one of the great institutions of the neighborhood--and the city. No sign was needed on this building because everyone knew that toiling therein was Chris the Baker. A blind man could have found his way there by the wonderful smell of Chris's bread baking in his wood-fired oven. Throughout the SIU-E interviews of the older residents, Chris and his bakery and his bread were mentioned almost as often as the joys and benefits of the Clubhouse, which stood across Spruce Street from the bakery. And in its way, Chris's Bakery was as much a "community center" as the Clubhouse.

Millie Todoroff Chandler, whose father was Bulgarian and mother Hungarian, says in her interview that Saturday was the day Chris "donated for the entire neighborhood. He baked bread; he gave it away to everyone....In the summer," she continues, "we didn't want to heat the kitchen. My dad would make stew and take it there on Saturdays [to be cooked]."

I don't remember Chris making cakes or donuts or anything sweet. But what tasted better than his Hungarian bread (*kenyér* in Hungarian), which he rescued from his oven mid-morning at just the right moment on wide, long-handled paddles? Mary Asadorian asserts that Chris's paddle was "so big that that you could put a child on it and shove it [into the oven]." Later in the day, he made a darker bread in a round loaf, and last would come the pita, or "pocket" bread. Each European nationality was served its own particular staff of life by Chris, who was, I think, Macedonian. (I assume Mexican mothers crafted their own corn tortillas as they did their wonderful home-made tamales, which were still carried into Ernie and Annie's a few years ago in large covered baskets by a mother and daughter team dressed in traditional Mexican outfits.) This scrawny baker in white apron with a cleverly folded piece of newspaper for a hat seemed like a very old man when I was a child. Long after we moved to the outskirts of Granite City on Pontoon Road in the Nameoki area when I was in fourth grade, Dad and I were still bringing warm bread home from Chris's every Saturday wrapped in newspaper. However, by the time I graduated from high school, the bakery was a memory: a memory enhanced by smell and taste, a memory vivid and unforgettable.

CHAPTER 26

Uncle George's World

IN 1948 WITH MY SISTER Janice on the way and the service station closed, the Veizer family needed a larger house than the one on Poplar Street. In what I suspect was a coup for my mother, we moved from Lincoln Place to the 2600 block of Grand Avenue when I was five years old. We now lived less than a block from beautiful and spacious Wilson Park, sometimes called "the crown jewel of Granite City," two blocks from Niedringhaus Elementary School, considered the best in Granite City, and less than a block from my mother's beloved Third Baptist Church. Nevertheless, the family, especially my dad and I, stayed closely connected to Lincoln Place. I received my pre-teen haircuts, as I had my very first, in Johnny the Barber's chair. While I was waiting, I would closely examine the fascinating calendars on the wall: one had pictures of all the U.S. Presidents above the tear-off sheets for the months and another had images of each state with its capital highlighted. Hair piled up under the barber chairs while I examined the calendars. The sweet smells of lotions and powders and the keen odor of astringents filled the air, as did the clipping, snipping, and buzzing of barber tools. The sounds of Hungarian, Bulgarian, and English mingled. It didn't seem strange to me at all though I regret I never learned many words in any of the languages.

The next stop on these Saturday mornings was usually Vartan's Market, where Nellie Vartan always made over me while slipping me a piece or two of candy. Then we would spend a few minutes at

Sim's Place where Dad gathered the latest neighborhood news and I could have a bottle of soda--a Nu-Grape or a Frosty root beer--or an ice cream bar, but not both. Then we would stop at Chris the Baker's. Uncle George's house on Spruce Street was always our final destination. If George's freshly polished Cadillac was in the graveled driveway, we would go around to the back door, unless Dad noticed him working in his front-porch office. Either way I always ran down the driveway to look into the Caddy to marvel at how clean it was, to examine the colorful turning knob attached to the steering wheel, and to see if there were any new novelties on the dashboard: a hula dancer, a swaying palm tree. Our family cars were boringly utilitarian. Although some sported antennas, they never had radios. In making his car deals, Dad would have the radio removed to save a few dollars, but he insisted that the car would not look right with a plastic cap where the antenna should be. The customer is always right, you know, so he got his useless antenna.

Uncle George, however, always had a Caddy, and the one I loved best was his snow-white '57 El Dorado. Its lines were similar to and as classic as the '57 Chevy Bel Air's. That highly-polished '57 El Dorado was understated, yet elegant. It was bigger inside than it looked outside. And it was fit for a movie star or any other big shot, as Uncle George was in my eyes. He had succeeded Dad as alderman for Lincoln Place and West Granite and was a strong and popular representative of the interests of the people of Lincoln Place. As one of the SIU-E interviewees says, "His [Ronnie Veizer's] father worked in the license division and always helped everybody in Lincoln Place." Uncle George had a passion for face-to-face politics and wheeling and dealing that I think my father lacked.

Dad was interested in issues and ideas, so much so that the Socialist mayor of Granite City, M.E. Kirkpatrick, who served in that office for at least seventeen years, considered him his right-hand man when Dad was on the Board of Aldermen. He told me several times that the Mayor he so admired once confided to him, "John, you're really a Socialist. You just don't know it." Mayor Kirkpatrick, who owned the first electrical appliance store in Granite City, was the most important political figure in Granite City from his first election as mayor in 1911 to his death in office in 1942. He was elected ten times to two-year terms and served nineteen years as mayor. His first successful bid for the office in 1911 was significant enough to merit mention in an article in the April 19th edition of the New York *Times*, which also noted that three Granite City Socialists had been elected aldermen. The year before Mayor Kirkpatrick died, the Kirkpatrick Homes development on Nameoki Road, the first and only federal housing project in Granite City, was completed. The obviously popular mayor must have been an intelligent and effective leader. His politics seem to have been rational and practical, not radical. He managed to forge ties with factory owners, union officials and others to ensure that Granite City grew and prospered during his thirty years of influence--and that it became a desirable place for working people. I wonder why no one has written a biography or a study of this amazing man's life. As academics like to say when they think they've stumbled across an understudied subject, "There's gold in them there hills." Maybe a local historian will soon go digging in that rich vein of our local history.

Uncle George's house was the province of Aunt Marie, who kept her domain as clean and bright as Uncle George did his Cadillac. There was a small stained-glass window in the kitchen that toyed with sunlight. A collection of fancy liquor bottles, probably gifts from other politicians and his constituents, commanded the tops of the cabinets. Each bottle was filled with a different color water. I'd never seen Uncle George drink more than a beer or two at the family barbecues he often held in his backyard; so I asked my father what had happened to the whiskey in the bottles. "He probably pours it down the sink," my father answered.

I'm not sure what did happen to the alcohol in those bottles, but Dad's explanation was not hard to believe. None of the Veizer brothers were drinkers when I was a child. Beer was for summer picnics; a little sweet red wine was for Christmas. I don't remember seeing any of the brothers drunk. Talk would inebriate them as nothing else could; alcohol was unnecessary. Hanging high in George and Marie's living room was a large baby picture in an oval frame of George, Jr. at six months lying on his belly in his birthday suit with head held high. The table next to the television held an elaborate clock with exposed works that their younger son Ronnie had brought back from the Far East when he was in the Navy. An ever more impressive succession of televisions in the living room provided entertainment when George and John did not. One of their early TVs possessed the largest round screen I ever saw. It was replaced by another with a multi-color scrim fastened to the TV and fixed over the black-and-white screen: voila! affordable color TV in the 1950s! Between those two rooms was an archway onto which Aunt Marie taped all the Christmas cards they had received that year. This collection seemed to be on display year round. Perhaps this colorful archway helped Aunt Marie remember to send cards to everyone in the family on their birthdays. In any case, she never forgot anyone's.

The main feature of Uncle George's backyard was a large brick barbecue pit. I suppose there were such things as portable barbecue grilles in the 1950s, but Uncle George was not having any of that. Did Sears make a grille large enough and sturdy enough for barbecuing a goat? In time the large brick barbecue pit was replaced by an even bigger one with an impressive brick chimney. It wasn't large enough for a steer, but it could have handled a large calf or a small pig handily.

Picnics at Uncle George's were highlights of my summer months. Almost all the Veizers would be there and sometimes some of the Vizers and the Wiezers. In his interview Jack Vizer, born in 1928, recalls a time when all the Vizer, Veizer, Wiezer and Wieser descendants gathered for picnics, but that was in the 1930s, I believe. Uncle George's barbecue was always excellent, and the potato salad, cole slaw, deviled eggs, and pigs in the blanket provided by Marie, my mother, and my aunts were delicious, but the family picnic was not all about food and drink.

At these gatherings I experienced my first taste of jijos, or bottle cap baseball. No one seems to know what language the word "jijos" came from. Obviously, this game was perfectly suited to poor children with limited play areas, which the kids of my father's generation had certainly been. After eating barbecue and all the fixings, the men and the older boys gathered in the cinder-filled alley behind George's house and chose sides. A pitcher would scoop up a handful of bottle caps and a batter would grab a sawed-off broomstick. The rules could not have been simpler. If the batter swung and missed one of the spinning, curving, diving bottle caps and the catcher caught it, the batter was out. If the batter hit the bottle cap in front of home plate, he was awarded a single. If the batter nicked the bottle cap and it landed behind the plate, he was out. A bottle cap caught in the field also produced an out, but batted bottle caps were even harder to snag than thrown caps. The bottle caps were, of course, bent to varying degrees when they were removed from bottles, so each cap was unique and each throw unpredictable. The caps were mangled even more when pitchers mashed an edge with a knuckle. Since my father had a strong hand for mashing and was perfectly ambidextrous, he was an especially deceptive and effective pitcher. And he was well-practiced: he often played at General Steel with other foremen on lunch breaks. At family picnics I always tried to be on the opposing side from Dad, of course, so I could have a hit or two to brag about at home.

There was also a bat-and-ball game with rules similar to jijos' that was unique to St. Louis and the surrounding area: cork ball. Corkballs were miniature baseballs, a bit less than two inches in diameter. They could be thrown at blinding speeds, and a good pitcher could produce a curve, a slider, or a knuckleball. The elegantly thin corkball bat and the little horsehide balls I still have were made by Rawlings, but I think Wilson made them also. In the 1950s corkball leagues competed on the girls' field hockey area behind the high school. Pitchers threw into little backstops to stop errant deliveries and damning foul tips. The most serious level of the game was conducted at night in well-lit cages behind taverns. The cages I recall were in Fairmont City and Belleville. Cork ball competition is not what it used to be in Granite City, but I read recently that there are still two cages and several leagues in south St. Louis. And some company is still producing balls and bats, which can be ordered online. It is hard to kill a good game.

At one of Uncle George's picnics I sneaked my first taste of beer--provided by Uncle George, of course. I did not like that first taste. That did not deter Uncle George from offering me some more later in the afternoon. My Baptist mother was ever observant though, as mischievous Uncle George and I well knew. "I didn't like the taste. Phooey!" I told her after we returned home. That did not give her the pleasure I thought it would. She just frowned and shook her head at me or Uncle George or the Veizer in both of us...which, by turns, annoyed and charmed her.

George and Marie Veizer with George, Jr., 1928

CHAPTER 27

The Veizer Exodus
from the Hollow

BEFORE UNCLE JOE AND AUNT Margie purchased our house on
Poplar Street in 1948, they lived in temporary housing within the
Granite City Army Engineer Depot, right next to Lincoln Place.
Since there was a severe housing shortage after World War Two,
shelter was provided at the Depot for former members of the Armed
Forces. Soldiers, sailors, and Marines were coming home with pent-
up energy, and the Baby Boom was gaining momentum. The Depot,
which contained 114 buildings--mostly large warehouses--on 895
acres of former Mississippi River wetlands, lay behind a fence that
ran along Cedar Street, the western boundary of Lincoln Place.
(Cedar Street and the houses on it disappeared in the 1980s when
Illinois Route 3, now called the Great River Road, was rerouted and
expanded to four lanes.) I was three or four years old when Uncle Joe
and Aunt Margie lived at the Depot. The sight of their cozy quonset
hut, a metal half-cylinder, was astonishing and as unforgettable as
Uncle George's white Cadillac. (Picture a dull brown A.O. Smith
silo sliced longways.) My cousin George--or "Junior" as I continued to call him even when he was in his 80s--and his new bride
Mary Catherine then lived near the southern boundary of Lincoln
Place, the fence that kept mischievous kids out of the General Steel

railroad yard. As their families grew rapidly, Uncle Joe and Junior both bought new houses north of Granite City's high school.

Around that time Ronnie, Junior's younger brother, returned from his four years in the Navy. While he was waiting for the opportunity to become a full-time police officer in Granite City, he was injured seriously when he drove his Nash sedan into a telephone pole on Nameoki Road. As I mentioned earlier, he wooed his nurse from his hospital bed, undeterred by injury, medication, or prolonged physical inactivity. They were married in 1955, and in short order started their family, joining the other young Veizers north of the high school. Between 1948 and the mid-1950s, there was quite an exodus of Veizers from Lincoln Place. Soon only Uncle George and Aunt Marie remained, and there on the 1700 block of Spruce they would live for the rest of their lives.

CHAPTER 28

My Nameoki Aunts

AFTER MY FAMILY MOVED FROM Lincoln Place, first to Grand Avenue for four years and then to Pontoon Road in 1952 (just two years after the village of Nameoki voted to become part of Granite City), Mom was still under orders from Dad to call in a list of grocery items to Vartan's Market every week. Dad never forgot the generosity of the Vartans during the Depression. The family grocery tab had mounted during the Depression years, and the Vartans had waited patiently for the Veizers and many other Lincoln Place families to pay. I'm sure Lovacheff's, Mitseff's, and the other groceries in Lincoln Place did the same for their regulars. So more than twenty years after the Great Depression, early every Saturday morning, Mom would phone Vartan's and recite her grocery list to Nellie Vartan. Around noon, Vartan Market's ancient green panel truck would pull into our drive-way with the Veizers' box of groceries. A succession of Lincoln Place teenagers carried the groceries in over the years--Mercy Mendoza and Joey Ybarra I remember best, since they were and still are good friends of mine.

When we moved to Nameoki in 1952, we lived just a few blocks from Dad's older half-sisters, Anna and Katie, who both lived alone: Anna in a neat little white house on Ferguson and Katie in a small trailer across the street. Anna's younger daughter Anne Giese, her husband John, and their son Jimmy lived a half-block block down the alley from us on Venice Avenue. John and Jimmy were expert auto mechanics and were often found in the garage working on one of Jimmy's racing cars. Jimmy's last car, a red Porsche, won many races at the Wentzville, Missouri, track without suffering an accident. When he retired from racing, Jimmy won even more trophies with his immaculate red Porsche in auto shows all around the Midwest.

The back yards of Dad's older sisters were beautifully kept gardens, extravagant in size and color. Numerous vegetables grew near the flowers in Anna's lot. In later years Katie moved to one of a long string of small apartments near Nameoki Road and across from the Kirkpatrick Homes called, I think, the Kimberly Apartments. When she lived there, more than once she won an award for the "Most Beautiful Garden." She loved that small apartment and garden so much that she called it "her heaven on earth." Flowers and food were what my aunts loved and what they shared with those in their world.

Aunt Nonnie (Anna) had a fully modern kitchen in the rear of her house next to the basement stairs. However, when she wanted to cook seriously--to prepare pigs-in-the- blanket, chicken paprikas, goulash, or other Hungarian specialities, she walked down those stairs and stoked up the wooden stove in her basement. Of course, this seemed a bit strange to a teenager. Once when Aunt Nonnie was cooking in her basement, I hesitantly asked her what the bright, white kitchen upstairs was for. She just laughed, for her a friendly cackle. "It's nice, isn't it?" she said. There were things I never did ask her about: for example, her pierced ears and their ruby studs. In those days that alone made her exotic in my eyes, practically a gypsy. Aunt Nonnie was, as my British friends like to say, "tough as old boots"; she was small and thin, but she still looked as if she had the energy to work in the landlord's fields two days a week as she told me she had been obliged to do when she was a young woman in Hungary. Every Christmas Aunt Nonnie gave me a crisp new dollar bill in a bank envelope with an oval cutout that exposed the face of George Washington: "Kit" was scrawled on the outside. My mother was proud of my good manners when I did not correct Aunt Nonnie's spelling. However, after I began studying the Hungarian language, it did not take me long to realize that "K-I-T" would be the exact spelling of my name in Hungarian (if there were such a name), for in Hungarian the letter "i" denotes a long "e" sound and there is no "th" sound at all. My grandfather, whose English was never very good, and whose hearing was no doubt impaired by all those years in General Steel's core room, always called me "Pete." That was as close as he could come to pronouncing a name he had never heard in Hungarian. This inspired my older cousins to dub me "Piccolo Pete." (By the way, my mother must have chosen "Keith," since my seldom used first name is the same as my father's, John. Neither he nor his brothers had a middle name.) As with my name, the first American Veizers usually did as well as they could with what they had to work with. So, since my childhood I've never been fussy about the pronunciation of my first or last name. When a friend from the homogeneous culture of north Mississippi dubbed me "Beasley" because he could not handle anything so foreign as "Veizer," I accepted his sincere effort and answer to "Beasley" in some quarters to this day; I also accommodate my Cajun friends who insist on "Vee-zee-ay."

Aunt Katie was not so strong or tough as Aunt Nonnie, but who could blame her? She had been confined in the county TB sanatorium for ten years; her husband had divorced her while she was there; and she suffered bouts of serious depression after she was cured of tuberculosis. She overcame the depression, but not too long after that her daughter Mary, whom my Dad always spoke of as the most beautiful of the Veizer women, was diagnosed with terminal cancer. Mary was in her late thirties or early forties, married to Bill Ziegler an insurance agent in Joliet, and the mother of three sons; Skipper, the oldest, was my age. There were fears within the family that revealing Mary's grim prognosis would leave Aunt Katie sunk in deep depression with no will to live. In time, though, her daughter's condition was explained to her, and she was able to spend time with her before she died. Everyone in the family was relieved when Aunt Katie did not relapse into depression. In fact, she did more than survive. She retained the aura of gentleness and kindness I noticed in her the first time she ever patted me on the head and smiled into my face, shaking her head in a kind of wonderment while making a soft "tsk-tsk" sound that was unique to her.

A couple of years after I graduated from high school, I came to know a younger acquaintance of Joey Ybarra's who had grown up on the street where Aunt Katie lived. Both his parents had full-time jobs, rather unusual in the 1950s, so he had to have in-house child care from his early years. When he realized that MY Aunt Katie had been HIS babysitter for many years, he was deeply moved, almost to tears. She was, he told me, one of the most wonderful persons he had ever known. After that, the first thing he always asked me was "How's your Aunt Katie?"

CHAPTER 29

Aunt Mary and Uncle Julius

AUNT MARY WAS THE OLDEST of Erzsébet and József's children, the only one of their five living children born in Hungary. According to Ellis Island records, she was two years old when she arrived in the United States with her mother in 1906, seventeen months after her father arrived. She couldn't have remembered much, if anything, of Kompolt, but for many years I had the idea that she could read and write Hungarian and had maintained a correspondence with someone in Kompolt. I learned recently from her grand-daughter Mary Ann that my Aunt Mary could read a little Hungarian but could not write it.

Among my father's photos are two small pictures of an elderly woman surrounded by many younger people. On the back is written "Merry Christmas and Happy New Year, Ilona" in Hungarian. Aunt Mary had, as I recall, given copies of these photos to my father, which was what had given me the notion that there might be a bundle of letters to Aunt Mary from relatives in Kompolt. Many years later when I sent copies of the photos to Elemér and Erzsébet Vizer in Kompolt, they identified the elderly woman as Ilona Keksz and knew just where the photos were taken, but they did not know her maiden name so I was not sure of her relationship to the family. A few years later when I skimmed through the old Kompolt church ledgers in September 2013, I found only the 1880 birth record of Grandma Bech and two siblings, one on either side of that date. (I recently found out that Grandma Bech had four brothers--József,

Pál, András, and László. Four other siblings died in their early years.) The mystery of Ilona was solved by Emöke Abasári's research. Ilona Keksz was Grandma Bech's youngest sister. She was born nineteen years after her. By the time of Ilona's birth in 1899, the municipal government was keeping official records of births, deaths and marriages instead of the parish church. Ilona was much closer in age to her niece Aunt Mary than to her sister Erzsébet. She was only seven years old when Mary and her mother left Kompolt for the United States in 1906. This knowledge helped me correct another error. In my memory, my father's sister who had died of diphtheria was named "Dorothy." When Mary Ann informed me that her name was actually "Helen," I realized that she must have been named after Gáspár and Anna Bech's last child, Ilona—"Helen" in English.

My father spoke more Hungarian to his sister Mary than to anyone else. They used Hungarian to talk of serious matters, just as their parents had used German to talk past them when they were young. And there were many serious matters for my father and Mary to talk about, matters that children need not have been burdened with. Multiple tragedies haunted Mary's family after her two children reached adulthood.

The first blow came in 1954 when I was eleven years old. Aunt Mary's daughter Mary Ann had married her high school sweetheart Donald Deems when he returned from the Korean War. I remember the lengthy wedding ceremony during a full mass at Sacred Heart Church and the wedding reception in the Toths' back yard on a perfect summer afternoon. A year or so later, Donald, Jr. was born, and the family moved into a new house a couple of blocks north of Nameoki Road, not far from where Uncle George's two sons had moved. The Deems family had not lived there very long when one morning in late autumn Mary Ann noticed a gas smell. Someone from the utility company came out, checked the gas lines, and told her there was no leak, that everything was fine. Late that night the house exploded, killing all three of them instantly. Investigators speculated that Donald had either flipped a light switch in the middle of the night or struck a match to light a cigarette, supplying the fatal spark to the natural gas that had seeped into the house. This incident and the family's funeral were front page news in the Granite City *Press-Record*. Other residents of this large new sub-division were on edge for a long time, but there were no subsequent gas explosions.

Mary Ann's older brother, Johnny Toth, was the first college graduate in the family. He was a Marine during World War Two and after the war attended St. Louis University on the GI Bill, majoring in accounting. My father was as close to Johnny Toth as he had been to George, Jr. Their fathers were not outdoorsmen or enthusiastic sportsmen, so my father, not having a son yet, took them to ball games and taught them how to fish. I don't think Johnny, who was named after my father, took to the outdoors as George, Jr. did. However, he always enjoyed being with my dad, and he became a well-informed sports fan, always up on the latest stats, a man after my own heart.

Before I reached high school, Dad was for several years captain of the #10 Building bowling team in the General Steel Castings League, which competed on Monday nights on the ten lanes of the Madison Bowling Alleys. This team was always at or near the bottom of the standings, far behind John Harshany's Open Hearth, Don Pindell's Machine Shop, and Larry Biondo's Accounting Department, the three teams always vying for first place. In spite of the losing ways of my father's team, I would not have missed Monday night bowling for the world. I could buy a big paper bowl of popcorn for a dime if I could extract ten cents from my dad, and when one of the three "beer frames" came around I was always offered a bottle of soda. The beer frame worked like this: the low scorer on the first ball bought for everyone on the team. The byplay of the men razzing each other was funny, though much of it whizzed over my head. I was the only kid in Madison Bowl on Monday nights. That did not bother me at all. I amused myself trying to figure out what the barbs really meant and enjoyed the "bowling alley discords," as I entitled one of my enthusiastic high school essays: the explosion of pins when a ball hit the pocket just right, the solid knock of a single pin picked off, and the clank of the manual pin-setters--each a distinctive tone in a rough musical score.

It never seemed to bother Dad that his team was last in the league standings and that his single-game average, usually between 125 and 130, was near the bottom of the weekly mimeographed list compiled by Larry Biondi. Dad's name was usually third from the bottom, just above Milton Haley, another member of #10 Building, and Johnny Toth, who was a regular substitute. Because of shift work, Dad's team was often short a man on Monday. Johnny, still a bachelor, was usually available when Dad called him. Johnny always showed up neatly dressed, then rented a pair of shoes and found a house ball to his liking. Like Milton Haley, Johnny bowled a ball that "backed up," losing force and fading to the right in the crucial moments before it hit the pins. Dad's ball was even slower than theirs were, but he threw the biggest hook in the league. It started in the middle of the lane, teased the right gutter just past halfway, and then it was destination unknown...if it escaped the opposite gutter. Maybe it was the uneven wax on the lane, maybe it was the inconsistent spin he applied, maybe it was the distraction of running the team and worrying about having five stalwarts every week, but Dad's hook seldom hit the pocket and more often that not missed the spot to pick the spare.

I don't say "never," because Dad sometimes mysteriously--and to the high-average bowlers, suspiciously--found his form during the annual end-of-the-season tournament when the General Steel bowlers competed as individuals. More than once Dad bowled nearly 200 pins above his three-game average. When his huge handicap was added to his huge scratch score, the Harshanys, Pindells, and Biondos were far behind, and Dad came home with cash, a new bowling ball, or a colorful pair of new bowling shoes.

Clear-headed St. Louis University business major Johnny Toth profited from bowling in another way. He was the first person I knew, or heard of, who actually owned stock in a publicly traded company. He bought shares in the Brunswick Corporation, developers and purveyors of the first automatic pin-setting machine, which revolutionized bowling. Johnny had the foresight to buy this stock while nimble young men from Granite City and Madison were still dodging balls and pins in the darkness at the end of the lanes. In a few years, twenty- and thirty-lane bowling palaces appeared in Granite City, all over the St. Louis area, and from one end of the country to the other. Johnny profited. However, he did not get rich off his shares. And he had to put up with my asking him every time I saw him how Brunswick Corporation was doing.

Two or three years after his sister's family was killed in the explosion, Johnny met and married Nancy, a sweet and lovely girl from a German-American family in south St. Louis. He had by then earned his B.S. degree in Accounting and had acquired a good job with a rapidly growing finance company in St. Louis. To attend their wedding reception, I entered for the first time the original Rose Bowl, which was, in my youthful eyes, the most elegant bar and restaurant Granite City had to offer. It was located across Nameoki Road from Granite City High, and at night a red neon rose on a long green neon stem promised a luxury offered nowhere else in our little city. The fact that some local teachers and coaches were rumored to frequent the Rose Bowl only added to its glamour.

Not long after their wedding, Johnny and Nancy moved to a new home in Bellefontaine Neighbors in north St. Louis County. Mary Ann, their first daughter, was named after Johnny's sister who had perished in the fire. Little Mary Ann, who to me always looked so much like her namesake, was followed shortly afterward by another girl, who was given the same name as my younger sister Janice. When Johnny and Nancy's daughters were still very young, Nancy was afflicted by a vicious disease that generated tumors. I don't know if it was a form of cancer. I never heard it called that, but people seldom uttered that dreaded word in the 1950s. Little effective treatment existed then for most forms of cancer: people regarded it as a death sentence, and it usually was. Whatever the tumor-causing condition was, it was unrelenting. Yet Nancy's spirit held up through several operations and other treatments, and I often saw her at Aunt Mary's house between these episodes.

The tragedies that tested Aunt Mary were far from over. A few years after Johnny became a widower, he suffered a massive heart attack early one morning at his office an hour before anyone else came to work. He survived it, though, and continued working at the finance company, where he was quite successful. Less than ten years later, he suffered a second serious heart attack, again at his job site in the early morning hours. He had come in to work early, as he often did, and no one was there to help him or to call for an ambulance when he collapsed. The lack of timely intervention intensified the damage to his heart. He did survive once again, continuing to work for a while as I recall, but his health and strength continued to decline. He was confined to a bed in Jefferson Barracks Hospital for the last months of his life.

My mother admired Aunt Mary and how her religious faith and strength had supported her in the face of her misfortunes. I believe Mom felt that she herself might have fallen short of faith and strength if she had suffered to that degree. Perhaps not. Her faith, like Aunt Mary's, was quiet, unobtrusive, and strong.

Aunt Mary's husband, Julius Toth, was one big Hungarian, compared to her three brothers anyway. He was certainly over six feet tall, as easy-going as he was large; Aunt Mary was no more than 4'10". I remember hearing once that Grandpa Veizer had arranged the marriage, which was not that unusual among first-generation Hungarian-Americans. Julius Toth was indeed Hungarian, but he was born in the area of the Austro-Hungarian Empire that is now part of the Czech Republic or Slovakia. He had lived for a while in Connecticut before he came to Granite City to become a "molder" in the Commonwealth core room. Highly skilled molders like Julius took cores--black sand shapes that had been baked and hardened in the core room oven--and connected them to each other to fashion the molds into which molten steel were poured to form rough castings. Grandpa Veizer was a laborer in the core room. This might have been where they met.

Entering the Toth house on Hodges Avenue was to be enveloped in a wonderfully fragrant atmosphere consisting of Uncle Julius's pipe smoke and Aunt Mary's cooking and baking. The prevailing odor went from sweet pipe smoke to well-spiced food as one walked from the front to the rear of their little house. Uncle Julius had a wooden rack for six pipes on a table next to his easy chair, which seemed to be a part of him. In the middle of the rack was a round silvery container with a tight-fitting lid that kept his tobacco fresh. Uncle Julius was the most pleasant of fellows, often laughing deep in his chest at the antics of the children who loved to gather around him, but he seldom spoke. When he did, he formed his words around the stem of his pipe and his dwindling number of teeth into very short sentences. He had a cigar box full of coins from the world over which he would allow me to fumble through for as long as I wished. Julius was so imperturbable that he used to allow his daughter Mary Ann and my sister Shirley to put his hair in curlers, not that he had all that much hair. Since he seldom moved one way or the other, he was the perfect beauty shop customer.

For years and years Uncle Julius had a light green Chevy pickup truck. He drove it to work, he drove it to church, and then he drove it home and put it in his sturdy and well-maintained one-car garage. When their garage was built, the Toths had the foresight to install a regular door on the passenger side and also to lay a cemented path to the back porch so Aunt Mary would not have to shinny past lawn mowers, oily rags, and sharp-edged tools to get out of the garage, possibly tearing or dirtying her clothes.

Aunt Mary, like her older half-sisters, was an excellent gardener. She grew some flowers around the border of their house, but most of her backyard garden was divided into long, neat rows of vegetables. I especially remember her bib lettuce. During its long season, my dad and I could not leave Aunt Mary's house until she picked a shopping bag full of fluffy green stuff for us. When we returned home, my mother would slow-cook that pile of lettuce with bacon drippings until it could fit in a bowl. Like so many kids, I did not like salads, but I made an exception for that kind of salad and have evaluated all salads since by that standard. I suppose the rapid transformation from garden to dinner table broke down my resistance. That and the wonderful smell of bacon. What the Toths did not or could not eat fresh, Aunt Mary preserved, lining the walls of their little storm cellar with Mason jars: colorful swirls of pickled peppers, tomatoes, cucumbers, and watermelon rinds.

Mary, Julius, Mary Ann and Johnny Toth circa 1950

Mary Veizer Toth, 1922

Johnny and Mary Ann Toth, circa 1935

CHAPTER 30
Dad's Fancies

OUR GARAGE ON PONTOON ROAD did not have a side door, but Mother managed without one, and since she was in and out of the driver's side at least as often as Dad, a side door would not have helped her avoid the clutter in the garage. My mother was not a complainer, though my father's behavior often seemed calculated to provoke--almost require--complaint. I am sure I filled the role of complainer more often than Mom did, no matter the consequences. However, there was one thing about our garage Mother did not like and would even go so far as to complain about: the longhorn steer skull that Dad nailed above the garage door as soon as Uncle George presented it to him. Since our driveway was almost perfectly aligned with the last hundred yards of stylish Terrace Lane, anyone coming from that direction could not only see the longhorn skull but had time to contemplate it, or perhaps admire it, while they paused at the stop sign. I don't know what "they" thought and neither did Mom, but I know she did think about what they might think. Dad, of course, did not give a damn what they thought and sometimes said so, or sometimes he said he thought they would think good, maybe great, or at the least interesting things about a man who hung a longhorn skull above his garage door. How many steamy river's edge summers and how many bitter Midwest winters can a longhorn skull stand up to? I'm not sure, but the horns were hanging above that door many years after I left for the University of Illinois in 1961, long after Mom had grown tired of complaining about it.

One of Dad's more ambitious projects, though he did not actually build much of it, stood between our house and its garage: our seldom used patio (or "potio" as Dad persisted in pronouncing it in spite of my enlightened corrections; "mull" for "mall" was another one of his maddening idiosyncrasies). I suppose the idea was for the family to sit out there and have a meal in nice weather or listen to baseball games on the massive old Crosley console radio that had moved with us from Lincoln Place to Grand Avenue to Pontoon Road. After the patio was flat-roofed, aluminum-screened and linoleumed, Dad bought some outdoor furniture for it: brown- and green-streaked plastic cushions attached to sturdy black steel tubing. On first inspection the patio seemed a fine addition to Chez Veizer; but everyone in the family except Dad soon realized--and had to admit--that in spite of the multitude of screens, hardly any air passed through them. The garage blocked off most of the flow, and only a perfect southern breeze, usually hot, dust-laden blasts in the summer, found the deeply inset front doorway. As Casey Stengel famously said of the new Busch Stadium after a brutally hot All-Star Game in 1966 when the temperature reached 105 degrees: "It holds the heat well." That was equally true of our patio. There were bamboo shades on the patio windows to absorb some of the glaring afternoon sun, but there was no overhead fan to move the thick air, and not enough cross ventilation to stir a feather or dry up the smallest drop of sweat. Our house on Pontoon Road was not air-conditioned either, but at least it was provided with window fans and a television.

The family gave up on the patio quickly and quietly after a few uncomfortable summer evenings. Little was said about it during the many years it stood there as a two-doored barrier between the garage and the rear porch of the house. Its two permanent--and legendary--inhabitants were trophy bass that Dad had caught: one was a five-pound largemouth enticed by an irresistible Crippled

Shad in nearby Lake Hillsboro, and the other an even more impressive smallmouth bass done in by a Lazy Ike on a weekend trip to Bull Shoals Lake in northern Arkansas. More than once when I was trying to get through all those doors late at night as quietly as I could, I thought with admiration, "These trophies deserve a place of their own." Then I dug the back door key out of the gaping mouth of the largemouth bass and continued my midnight creep.

CHAPTER 31

Uncle Joe

I'VE MENTIONED MY FATHER'S YOUNGER brother, my Uncle Joe earlier. He must have been in uniform when I first saw him because a
military image always comes to mind when I think of him. Joe was
a man made for a uniform: dapper, neat as the sharp creases in his
pants, never a hair out of place; in short, always ready for inspection.
My dad could be dressed up well--usually with Mom's help--and
always was for the funerals of friends and co-workers that seemed
to take place so often during my adolescence. As the years passed,
though, Dad seemed to care less and less about his appearance while
sitting on the front porch. A ribbed t-shirt was good enough for one
of his lengthy cigar-smoking sessions there, and on especially hot
and humid nights he favored shirtlessness. He relaxed on that porch,
watching traffic rumbling up and down Pontoon Road and coming straight at him on Terrace Lane. He waved at people he knew
or thought he recognized and those who honked. On the porch he
seemed to know nothing of time. Sometimes I sat with him and
wondered what he was thinking about while sitting on the steps of
that concrete porch. And I always will wonder.

I was once told that Uncle Joe's nickname in Lincoln Place was
Cheenchy Joe. Whether he deserved to be called "chincy" or whether
just being Hungarian was enough to merit the tag, I don't know. As
Andy Matoesian says in his interview about, what he calls, the most
popular method of Hungarian suicide: "Hungarians save the price of

a bullet and the rope can be re-used." Leon Sanasarian, who bought Yonch's Tavern in the 1960s, and others frequently echoed this droll observation for my benefit throughout my years in Granite City. But Uncle Joe was certainly generous with me. He gave me his Army dress hat and called me "General Eisenhower." Often I dragged the hat out of Mom's cedar chest and marched around the house in it. I loved that hat with its shiny black brim, its brown wool sides and drum-flat top, and especially its smooth silky lining. I cherished a picture we had of Uncle Joe in that very hat standing with some friends next to palm trees, bamboo clusters and other tropical plants. For a long time I believed that photo was taken at Guadalcanal or Iwo Jima or some other battleground in the Pacific. One day when I was fishing photographs I loved out of the bulging shoe box where they were kept, my mother told me that Uncle Joe had never left the United States and that the photo had been taken in a photographer's studio in Biloxi, Mississippi. I was beginning to realize that all was not as it seemed, that Santa Claus was a two-headed person named Mom and Dad.

Uncle Joe married Margaret Magyar, the attractive and stylish daughter of one of Grandpa Veizer's best friends in Lincoln Place. The story I heard was that the old friends had long wanted to match up two of their children in marriage. They got their wish after Uncle Joe returned from his WWII service and married Margie. Not long after that Grandpa died.

Joe and Margie Veizer, circa 1940

CHAPTER 32

The Veizer Genealogy

My grandfather died when I was only three years old, but I remember distinctly his scratchy grey sweater, his equally scratchy whiskers, and his even scratchier, heavily accented voice calling me "Pete." I think I squirmed around a lot when I was in the lap of all this scratchiness. That might have been why Uncle George conjured up the ineradicable notion that I had a worm up my butt, and he had just the pair of pliers to pull it out.

Recently I was contacted online by Louis Takacs, a grandson of one of Aunt Margie's sisters. He lives in the Netherlands now but was raised in St. Louis. His father was a Hungarian refugee who came to the United States in 1956. Louis, who has dual American and Hungarian citizenship, was kind enough to send me online photocopies of the Kompolt church's registers, hundreds of pages of the births, deaths, and marriages in Kompolt from 1819 to 1895, an online replica of the ledgers in Dr. Artner's office. These documents led me to the names of my grandfather's parents, Ferenc Vizer and his wife Mária Krisztián, names which I do not think my father knew.

Grandpa Veizer was 78 years old when he became ill and had to move in with Aunt Mary. For several years he had been living on a place we called "Grandpa's farm." The farm was near Maeystown, Illinois, in Monroe County, ten miles south of Waterloo and only three miles or so from the Mississippi River. He lived in a tin-roofed shack near a pond full of sunfish and turtles. His pet pig followed him when he went to town for mail or provisions. Except for a fifth or two of whiskey every week usually delivered by Aunt Mary and Uncle Julius, he required few comforts. He was a happy old man. My older cousin Ronnie used to stay with him in the summer when he was an adolescent, and some nights he would tell Ronnie, "Fix your dinner and go to bed. I'll be back in the morning. I'm going to see the 'widder' woman." Ronnie's widow Willie recently told me that when a visitor brought Grandpa a bottle of whiskey--the usual and expected offering--Grandpa would hide it in the cistern in case another visitor came along with another bottle: the appearance of demand needed to be kept up in order to maximize the supply.

Grandpa's old friend Mr. Magyar lived into his late 80s or early 90s. I remember his coming by the house with Uncle Joe one afternoon when I was in high school. Like Grandpa, he was a tough-looking little guy with rough, strong hands who spoke "broken" English. Unlike Grandpa, he had a faded blue identification number tattooed on his forearm that, as I recall, was from his time in the Austro-Hungarian army. I recently learned from Julianna Puskas's book about Hungarian immigrants that these tattoos were intended to discourage soldiers or those eligible for military service from emigrating, though a tattooed youth with some financial resources could leave Hungary after paying a heavy bond.

CHAPTER 33
Uncle Bill

UNCLE JOE DID NOT SEE combat in World War Two, but one of my uncles did: that was Bill Vivod, Aunt Betty's first husband, whose family had also come from Heves. Unlike nineteen thousand other American soldiers, Bill survived the Battle of the Bulge, the German army's desperate counterattack during the brutally cold winter of 1944-45. He and Aunt Betty, the youngest in the family, lived on Walnut, across the street from the high, red brick vista of American Steel Foundry. Theirs was a long white shotgun house with a delightful side porch so long that I could reach full running speed before I ran through the kitchen doorway. For my fourth birthday Uncle Bill bought me a marvel of a gift. Although I wore it out before I could form a lasting memory of the wonderful whole, the magic inside was a water pump that I could activate by rocking an armature back and forth. I can still remember the changes in pressure as water coursed through different parts of the pump. Was it an oil well? or a fire truck? or a water tank for servicing steam locomotives? No matter. I've been fascinated by moving water ever since.

Uncle Bill had a massive chest, which shows well in the picture I have of him in uniform. He had a reddish face and a kind manner, the only adult I can remember who would get down on his haunches to talk to me. He would have been as good a father as he was an uncle, I think. Like so many men who returned to Lincoln Place after WWII, Bill went to work at "the Commonwealth," as it was still called by most Lincoln Place residents. He was a chain man in #6 Building, not far from where my father worked in #10, also an area for finishing castings. As a chain man, Uncle Bill took orders from the crane man, who rode the building crane on its high tracks from one end of #6 Building to the other. Uncle Bill's job was to safely and securely attach the hooks at the ends of the chains hanging down from the crane to the casting after it had been worked on by grinders, chippers, burners, welders or "press men." Burners used acetylene torches to cut off risers, excess steel that rose out of the mold, and to burn out weak spots in the frames marked by inspectors. Chippers used small but powerful pneumatic hammers--hand-held jack hammers--to chip rough spots from the castings. Welders filled in the cracks that resulted from cooling, and they also strengthened the weak spots that showed up in X-rays. The grinders used powerful sanders with carborundum wheels to smooth the rough spots where the risers had been cut off, where the chipping hammers had battered, and where the welds had been made. When a casting was hooked properly and was safe to lift, the chain man gave a signal to the crane man, and off went the huge locomotive or railroad car underframes to the next work area. (Even after steam locomotives were phased out in the United States, General Steel continued to produce massive steam locomotive underframes for the wide gauge tracks of South Africa.) After the surface was "finished," the crane man had to move the castings to the monstrous press machines that straightened the slight warping that often developed during the cooling process.

One day when a twenty-ton railroad underframe was being lifted, it swung slowly toward Uncle Bill. He was trapped between a large structural beam and the corrugated steel wall. The casting pressed lightly against his abdomen before he could get out of the way. He thought he was fine, my dad told me, and he walked away under his own power. But two days later he died in the hospital of massive internal bleeding. My dad used to say with a shake of the head, "Bill survived the Battle of the Bulge to be killed in the Commonwealth."

I don't think Aunt Betty ever recovered from the shock of losing her first love.

Fifteen years later, during the summer before my junior year in college, I was working in #6 Building. On my first day, I was given a broom and a shovel. About an hour into my new job, I heard a crash at the other end of the building. A boxcar-end weighing at least a ton had fallen off its awkward stack and crushed the foot of the chain man. The foreman promoted me immediately to "chain man" and I received a fifteen-cent hourly raise. Before the stretcher and ambulance arrived, the shift foreman hurriedly told me that rubbing my belly as if I had just enjoyed a full meal indicated to the man up in the crane that it was safe to lift a load. That was the only instruction I ever received as a chain man, though the crane man would sometimes give me hand signals when he thought a load was not balanced well. I thought of Uncle Bill often and stayed on my toes. "Don't ever tell your mom what you're doing," my dad told me more than once. "And don't mention it to Aunt Betty either."

Elizabeth Veizer Vivod and Bill Vivod, circa 1940

CHAPTER 34

Miss Bessie's Nursery School

NOT VERY LONG AFTER UNCLE Bill died, my family moved from Lincoln Place to a larger house on Grand Avenue near Wilson Park to accommodate a third child: the darling of the family, Janice Sue. Janice arrived in the world shortly after we moved in. In the new house the baby had her own nursery room: bright-colored walls and Mother Goose linoleum on the floor. Each two-by-three foot slab of linoleum contained a colorful illustration and a few verses from one of those classics. I doubt if baby Janice noticed the floor much, but it fascinated me. I used to lie there studying the images and sounding out the words of the nursery rhymes.

Our first year on Grand Avenue, Shirley attended sixth grade at Niedringhaus School, and I was sent off to Miss Bessie's Nursery School for the morning session since there were no public school kindergartens in Granite City then. Every weekday morning, Mr. Tom, Bessie's husband, would drive up in his long green Studebaker. Where the back seat should have been stood eight or ten of my class-mates. There was little to hold on to, but since Mr. Tom was the slowest driver that can be imagined, handholds were unnecessary. It took a long time to travel the five blocks to Miss Bessie's nursery school, which was conducted in the kindliest fashion on the second floor of their house. We sang, and we slept on towels, I think. We must have learned something or absorbed something; however, I cannot recall any details except the names of two of my classmates:

Howard Helman and Margaret Ann Cariss. I learned not long ago that my cousin Pat lived across the alley from Miss Bessie and attended the afternoon session. Our "graduation ceremony"--minus the now obligatory gowns and mortarboards--was conducted in the auditorium of the YMCA. I bungled my recitation, a cute enough lapse to get a laugh. If I had really been going for laughs, though, I should have emulated the even more nervous young man who darkened the front of his pants mid-recitation. My hand was shaky, but I kept my powder dry, and I moved on to first grade at Niedringhaus School.

CHAPTER 35

Aunt Betty's Gifts

Two days before our second Christmas on Grand Avenue, Aunt Betty gave me an early Christmas gift, which I immediately unwrapped. I begged Mom to let me put on my new cowboy chaps and Red Ryder gloves. Since December 23 was a very cold day, the coldest of the year, she allowed me to put the chaps on over my pants. She was surprised that I was excited about wearing gloves. I had always refused to protect my hands even on the coldest days. My reasoning, as I recall, was that I could make a better, harder snowball bare-handed. Besides, hands dried out and warmed up much faster than gloves did. But I had never possessed a pair of gloves with long stiff cuffs sporting lengthy plastic fringes. I showed off my new regalia to a friend across the street, and we soon decided that the most comfortable place to be on that bitterly cold day was next to a small smoldering alley fire.

An open alley fire, or one in a 35-gallon steel drum, or a smoldering fire in a concrete block ash pit were common enough sights in those days. Piles of leaves big enough for a kid to hide in were commonly burned in the gutter in front of the house, carefully tended, of course, by a dad or mom with a rake. At that time most Granite Cityans spoke of factory smoke as a sign of prosperity, not air pollution. This was true even in the parts of town where houses were darkened with soot from Granite City Steel's blast furnace when the wind was favorable. On that frozen day my friend and I sat on cold gravel and hardened mud in the alley and stretched out our legs, surrounding the little fire. I relaxed, enjoying the warm toastiness and thinking of campfire scenes from the Hopalong Cassidy movies I watched every Saturday morning. I can't remember what I noticed first: the sharp pain deep in my leg or my smoldering pant leg. Numbed by the cold, I had slow-roasted my leg to the third degree. As soon as I jumped up, the lower left legging of my new chaps burst into flame. My good fortune was that I was wearing gloves for the first time in my life. With my well-protected hands I was able to beat out and smother the flames as I instinctively rolled on the damp ground. My friend ran away shouting wildly to his own house, but he did scream loud enough to alert my mother. Mom rushed out to the alley and immediately called Dad at work. That is who I was screaming for, the dad who could make everything OK. He sped home from the Commonwealth and took me to the emergency room at St. Elizabeth's Hospital.

Two days later it was Christmas. Since we were in a new location, our home was family headquarters that holiday season. I greeted my aunts, uncles and cousins with my lower leg wrapped in yellowing gauze. I remember enjoying the attention of all the Veizers who shared our Christmas on Grand Avenue and then telling them over and over, "It don't hurt." To prove it, I shot and rebounded my new basketball for hours. My new basket was attached to the top of a closet door in the hallway. On that day at least, no one complained about the loud "ding" produced every time my ball found its way through the rim and depressed the bright orange tongue of the dinger.

I was deemed ready to return to my first-grade class on the first school day after New Year's Day. That day or the next I was punished for disgusting the girl sitting behind me by lifting my leg and exposing enough ooze and scar tissue to make her scream. My way with the fairer sex has not improved much since then. When I was six years old, the scar tissue extended from my ankle to my knee.

Now it only ascends to the first bulge of my calf muscle, proof that in one respect, at least, I have grown up.

As radiant and energetic as she seemed that Christmas, her first as a widow, I knew that Aunt Betty must be lonely and unhappy. She hugged me harder and more often than she ever had. Uncle Bill had been a devoted husband, a hard worker, and in addition a genial, easy-going Magyar--not the usual thing according to my memory. Since Aunt Betty was the baby of the family, only in her teens when her mother died, my father and Aunt Mary, whom she had lived with after Grandma Veizer died, worried about her and looked out for her. In the early 1950s Aunt Betty was married briefly to a man who was running what was left of the Bella Vista, an old roadhouse on Long Lake. (By the way, a wonderful memoir entitled *Christmas at Long Lake: A Childhood Memory* was published a few years ago by Rick Skwiot, who lived in an drafty old camp on the lake in the 1950s.) A few years later she met Chris Reynolds, a widower from Belleville who had a teenage son named David. Chris was a salesman for Krey Packing Company by day. At night during the racing season, he was a betting clerk at the Fairmont race course. In the early 1960s, Betty and Chris (whom Aunt Mary always called "Christ" with a short "i") bought a house on Clark Avenue in Granite City.

I know they lived there by New Year's Day in 1964 because it was in their basement where I glumly watched the University of Illinois football team win the Rose Bowl. Dick Butkus, Wiley Fox (my one acquaintance on the Fighting Illini's football roster) and the rest of that stellar squad of thirteen high NFL draft picks dominated the University of Washington and won it for the Big Ten by the score of 17-7. I was glum because I was not AT the Rose Bowl. I had saved the money to go to California from my meager earnings filing journal articles on the crowded shelves of the University of Illinois Physics Library and had transportation worked out with some of my friends at U of I, where I was a junior. However, my father had stopped my travel plans by invoking The Holiday Rule: the family had to be together during holidays. No son could be out risking his life on a road trip to California and back. I didn't follow the logic, but I had not the will to defy him in this. My pathetic revenge was to squander all my Physics Library savings in the bars and night clubs of Granite City, Madison, and St. Louis's Gaslight Square. And then to quit my dull job as soon as I got back to Champaign-Urbana. This may have been the beginning of the end of the American Work Ethic: what good was making money if you could not spend it as you liked?

Aunt Betty's luck was to turn bad again when her husband Chris died of a heart attack in the early 1970s, not too long before my father passed away. In the last year of my father's life, when his breathing was so difficult that he had to sleep sitting up, he was often at his sister Betty's, unclogging a drain or changing a fuse, starting her car on a cold day or digging it out on a snowy day. My mother's concerns for his health and safety were ignored as Dad went to the aid of his little sister, who, he understood, needed more than his handyman skills. She was lonely, left adrift once again, and needed to know that someone cared, that she still counted for something, that something in her life could still be fixed. After my father died, Johnny Toth, Aunt Mary's son, who was far from healthy himself, was called into service every week for years to bring her groceries. And then Johnny Toth went to the Veterans' Hospital for the final time. In her last years Aunt Betty seldom left the house and often would not answer her door or her phone. She had a standing order for a pizza delivery every day at noon. She chose to live in the basement of her home, below her neat and well-furnished living room and bedroom, until the end of her life.

CHAPTER 36

Dad's Forced Retirement

IN 1965 DAD WAS STRETCHERED out of General Steel when his lungs hemorrhaged and he began to cough up blood. He had worked there since 1922 when he was fourteen, except during the worst years of the Great Depression. He was only 56. He proudly wore on his wrist a golden Bulova watch awarded for twenty-five years service. For thirty-five years of service he sported in his lapel a gold pin shaped and designed like the General Steel shield. With raspy voices raised to overcome the deficiencies of their "Commonwealth ears," my dad and his retired friends occasionally gathered in a local bar, sharing beer, home grown vegetables, fish from their latest trips, and endless stories. Here they did not have to shout over the din of the factory directly into the ears of their listeners, but they spoke just as loud anyway out of habit. No matter where conversation began it always reverted to their work, their workplace, and other workers. They laughed at themselves and called their lengthy tale-telling sessions "Drilling Underframes." Not all of my father's co-workers developed tuberculosis like my father, but all of them developed silicosis to some degree.

With the introduction of pneumatic hammers and sandblasting at the turn of the twentieth century, the incidence of silicosis increased rapidly. More than 400 workers died of dust and sand in their lungs during and after the construction of a tunnel in West Virginia the early 1930s. The Hawk's Nest Tunnel Disaster still is remembered as America's worst industrial catastrophe. When sputum tests showed that my father had tuberculosis, X-rays were taken of his lungs. However, those lungs were so clouded with microscopic black sand from the foundry that the dark images on the X-ray were useless to his doctors, who were trying to locate the infected places on his lungs. Silicosis increased a worker's risk of TB while increasing the difficulty of treating it. Several of my father's friends and co-workers had already died of this deadly combination.

Fortunately for Dad, the Madison County Tuberculosis Sanatorium on the outskirts of Edwardsville was still open and a bed was available. Soon after his collapse at General Steel he was admitted to the county facility, as his sisters Anna and Katie had been many years before. He was also fortunate that several miracle drugs, and the first ones that could be taken orally, had been developed to treat tuberculosis in the 1950s and the early 1960s, making a relatively fast cure possible for the first time. Earlier generations of drugs had been too toxic to be effective, and recovery by strict bed rest, a chilled environment, and pneumothorax--or collapsing the lung--was excruciating. And this treatment took years. Of course, at first my father did not like the regimen required: bed rest and 20-30 pills a day. However, the positive effects of the four different pills he had to swallow every few hours were apparent within his first month there. He began to feel better than he had in a long time.

Like many people in Granite City, he had probably first been infected by the TB germ through close contact with family members, friends, or fellow workers. He had been carrying the bacillus in his body for a long time but had not realized it. While he was young and in good health, the TB germ was dormant. Ten years before his last day at the foundry, however, he had lost more than forty pounds in a few months; his weight plummeted to less than 110 pounds. He could not sleep; he looked like walking death. Finally he went to the doctor, but instead of the cancerous tumor he expected to hear about, the doctor found a hyperactive thyroid gland. The removal of the gland in his throat was a routine operation. He recovered his health and his lost weight rapidly--except that the throat incision from the thyroid operation refused to heal. The presence of the tuberculosis germ in his blood was found to be responsible for the slow healing. He was prescribed INH (Isoniazid), the first of the TB miracle drugs. This little white pill suppressed the tuberculosis germs in his system, and his neck wound healed. He was supposed to continue taking INH pills every day, but after a while he began complaining of its terrible side effects-- which might well have been the effects of aging--and would not take his pill regularly in spite of Mom's best efforts.

Obviously, Dad was not the most cooperative of patients, nor had his behavior in previous visits to the hospital been angelic. He didn't like needles; he didn't like people fussing about him; he didn't like being confined. And he did not like nurses and aides--women!!-- seeing him half-dressed and in a weakened state. Nevertheless, his charm and genuine interest in others elevated him well above "worst" patient statue.

He had a rough affection for our old family doctor, Jacob Schermer, but he did not automatically trust those in authority, quite the contrary. I spent many hours listening to Dad summarize stories in the St. Louis *Post-Dispatch* about the misdeeds of doctors, judges, religious leaders, and what are now called "CEOs." During one visit to his doctor Dad questioned a charge on a hospital bill, and Dr. Schermer made the mistake of saying, "What are you worried about, John? The insurance is going to pay for it." That casual attitude toward responsibility and a number on a bill (all money was real to Dad) infuriated him. He was not going to be a passive party to what he thought might be some kind of scam, and he made that absolutely clear to the doctor.

The only thing Dad complained about at the sanatorium during my visits was having to force down so many pills every day. He enjoyed most of the other patients: a fresh new audience always perked him up. And he made new friends among the patients and nurses. Perhaps his hospital stay, long as it was, was easier because there were no needles or IV drips, and he was not in pain or discomfort after the first couple of weeks there. Most important, he developed a great respect for the doctor in charge of the sanatorium, an intelligent and humane pulmonary specialist from the Dominican Republic. One of the doctor's longtime friends was fellow Dominican Julian Javier, the second baseman of the St. Louis Cardinals, who had won the World Series in 1964, the year before Dad entered the sanatarium, and would again in 1967. On one of the Cardinals' open dates, Julian visited his old friend and spent some time with the patients in Dad's ward. The St. Louis Browns had moved to Baltimore more than ten years earlier to become the Orioles, so Dad had once again become a Cardinal fan, enjoying the heydays of Lou Brock, Curt Flood, Bob Gibson, Ken Boyer, Julian Javier, and Granite City's own Dal Maxville, whose father worked at General Steel. That day with "Hoolie" was a highlight of Dad's long stay in the sanatorium, almost as memorable as the day he was released and Mother drove him home, six months after he was admitted.

Although Dad felt much better than he had six months before, he was unable to return to work at General Steel. He retired with a small pension from GSI, Social Security disability, and Illinois State Workman's Compensation for his wasted lungs: a check for $10,000. He was never again as active as he wanted to be. He would go on fishing trips occasionally, but struggling up even a small bank on a lake or stream so taxed his lungs that he returned home exhausted. When pushing the lawnmower became too strenuous for him, he would sit on the porch and supervise Mom. More and more often, he could not sleep in a bed because lying down made breathing difficult, stressful. What sleep he managed was achieved sitting up in his living room easy chair.

His life would have been bleak indeed were it not for my mother's patient love and understanding and his grandchildren. My father was forty when my younger sister Janice was born: Dad then gave the first signs then that he would be an enthusiastic and indulgent grandfather. As happens so often when children's births are spread out, all the rules seem to change for "the baby." My older sister Shirley and I used to marvel at the affection he showed for "Looly Flooly" as he liked to call her. She was so sweet and pleasant a baby and child that my older sister and I could not feel jealous of her. Moreover, she showed no signs of being spoiled. We did envy her the spell she cast on our father. For all she knew Dad had always been a soft touch, a gentle hand, and a welcome lap. Ten years later, when Shirley made Dad a grandfather by giving birth to Suzy and, shortly after that, to Johnny, he was in his early 50s and prepared to be an extraordinary grandfather.

Grandpa made up stories for his grandchildren and narrated them in mesmerizing style. Every month there was a visit from Shirley's family, or we made the three-hour drive to Champaign. One Christmas Eve when Suzy and Johnny were too excited to go to sleep, their Grandpa Veizer told them that Santa Claus would not leave their gifts under the tree if they were not in bed when he arrived. This information did little to calm them down. A few minutes later Dad sneaked out of the house with a cowbell that he'd hidden away and some jingly bells. He must have mounted a ladder, too, for scraping on the roof accompanied the bells. I do not think he ho-ho-hoed because his raspy voice would have given him away. The bells and the sound of Santa's sleigh on the roof proved to be enough of an alarm. I will never forget the looks of astonishment on Suzy's and Johnny's faces while they froze for a second, then squealed before sprinting to their beds. Three years after my father was released from the sanatorium, there would be two new grandchildren to entertain.

Christine was Shirley's late baby, and Eric, born on an Army base in Hawaii, was Janice's first. They were about a year apart, and they came along at just the right time to raise Dad's spirits. He was not well, but you would never guess that when the grandkids were in the house. There were new stories, the most memorable about an old Indian chief who lived in the house. Dad never tired of relating the old Indian's adventures in the basement, in the closet, in the attic. The wily chief kept just out of sight. Every brush of a branch on the side of the house, every click of the furnace was a sign of Boola Boola's presence. Sometimes Dad caught a glimpse of him, but the Indian was always a little too fast for the children. Christine lived in Champaign, but "little ol' Eric," as Mom loved to call him, was at the house for hours every day after Randy, his father, finished two years in the Army. While Janice worked and Randy worked and took classes at SIU-Edwardsville, Eric spent the day with Dad and Mom. Christine would visit at least one weekend a month, always hungry for new stories. After a month of entertaining Eric, he would have a full and well-rehearsed repertoire. No one in the family will ever forget the sight of Dad in his easy chair with mellow, enchanted Eric on one knee and wide-eyed wiggling Christine on the other.

As the effects of the silicosis worsened, the difficulty of breathing put a strain on Dad's heart. He was told he had less than 30% lung capacity. In the late summer of 1974, he was admitted to the hospital with congestive heart failure. Though he recovered quickly and returned home, I received a call a few weeks later from my mother. Dad was in intensive care at St. Elizabeth's Hospital again, not expected to survive. I rushed home from New Orleans to be with him.

When Mom and I arrived at the hospital, she went into the Intensive Care ward, then came out and told me I should go in alone to see him. He did not look too bad. He had not lost weight; his color was good. Because he had a tube in his throat for oxygen, he could not speak. I could, but it was difficult for me to utter anything other than "Dad, I love you." Even before I said that, he grabbed my hand and smiled a radiant smile, the most radiant smile I have ever seen. It was like one of those animated drawings of the sun looking down on the best and brightest of days. "Life was good," the smile said to me. That was my father's last gift to me.

I drove back to New Orleans the next day for a new-teacher orientation session. A few days later Mom called and said that he was doing better, out of intensive care and in a single room. The oxygen tube had been removed from his throat, she told me, and he was going to come home in a few days. An hour before dawn two days later, Mom called again. Dad's heart had given up its struggle.

CHAPTER 37

A Search Begins, My
First Visit to Hungary

IN THE SUMMER OF 2003, twenty-nine years after my father died, I fulfilled an oft-delayed promise to myself by traveling to Hungary and spending more than three weeks there. Although some of my father's Beck relatives in New Jersey had managed to visit Hungary and Kompolt in the 1960s during the Cold War, no one that I knew from Lincoln Place had visited there since Matilda Wiezer in 1938. As interested as my father was in all things Hungarian, he had shown no more desire to visit the Old Country than to return to the Great Northwest.

Most of my time in Hungary was spent in its fascinating and lovely capital city Budapest. I found a small room in Pest on Rákóczi, a boulevard that leads to the Erzsébet Bridge, which spans the Danube and connects Pest and Buda. For two weeks I traveled from one end of Pest to the other. I walked along the Danube past the magnificent Parliament--the largest such building in the world. I strolled halfway across the historic Chain Bridge to descend to Margitsziget, a two-mile long island-park in the middle of the Danube. I took a long trek to huge Heroes' Square in eastern Pest dominated by a dozen larger-than-life statues--great figures of Hungarian history--and to the spacious City Park behind it. One night I searched for and found the Bábszinház, the puppet theatre, to attend a folk dancing program.

My one sweaty subway trip took me to Újpest to see their soccer team play Debrecen. My lengthy walks in Pest almost always ended at Fekete Szakáll (Blackbeard's), a small restaurant near the beautifully restored Jewish Synagogue. When the weather was good, as it usually was, I sat at an outside table eating *hal* (fish) or *csirke* (chicken), or *töltött káposzta* (stuffed cabbage) and drinking a Hungarian pilsener. Láci, their neat and trim waiter with sharp features and a full head of hair, reminded me of Uncle Joe. Ferenz the chef, who looked enough like Láci to be his cousin, had one answer when I asked about something that was not on the day's menu: "Tomorrow!" And the next day I would be dining on *paprikas*, or goulash, or whitefish from Lake Balaton. Fekete Szakáll prepared me well for the friendliness and hospitality I was to encounter later in my Hungarian journey.

I spent two days walking up and down the hills of Buda on the western side of the Danube. (The two old cities joined to become Budapest in 1873.) The Buda hills guaranteed good exercise but also the prospect of relaxing after my walks in one of the bath houses fed by some of the many hot springs bubbling under the hills. The most famous and elaborate of these is Gellert's, which has several pools, each with water of a different temperature plus an outdoor pool at normal swimming pool temperature where families tend to congregate. The beautiful interior of Gellert's is highlighted by intricate mosaics and numerous statues representing the 19th century's ideals of grace and beauty. Gellert's was designed to provide one of the most relaxing atmospheres in the world, and it does.

In the middle of Buda's Castle Hill District sits Fisherman's Bastion, which occupies the site of the defensive walls of Buda. Two furious last-ditch battles were waged there. The first was against the Turks in the 17th century. The second was fought at the end of WWII between the last remnants of the German occupying force and the Russian army, which "liberated" Budapest from the Nazis only to secure it within its own sphere behind "the Iron Curtain" in 1949. Budapest suffered tremendous damage during the 1945 siege by the Soviet Army. Street-by-street and house-by-house bat-tles persisted for six weeks. Eighty per cent of Budapest's buildings were destroyed or damaged; all the bridges over the Danube were destroyed; and thousands of civilians were killed in the bombing, the crossfire, and in attempts to retreat behind the German lines.

A few months before the destructive Russian siege, German troops had moved into Hungary in force when it was discovered that the leaders of the Hungarian government, who were supposed to be in league with Germany and the other members of the Axis, were attempting to work out in secret a separate truce with Allied forces. These leaders were arrested by officers of the German Army's SS and replaced by puppets from the Arrow Cross, the Hungarian Fascist party. The Germans, who had long been critical of the Hungarian government's foot-dragging when it came to the deportation of the Jewish population, especially from Budapest, immediately autho-rized the rounding up of Jews, marching them to box cars destined for death camps. According to Lucy Davidowicz in *The War Against the Jews*, the German's haste was such that troop trains were often sidetracked to make way for trainloads of Jewish people. In a matter of months, according to the Third Reich's own scrupulously kept records, 400,000 Hungarian Jews were transported and extermi-nated in concentration camps like Auschwitz and Sobibor. Thanks to the efforts of Raoul Wallenberg and others, a few thousand Jewish people did survive this last surge of the Holocaust. Today the Jewish population in Budapest is slowly growing with emigrés from Israel, the United States and elsewhere.

Today, Budapest shows few scars from World War Two. Bridges and buildings have been reconstructed; transportation has been restored and steadily improved. Only a few bullet holes and blast marks remain from the violent but brief Revolution of 1956. After the initial withdrawal of Russian troops from the city in late October 1956, the revolutionaries waited in vain for help from the United Nations and the United States. What arrived instead after Hungary's brief taste of independence were Russian tanks. In the subsequent fighting 1500 Russian troops and 20,000 Hungarians were killed; before Soviet domination was restored, 190,000 Hungarians escaped across the border to begin new lives in the free world. The United States alone took in more than 30,000 refugees, and many more were resettled in England, Canada, Australia and South America.

After two weeks in Budapest, I boarded a train for northeast Hungary and made the two-hour journey to Eger, the county seat of Heves and the closest city to Kompolt. Rolling my luggage down the main street in the old section of Eger, I noticed a newly refurbished hotel called the Szent János. Considering that use of my father's name a good omen, I secured a room and checked in. For the next three days I wandered around Eger, one of the first Magyar settlements in Central Europe and the heart of one of Hungary's wine districts. Eger is also a religious center, sometimes called the "Rome of Hungary" because St. Stephen established a bishopric there in the 11th century and in 1814 it was made an archbishopric see. For all these reasons and because of its historical importance as the site of a fort where the Hungarians fought off the Turks in the 16th century, it is a popular year-round tourist destination. The remains of the fort are manned by "soldiers" in period uniforms and tours are conducted in the summer months.

Surely one of the factors that keeps Eger's history alive is the legend of Bull's Blood wine, called in Hungarian "Egri Bikavér." The Turkish soldiers besieging the fortress in 1552 supposedly came to believe that the staunch defense by the Magyar defenders was fueled by bull's blood, which the Magyars were consuming in copious amounts on the ramparts: "Hungarian courage" as it were. In 1596 another Turkish army, larger and, perhaps, less intimidated by the "bull's blood" myth, succeeded in capturing the castle and the city. The Turks held sway in the region and in much of Hungary for nearly 150 years. The Turks are long gone, but the only minaret in Hungary remains, towering above tourist shops and small cafes.

When I was in Eger at The Valley of Beautiful Women in 2003, Bull's Blood wine at fifty cents a glass was still fueling the afternoons and evenings of residents and tourists alike.

The central feature of The Valley is, oddly enough, a hill. Tunneled deeply into the base of this hill are numerous wineries. Many of them have restaurants or bars in their forward sections and all of them have counters in the rear where bottles of the house vintages can be purchased. In late afternoon four- or five-piece gypsy ensembles begin to play, featuring a swaying maestro on violin and a lightning fast maestro on an ornately carved cimbalom, the Hungarian version of the hammer dulcimer. I am a person who can be carried away by wine or song, so I was doubly transported. The "women" part of the old equation was supplied by the girlfriends of two Aussie backpackers. The five of us closed down the Valley, for that night anyway. Without the backpackers' keen sense of direction, I might still be wandering the outback of Heves. Once we were back on the main street of Eger, I invited the two Brits who had joined our party at some point in the night to my hotel. The Szent János contained a lovely patio and had had the foresight to fill the mini-refrigerator in my room with beer and wine, so our conversation continued into the morning hours. As so often was the case during my first visit to Hungary, my timing--or good luck--was perfect. The first complaints about the noise we were making on the patio came just after the little refrigerator was emptied. Better yet, not a word of complaint was aimed at me by hotel management. Between my first and second nap that day my little refrigerator was promptly refilled, the sight of which, I must admit, was not as appealing when I woke up as it had been the night before.

CHAPTER 38

Kompolt at Last, July 2003

AFTER A MUCH NEEDED RECOVERY day I made plans to visit Kompolt, my ultimate destination. I had learned that every hour or so, a bus left the central station in Eger for Kompolt and some other villages on the road to Miskolc. The next morning at 8:30 I grabbed the Veizer family photo album I had assembled, which I hoped would be my entree to Kompolt, and climbed the steep hill to the bus depot. Since none of the buses displayed "Kompolt" on their marquees and several of them were idling, I had to extend my communication skills to the limit to discover the correct one. I climbed onto a half-full bus and found a seat to myself near the middle exit. After the bus stopped at a few isolated spots to let a person or two off, I realized that I had seen no signs along the road for Kompolt or any other village. "Had we passed Kompolt?" I asked myself. "Was I on the wrong bus?"

Across the aisle from me was a kindly-looking elderly lady who had evidently made an early shopping trip to Eger. In her lap were a small bag of groceries and some flowers in a box. I pinned my hopes on her. I scooted over in my seat and gestured to her. When I gained her attention, I said "Americai vagyok." ("I am American," a good excuse for not knowing much) and "Kompolt." Then I showed her my passport, which she examined. After a moment she looked at me and exclaimed, "Elemér Vizer! Elemér Vizer!" "No, Keith Veizer," I said. She pointed to herself and said, "Erzsébet. Erzsébet

Fehér." Then she said "öt," the word for "five," and pointed at her watch. Five minutes later she held my hand and led me off the bus in Kompolt.

As we walked she smiled and laughed gently to herself, murmuring "Elemér Vizer" and shaking her head. A brisk five-minutes took us to a small white frame house which reminded me of Aunt Anna's house, the kind of dwelling we used to call a "Cooper Home" in Granite City. As in the sections of Nameoki built for WWII veterans, these homes in Kompolt were lined up ten or twelve to a block. Ms. Fehér went to the front door and knocked. A lady about the same age as my guide answered the door, and obviously they knew each other well. After a little back and forth in Hungarian, I was introduced by one Erzsébet to another, Erzsébet Vizer, Elemér Vizer's wife.

Erzsébet Vizer motioned for me to come into the house. Soon I was presented to Elemér, who had been in the back yard tending to his garden. He motioned for me to sit down at the dining room table, and I opened the photo album and gestured for him to page through. Erzsébet had already put some cheese and bread on the table for me, and now she was in the kitchen cooking up some scrambled eggs. Elemér poured shots of rum for both of us before he opened my album.

While Elemér looked through the photos, I noted that he had a barrel chest like most of the Granite City Veizer men but was a few inches taller. His face was flushed and round. Erzsébet reminded me most of Aunt Katy, both in her looks and her manner. After eating, I met their granddaughter, ten-year-old Franciska, who was with them for the day. Then Elemér's brother, László, who lived down the street, joined us. Franciska's brother, fifteen-year-old Daniel, who was studying English in school, stopped by briefly with a friend.

Elemér and Lajos were interested in the old photos, but they did not recognize anyone in them. Then Elemér made a phone call. Shortly after that the three of us were on our way to the main office of the primary employer in Kompolt, The Plant Improvement Institute. This business, established in 1918, develops grain and grass seeds for specific climates and soils around the world. Elemér had worked there for most of his adult years, retiring as chief accountant. When we arrived at the Institute, Elemér introduced me to its CEO, Alájós Fehér, who speaks several languages including English. He served as our translator for more than an hour while I asked questions about the history of Kompolt and the Vizers.

I learned first through Alájós, and later from other sources, that beginning in late 1944 when the Soviet army reached northeast Hungary, thousands of Hungarians, especially those of German descent, were deported to the Ukraine and elsewhere in the Soviet Union to be used as forced labor. This was done by authority of the Paris Treaty, an agreement among the Allies--England, the U.S.A. and the Soviet Union--in 1943. The massive infusion of labor from citizens of the Axis nations was intended as war reparations for the Soviets, who lost more than twenty-five million soldiers and civilians during World War II according to *The Historical Encyclopedia of World War II*. After the war was over, the Soviets continued to round up residents from other parts of Hungary, Germany, Romania, and the other members of the Axis powers. No research on this subject was possible until the dissolution of the Soviet Union, but the Red Cross estimates that some 874,000 men and women were deported. Some were imprisoned but most were used for forced labor (ironically called *malenkij robot*, "a little labor"). Many men and women died in transit, and over the next few years approximately one-third of the laborers died in the camps themselves from malnutrition, exposure, and disease.

There is a plaque on the side of the Catholic church in Kompolt. It contains the names of seventy-one citizens of Kompolt who were transported to work camps in December 1944 and January 1945:

eight Vizers are listed, including Lajos Vizer and his father Elemér, Sr. There is a monument in front of the church which memorializes the names of those who died before returning: among the twelve who died are four Vizers. Those who survived the work camps were brought back to Kompolt in flat-bed trucks thirty-two months after being seized. There was a joyous ringing of church bells then for these men and women who, according to Emöke Abasári, were "nothing but skin and bone." Some, like Elemér and Lajos Vizer's father, did not recover their health and died not long after returning. Many others suffered from physical and/or mental problems for the rest of their lives.

For many others with German roots in Hungary there was no returning home. In *Iron Curtain, The Crushing of Eastern Europe*, Anne Applebaum states that the Soviets ultimately deprived 185,000 German-Hungarians of house and property and resettled them to East Germany. In Kompolt, however, perhaps because of their families' presence there for two hundred years, most of the residents whose ancestors came from Germany were allowed to remain. However, after the Communists gained full control of the government in 1949, it seized their lands to create communal farms.

It was Daniel Vizer who would establish contact with me a few months after I returned to the United States and provide me with my first written information on the history of Kompolt. Over the years I communicated with him regularly online. About a year after my first visit he translated for me a document with some information on Kompolt in the Middle Ages and also provided me with a list of the German families that had settled Kompolt in 1754. (See the Appendix II for the complete list of family names.) Although the area around the village had been settled since at least the 12th century, in the middle of the 18th century it was a desolate area, depopulated by almost two centuries of conflict with the Turks. In

1754 after the Habsburg's armies pushed out the Turks, eighty families of Catholic peasants from Alsace in southern Germany, three of them named Wieser, were allowed to resettle the land around Kompolt. This land had been granted to Lord Antal Grassalkovich, one of the most important men in the Austro-Hungarian Empire. One of his palaces still stands in Kompolt not far from the Kompolt church.

Since serfdom did not end in Hungary until 1848, these eighty heads of family were technically "bondmen," allowed to settle and farm the land under certain conditions. Initially each family was allowed about twenty acres of land with additional pasturage, also land for a house and lumber to build it. They were also granted six tax-free years, but they were required to provide clearly established quotas of corn and other grains, chickens and eggs, etc. to the owner of the land, Grassalkovich and his descendants. To me this arrangement sounds rather like sharecropping in the southern United States, a system which emerged after the Civil War. As the population in the village increased in the 19th century faster than the land available, some children in large families had to move beyond farming. Some sought education or a job in the towns or cities. Some made advantageous marriages. Many emigrated to America, some with the idea of earning money to buy additional land when they returned to Hungary. However, a majority of these emigrants ultimately decided to stay in America.

After we left the office of Alájós Fehér, Elemére, his brother, and I walked to the Kompolt Catholic church to look at the three memorial stones outside the church. One listed the names of soldiers from Kompolt who had died in World War One. Another listed the names of local soldiers killed in World War Two. The third contained the list of those I mentioned earlier: casualties of the Soviet forced work camps. One of these four Vizer names was "Jakab Vizer," whose identity I was to learn a few years later.

A Memorial to those "Dragged off and Sacrificed" in 1944-45

In the nearby cemetery were, as Elemér and Lajos said repeatedly, "sok (many) Vizer." It was not difficult for me to trace the evolution of the spelling of our family name as I took photos of tombstones in the cemetery. On the oldest stones, weathered and barely readable, the spelling was "Wieser," the original German spelling. By the mid-1800s, the spelling was usually "Vizer," for in 1848 German ceased being the official language in Hungary. Some of the more recent tombstones were engraved with variations seen in Granite City today: Veizer and Wiezer--but the great majority were spelled "Vizer." There were also gravestones inscribed with the family names of other Hungarian families in Granite City as they were spelled in Kompolt: Yuhász, Kovács, Majláth, Szűcs, Szeposi, Szuromi, Jéger, Dorogházi, Lenárt, Szigetközi, Fülöp, Jakkel and others. All these correspondences reinforced the information in the Ellis Island records: many, perhaps most, of those who emigrated between 1890 and 1914 from Kompolt and Hevesmegye, the county that Kompolt is a part of, settled in Granite City.

Near the cemetery were the long low houses of Old Kompolt where my grandparents and several generations of Vizers had lived. These very old houses have not been abandoned but are now inhabited primarily by families of poor Hungarians and Roma. Some of the one-story buildings still have small stables attached to them, similar to 17th and 18th century houses I have seen in New England. "New" Kompolt, where Elemér and Erzsébet live, is about a half-mile from the old village and seems to be about the size of Lincoln Place, with 2000 or so inhabitants. These modest but well-maintained houses lie along several streets that parallel the highway between Eger and Miskolc.

After our walk from the Kompolt cemetery through grazing land and playing fields to Elemér's home, I had about an hour left until the bus to Eger arrived. With my dictionary and phrase book at hand, I reopened my photo album trying to find a connection between Elemér and Erzsébet and the Vizers who had emigrated a hundred years before. I told them that I was from Illinois, which they had not heard of. "Is that near Texas?" they asked. They knew about Texas. And Houston. And Las Vegas. And Los Angeles. I think I was showing them a picture of my Aunt Nonnie—"Anna Krisztián," I emphasized because I had learned that "Krisztián" was Erzsébet's maiden name. I then added that Aunt Nonni had been married in the Kompolt church before she came to "Granite City." It was as if lightning had struck! "Granite City!" Erzsébet exclaimed. "My mother was born in Granite City!"

Over the next hour Erzsébet explained to me slowly that her grandmother, whose married name was Haydu, had immigrated to Granite City with her husband in about 1910. In 1914 she and her two-year-old Hungarian-American daughter returned to Kompolt for a visit. After World War I erupted later that year, travel across the Atlantic was impossible. Mother and daughter were stranded in Kompolt. Before the war ended, Mrs. Haydu died, probably in the Spanish influenza pandemic which killed millions of people around the world during and after World War I. Her American daughter, Erzsébet's mother, was raised by relatives and spent the rest of her long life in Kompolt. She married a man whose last name was Krisztián, also the family name of Grandpa Vizer's first wife. Even though Erzsébet's mother was an American citizen, she never returned to America. She died just a few years before my visit in 2003. After our mutual connection to Granite City was established, Elemér and Erzsébet's generosity and hospitality became keen interest and friendliness.

László, Elemér, Franciska, and Erzsébet Vizer, Kompolt, 2003

CHAPTER 39

Cousin Pat

AFTER I RETURNED FROM KOMPOLT, I tried to contact Matilda Wiezer Olsen a couple of times on visits to Granite City. My father had mentioned to me more than once that Matilda had visited Kompolt in the late 1930s. Now that I had been to Kompolt I wanted to compare notes with her. Mathilda Wiezer was the daughter of Leslie Wiezer (born László Vizer), and she was the mother of Patricia Olsen, who graduated from Granite City High School and the University of Illinois with me. Pat and I were both English majors; and we both wound up teaching composition and literature for forty years. I had talked to Pat's mother only once in my life. In that conversation she explained to me that the Vizers were originally Germans. I had long suspected this because I knew that our name did not look or sound very Hungarian. Whenever I had asked my father about this anomaly, he said that "*viz*" meant water in Hungarian, which is true, but....

Matilda Wiezer Olsen, 1938

When I knocked on Mrs. Olsen's door after I returned from Hungary, no one answered. On my next visit to Granite City, I discovered that her only son Bud was still living in the house for part of every year. Bud told me that his mother had resided in a nursing home in Edwardsville for several years, but that she had died a year or so before. He showed me some large family wedding pictures from the 1920s and 1930s that were stored in the garage and--what turned out to be more important--gave me his sister Pat's phone number in central Illinois. Pat and I had not seen or talked to each other since our college days, but we talked on the phone as if we had just bumped into each other in an off-campus coffee shop. Pat informed me that her mother had passed her last days happily primarily because she was able to speak Hungarian with several other elderly people there. Pat said that she herself spoke Hungarian until she was three years old because she and her mother lived with her mother's parents while Pat's father was soldiering in World War II. However, she had forgotten almost all of it. She only remembered that her grandmother had called her "kis ördög."

"So you were a little devil," I said, finding use for one of my scraps of Hungarian.

"I was," she said. "But Grandma said it lovingly."

"But she must have said it often for you to remember it so well."

My first telephone conversation with Pat lasted over an hour. I told her about my visit to Kompolt and promised I would send her copies of some photos I had taken there. She told me that she had many photographs from her mother's trip to Kompolt in 1938 and also family letters, documents, and portraits. She had been wanting to organize them, but she never found time to do it. I think my call provided a spark. In short order Pat joined *Ancestry.com* and worked out some of the genealogy of the Vizers, Wolfes, Groffingers, and others in her family line. Over the next year or two she filled four thick albums with family photos and documents, adding captions to each entry.

When I sent her copies of some pictures from a photo album my father had kept as a young man, Pat recognized a studio portrait of Jacob Vizer, Jr. He was the young man in the mystery photo that no one in my immediate family could identify. It was definitely, she said, her great-uncle Jacob who had returned to Kompolt with his father, mother and sister Maria in 1927. Pat's mother had told her what happened to Jacob. He was "dragged off and sacrificed" (*"Elhurcolt Áldozatok"* as the memorial tablet in Kompolt puts it) by the Red Army. Jacob died of pneumonia in a box car on the Romanian border in the waning days of 1944.

Jacob Vizer, Jr., circa 1925

As I learned later, the three other Vizers on the memorial stone--Anna, János, and Sándor--died in the Stalino work camp in the eastern Ukraine in 1947. And as the genealogy provided by Emöke makes clear, János and Sándor were brothers, grandsons of Jakab Vizer, Sr.'s brother Ferenc. They were Pat's cousins. János Vizer's history was particularly grim. After surviving the brutal winter fighting on the Russian front, he walked hundreds of miles back to Kompolt, arriving in November 1944. Weeks later he and his younger brother were collected by the Red Army and shipped to Stalino.

So the story had come full circle. Jacob was the handsome young man in my father's photo album, he was Pat's grandfather's brother who had returned to Hungary with his entire family--except for Pat's grandfather--to become a farmer in 1927, and he was the "Jakab Vizer" on the memorial stone for civilian victims of the Red Army near the Kompolt church. And there is one more interesting connection in this story. Two years ago, when I sent photos to Elemér and Erzsébet Vizer of Pat's family in Kompolt taken during the 1930s, they wrote back immediately that they had been neighbors to Jakab, his Hungarian wife Erzsébet Jakkel and their daughter Ilona. Jakab, they wrote, had worked at the Kompolt City Hall before he was taken by the Red Army. Jakab's only child Ilona had married László Fekete, whom they knew well. They had stayed in touch with Ilona and her husband after the couple moved to Salgótarján, about twenty miles from the Slovakian border. In addition, Elemér and Erzsébet said that they had worked for many years with Pat's other cousin, László Paradis (the child of Mária, Jakab, Jr.'s sister) at the Plant Improvement Institute in Kompolt. In 1962 Laszlo and his wife moved to Kiszombor, in the south of Hungary near Szeged, to continue his research on wheat. Then they had retired to Szentendre (St. Andrew), a beautiful small city on the Danube a few miles north of Budapest. Kompolt-Granite City connections were expanding rapidly.

Jakab Vizer, Sr. and family, Kompolt, 1938
1st row: Ilona, Katalin Wolf Vizer, Jakab, Sr., László Parádis
2nd row: Erzébet Jakkel Vizer, Jakab, Jr., Mária Vizer Paradi, Elemér Parádi

The author and cousin Pat Meller, Prague, 2013

CHAPTER 40

Our Trip, September 2013

My cousin Pat Olsen Meller, her husband David and I flew to Prague in early September 2013 to begin a two-week Road Scholar tour of Prague, Bratislava, and Budapest. On our Saturday night in Budapest we enjoyed a splendid Hungarian meal at Paprikás, a restaurant near our hotel, with Elemér Vizer's granddaugter Franciska Vizer and her boyfriend Krisztián Nagy. Both speak English well and agreed to meet us in Kompolt when we visited there the following week. After our Road Scholar tour was completed the following Thursday, we rented a car and headed east to Heves, where we planned to spend five days doing research on our ancestors. Fifteen miles or so before Eger and our hotel, we noticed a turnoff for Kal and decided to begin our research early. We thought that, at the least, we might acquire some sense of the lay of the land. On my one-day visit ten years before I had taken a bus to Kompolt, so I had seen only the parts of Kompolt I mentioned earlier and nothing of Kapolna or Kal.

Krisztian Nagy and Franciska Vizer, Budapest, 2013

We noticed the old Catholic church in Kal and stopped, but it was surrounded by a cyclone fence, and we could not find a way in. Driving a little farther, we spotted another steeple, which belonged to the old Catholic church in Kapolna. As we were admiring the exterior, a middle-aged couple pulled up to the side entrance of the church on their bicycles and unlocked the door. They noticed us and immediately invited us inside. The interior was impressive, in the baroque style with marble columns framing the altar. There were ceiling frescoes and some gilded ornamentation, all surprising to find in a small-town setting. They guided us to a small religious painting, which clearly occupied a place of honor in the church and tried to explain to us its significance. They seemed so proud to show us around. My limited grasp of Hungarian was of some use as I gathered that the old painting was from the eighteenth century and brought there from Germany. The old couple were as friendly and as helpful as they could be, a harbinger of what we unfailingly encountered over the next five days. When our informal tour was finished, they pointed us toward the Kompolt cemetery. After a few wrong turns, we spent the next two hours looking for the tombstone of Pat's great-grandparents and taking pictures of Vizer and Bech tombstones as well as others that bore Hungarian family names common in Lincoln Place and Granite City.

To our surprise we could not find the burial place of Jakab Vizer, Sr. and Katalin Wolf Vizer, Pat's great-grandparents, though we trudged down every row in the cemetery. Disappointed by our failure and tired after a long and stressful day, we drove on to search for our hotel in Eger, which turned out to be high above the city on the narrowest and steepest of roads. The driveway of the Palaccio Wellness Villa was even narrower. Dave had to nose in, back out, and turn sharply to bring our rental car to the imposing front gate. When the gate was opened for us, we were relieved to see that the secluded Villa was even more "Palaccio" than its online photos.

The next morning our first stop in our ancestral village was the Kompolt Falu Ház, a very impressive village hall considering that Kompolt's population is only 2,250. We identified ourselves to the receptionist as well as we could and offered our ancestors' names on slips of paper, communicating to her that we were looking for old records of births, deaths, and marriages. In a few minutes and with the Kompolt mayor's blessing, several clerks and secretaries were helping us search old ledgers going back to 1895, the year when Hungarian civil authorities assumed the record-keeping responsibilities which had for centuries rested with the churches in each community. Since my grandparents had been born well before 1895 and had departed Kompolt in the first decade of the twentieth century, I could not think of anything to look for in the municipal records. However, since Pat's great-grandparents had returned to Kompolt with two of their children in the 1920s, she and Dave had a great deal to research.

The polgármester, or mayor, of Kompolt Zoltán Balázs, invited us into his office where he offered us the use of his conference table so we could more comfortably examine the ledgers and then asked if we wanted coffee or other refreshment. When Pat ran into difficulty understanding the ledgers and the explanations of the clerks, the mayor telephoned Zuzana Finta, an English-speaking friend of the mayor who worked nearby, and she served brilliantly as a translator and explainer. Zuzana had worked at The Plant Improvement Institute as a hemp researcher and and because of that had known Láci Paradi, Pat's cousin, as well as Elemér Vizer.

While Pat and Dave scoured the ledgers with Zuzana, a Slovakian who had mastered at least three languages, I attempted a conversation with the mayor. Using my limited Hungarian, I communicated to him that my grandfather was a Vizer and my grandmother was a Bech. He brightened at that and told me that his mother was also a Bech. The mayor then astonished me by explaining that he knew a man whose hobby was researching the genealogies of the Vizer and Bech families. Then he went to his phone and made a call to István Tarnavölgyi. He said that István was vacationing at Lake Balaton but would be back Monday, our last day in Kompolt. István would be glad to meet with us late in the afternoon if we were available. I assured him we would be.

After Pat and Dave finished with their research, I asked the mayor if a chart of the Kompolt cemetery existed that could help us find Jakab and Katalin Vizer's grave. The mayor called in a clerk from another office. She copied down their names and some other Granite City Hungarian names that I was searching for and promised to meet us the next day at the Kompolt cemetery at one p.m.

The author and the Mayor of Kompolt, Balázs Zoltán, 2013

A few minutes later we were enjoying a fine lunch at an excellent restaurant near the highway entrance to Kompolt, marveling at our good luck. The mayor walked in with two friends, and we smiled and waved. If my Hungarian had been better, I would have approached their table, but I thought we had taken up enough of his time and hospitality. After the mayor and his friends left, we lingered over our wine talking about our next puzzle: finding the house where Pat's great-grandparents had lived after they returned to Kompolt from Granite City. When we finally asked for the bill, our waiter told us that the mayor had paid.

In the late nineteenth century and early twentieth century ledgers we had been examining that morning, there were no street names; each house had been assigned a two- or three-digit number. At some point in the twentieth century, probably in the late 1920s, Kompolt expanded enough to require street names. Fortunately Pat had a photograph of her great-grandparents' house taken in the late 1930s plus a street address: #10 Arpad. The photo of the house showed a cobalt-blue stenciled design on the side porch. Pat felt this design would be important in identifying old Jakab's house since we had not noticed a similar design on any house in a day of driving around the three villages. After a few wrong turns we came upon #10 Arpad. The resident of the house spoke little English but after looking at the photo he understood our purpose and let us into his yard and his house as Pat searched for identifying details. There were similarities in the shape and size of the house, but most of the older houses in Kompolt followed a similar design: a narrow front, a lengthy line-up of rooms perpendicular to the street all exiting to a broad side porch protected by an overhang. The kitchen was at the rear of these rooms, and extending beyond the kitchen often stood the remains of old stables and barns. To Pat's eye, something was not quite right. She did not see any trace of that distinctive pattern of tiles running down the side porch.

Jakab Vizer's house in Old Kompolt, 1938

At that time, as so often happened, a Hungarian who spoke some English came to our aid. (In most Hungarian schools English, French, or German language offerings were expanded as soon as the Soviets vacated Hungary. Most Hungarians under the age of thirty-five seem to have some fluency in English.) After the neighbor heard our story, she explained that the names of the streets had been changed after New Kompolt was constructed. In effect, she explained, the people in Old Kompolt had moved to New Kompolt and taken their street names with them. At least that was how I understood it. The old #10 Arpad, she said, was now #10 Deák Ferenc. The house at this address, she said, was located near the old Kompolt church and cemetery on the main street of the original village.

This church, like the one in Kal, is forebodingly fenced off, but as I found out recently, church services are still held there regularly. The fence was put up to discourage thieves and vandals. I have not entered the interior of the *Kisboldogasszony* ("Little Happy Married Woman" in my rough translation) Roman Catholic church in Kompolt, but some images I received on the internet show how beautiful and well-maintained it still is. Emöke Abasári explained that the demographics of Kompolt changed after the 1970s, and Old Kompolt began to take on a rather shabby appearance. Even the beautiful trees that lined both sides of the old village main street, the trees that are so prominent and majestic in old post cards, have disappeared. And the older people in Kompolt feel their loss as much as many New Orleanians feel the loss of the Claiborne Street oak trees that were cut down to make way for Interstate 10.

The house we were looking for was only a few lots away from the church. The current residents of #10 Deák Ferenc were friendly and welcoming also, fascinated by Pat's photo, which showed the appearance of what seemed to be this house so many years before. The grandmother of the family pointed out remnants of the distinctive stenciling on the side of the house, most of which had long before been painted or plastered over. This detail convinced Pat that #10 Deák Ferenc was indeed her great-grandparents' house. What remained of the house, however, was only about half the length of the house in her photo. The rear sections of the house--the stables and small barns and sheds--had been demolished. After we spent about a half hour there, Pat promised to send the Horvath family a copy of the old photo, and we headed back to Eger for some wine after a long and successful Friday. Now Pat had new questions that are still unanswered: where was the land that her great-grandfather had farmed? and where were the grain fields and vineyards that appeared in other pictures she had?

(In light of recent information, we are still not sure that this house was the one her great-grandfather lived in. "Ferenc Deák Street, we have been told, was never named "Arpad." The street acquired the name "Fő" (or "Main Street") in the early 20th century. During the Soviet occupation it was changed to "Hámán Kató," as I mentioned earlier. After the Soviet army withdrew from Hungary in 1990, the street was renamed "Deák Ferenc," after a nineteenth-century Hungarian statesman known as "The Wise Man of the Nation." In his later years Pat's great-grandfather moved in with his daughter Mária. This might have caused our confusion about the address of the house in Pat's photo.)

Before our scheduled rendezvous with the village clerk at the Kompolt cemetery on Saturday afternoon, Pat had scheduled a morning appointment with Dr. Peter Artner, the Catholic priest who keeps the old church records of Kompolt in his residence behind the Kal church. About a year before our visit Pat had established contact with the priest's mother through the Hungarian wife of a Road Scholar tour guide. However, Pat had not received a written response from the priest concerning her request to examine the Kompolt church records nor had he answered the telephone when she called long distance several times. Pat does not surrender easily. Buoyed by our successes at the mayor's office on Friday, she tried the priest's phone number one last time: she connected with him, and we were told we could drop by at eleven the next morning.

Dr. Artner was welcoming and his English was excellent. He explained that during the week he taught at a college in Budapest, which was why he had missed Pat's phone calls. He was very helpful in finding the hand-written pre-1895 volumes we were most interested in, translating key words, deciphering the sometimes puzzling penmanship, and explaining some of the symbols. Unfortunately, because of our appointment at the cemetery, we had only about an hour and a half for this research. Nevertheless, we learned a great deal in that time about our Kompolt ancestors.

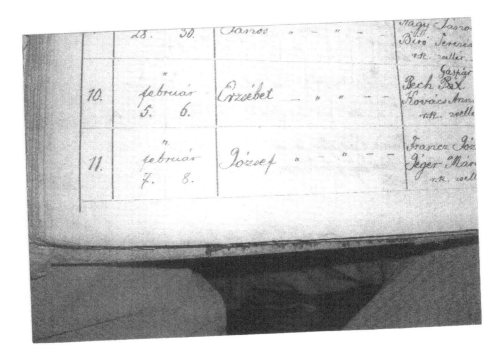

Erzsébet Bech's birth in Kompolt's church registry, February 5, 1880

Although Pat had done considerable research on her branch of the Vizer family on Ancestry.com, she quickly uncovered in the ledgers the existence of several siblings of her great-grandfather that she had not known about. When she found the birth entry of her grandfather Laszlo, the first-born in his family, she noticed it was unusual in that it contained scratch-outs and additions. Dr. Artner explained that Laszlo was born before his parents were married. In a flash, real life intruded on the faded records.

Up to this point in my life I have not been much interested in genealogy. It has always seemed to me no more than names and dates on a chart. I needed a shred of a story, a detail of character, a brush against or a collision with history to make a date and a name come to life. My father was adept at providing such details on anyone he had met and any place he had been. However, as interested as my father was in all things Hungarian, he never showed much interest in his ancestors. Perhaps he felt that the gulf of space and time could not be breached. I'm not sure my father even knew the names of his grandparents, all of whom spent their lives in Kompolt. If he did, he never mentioned them to me. The only detail he ever passed on was that his Vizer grandfather had worked in the stables of the Emperor Franz József. I was always skeptical of that. It reminded me of a story he told me that I had once believed: that before I was born, I was a star-polisher--the best one, too. Recently, however, I learned that a palace of Count Anton Grassalkovich, one of the most powerful men in the Habsburg Empire and the man who established and literally owned Kompolt in the mid-eighteenth century, was located not just in Heves but not far behind Kompolt's Catholic church. Originally, this palace had its own Hungarian staff, whose dwellings along a small river were a few hundred yards away from those of the peasants brought in from Germany to farm. A century later when my father's grandfather was alive, it is possible that he might have worked in the stables of the Palace. Until recently, that tidbit was the only detail I ever heard about my Vizer great-grandparents.

Opening the Kompolt church ledgers shelved in Dr. Artner's apartment, I made my first small step into the world of genealogy. I learned there that my grandmother Erzsébet Bech's parents were named Gáspár Pál Bech born in 1853 and Anna Kovács born in 1862. (The "Kovács" name is probably a direct translation into Hungarian of the German *"schmied"* meaning "blacksmith." Two families of Schmidts were listed among the original Kompolt families who arrived in 1754.) Gáspár and Anna Bech's daughter Erzsébet was born on February 5, 1880. That day I found that she had an older brother József born in 1878 and a younger sister Mária born in 1882. From my father I knew she had younger brothers who had immigrated to New Jersey, but I did not come across their names that day.

My father's uncles, the Bech brothers, circa 1920

In another ledger I found an entry listing the death of Paulina Krisztián Vizer, my grandfather's first wife and the mother of my father's half-sisters, Anna and Katalin (my Aunts Nonnie and Katie). In 1900 at the age of 30, their mother Paulina died of tuberculosis, the same disease that was to afflict her daughters in America. Then I discovered in the ledger than less than two years after Paulina's death on May 31,1900, my grandfather's second wife Erzsébet Bech gave birth to their first child József on February 28, 1902. My father always told me that this first József had died in Hungary, but I did not have time to search for a record of his death.

A few months after I returned from this second trip to Kompolt, I learned from Emöke Abasári that my great-grandparents, Ferenc and Mária Kristián Vizer, died during a cholera epidemic in 1873: Mária succumbed to the disease eight days after Ferenc. My grandfather József was only six years old. I am not sure who raised him. His parents were in their early forties when he was born. When they died, his older sister Magdi was eighteen; she married József Engel about a year later. Margit, who was fourteen when her parents died, married József Schlag when she was sixteen. Since the Schlag family had lived next door to József's parents and since another of Jószef's sisters, Mária, married József in 1888, I suspect that my orphaned grandfather was raised in the Schlag family.

As an orphan and as a man who had lost his first wife to tuberculosis in 1900 and his infant first son two or three years later, my grandfather József Vizer might have had more reason than most to leave behind the village of his birth in 1905.

The village clerk's motor bike was parked near the cemetery's maintenance shed when we pulled into the parking lot. The clerk stood near it with a sheaf of papers under her arm. She briskly walked us to tombstones bearing some of the Granite City names I had asked her to find. The sky darkened considerably by the time she worked down to the most important names on the list for us: Jakab and Katalin Wolf Vizer, Pat's great-grandparents. The clerk led us halfway up a gentle rise, looked closely again at her chart, and then pointed to a tombstone completely covered by thick clusters of ivy, one of about three in the cemetery that we had noticed in that condition two days before. Some of the vines were as thick as our fingers. On Thursday we had not been willing to spend the time and effort required to clear this vegetation from the tombstones. What were the odds? we had thought. But on Saturday there we were, tearing and pulling back tenacious vines and leaves, not resting until we could see Pat's great-grandparents' names clearly. Just before the skies opened up, we managed to take some photos of their tombstone. Then we made a wild run for our car as the rain pelted us.

Dave Meller and village clerk clearing vines from Pat's great-grandparents' tombstone

Through driving rain we drove back to New Kompolt searching for Elemér and Erzsébet Vizer's home. I possessed a vague memory of where Alcotmany Utca was from my walk there with Erzsébet Fehér ten years before: five minutes from the main road, a left turn, a house in the middle of the block on the main-road side. Street signs in Kompolt, though, are as random as they are in post-Katrina New Orleans. Nevertheless, I had a good feeling about the street Dave was slowly driving down, looking between the raindrops for a street sign. I was trying to read some faded lettering above a garage door when Pat spotted a line of people streaming out of a house that we had just passed: the Vizers had been watching for us, of course. Dave backed the car up, and in no time we were under umbrellas, surrounded by Vizers: Elemér, Erzsébet and Franciska, who had taken the train from Budapest with her boyfriend to help translate for us. Soon we were sipping wine Elemér poured while Erzsébet went from setting the table to asking if we needed anything to giving each of us another hug.

The meal that Erzsébet had prepared was memorable: vegetable soup, baked chicken, roast turkey, fresh-picked green peas, galuska (a gnocchi-like pasta), preserved apricots and cherries, sour cherry soup, and two or three kinds of dessert. All of the food except one of the desserts and two of the wines, we were to learn, had come from their garden, their fruit trees, and some chicken coops and vineyards within two hundred yards of their house. Recalling the Vizer's hospitality ten years before, I had anticipated this feast so I had eaten an uncharacteristically light breakfast that day. Franciska told me later that she had deliberately not told her grandmother the exact day we were coming until the day before so she would not exhaust herself making an even grander feast!

Elemér, Franciska, and Erzsébet Vizer with Pat Meller, 2013

After dinner Franciska's parents, Zoltan and Zsuzsanna Vizer, joined us. Zoltan is an engineer and, no doubt, has inspired Franciska and Daniel to follow in his footsteps. Pat and I hopefully passed around albums of old photos that we thought might contain faces the older Vizers would recognize. Pat had prepared an album full of photos of her relatives, and I had a stack of old family photos that I had recently copied from my cousin Jimmy Giese's collection. Some of them, I felt certain, were sent from Kompolt before World War II. However, neither Elemér nor Erzsébet recognized anyone in the photos other than the children of Pat's great-grandparents and Ilona Keksz, my grandmother's youngest sister. Once again I regretted that I had not started this research when some of my father's siblings were alive or before

Erzsébet's Granite City-born mother had passed away, which was not so many years before my first visit to Kompolt in 2003. With the help of Franciska and Krisztián Nagy--and Elemér's wine--we continued to communicate for several hours on a wide range of topics: from family history to engineering projects to soccer. Fortunately Dave, as the official renter of our Citroen, was the designated driver, and he resisted all temptations to drink. (By the way, the allowable alcohol level for a driver in Hungary is 0.0. This severity is made tolerable by excellent access to public transportation.)

Ilona Bech Keksz, my grandmother's youngest sister

The next morning we drove to the Kapolna cemetery. That is easy to write, but actually no drive in Hungary was ever simple for us. After wandering around looking for a sign to the cemetery, we stopped at a gas station, and a friendly old fellow took up our cause and led us to the cemetery in his rusty little Fiat. Kapolna's cemetery is, in many respects, the most beautiful and well-organized of the three village cemeteries. The entrance is marked by a low wall topped by some ironwork. Tall monuments bearing the names of soldiers from Kapolna killed in each of the World Wars stand near the entrance. A dirt path lined by many old trees divides the rows of tombstones equally; also, the plot of land is relatively flat in comparison to Kompolt's and Kal's cemeteries. Pat's main goal here was finding tombstones of Kroffingers/Groffingers and Wolfs. She had discovered a few Groffinger and Wolf stones in the Kompolt cemetery, yet none of the stones contained the specific names she sought. My goal here was again to search for Granite City Hungarian names and to take note of how many Germanic names were present.

Almost before we could begin our search, a woman noticed Pat and Dave speaking English and approached them, asking where they were from. When they answered, "Illinois," she said that she had recently returned from a visit to St. Louis and--yes--Granite City, where her father was born. The lady in the Kapolna cemetery was grieving the recent death of her husband, a military officer, and she walked away quickly before I could ask her for her father's name, which I suspect I would have recognized. In our thorough examination of the tombstones in the Kapolna cemetery, Pat found a few more Groffingers. I discovered a handful of Vizers and a Bech or two. The Bader name, obviously Germanic, was numerous and prominent on the most impressive burial vaults, but on the whole, there were fewer Germanic names in Kapolna's cemetery than in Kompolt's. We also noticed with relief that there were no tombstones completely covered by leaves and vines to torture our imaginations and consciences. After our thorough survey we thought we had earned a break. After all it was Sunday and the weather promised fair: we headed for The Valley of Beautiful Women. It was my first trip there in ten years, but this time I had adult supervision.

The "Valley," a collection of more than fifty wine houses and restaurants, is located on the outskirts of Eger. While we ate and drank at one of the restaurants, we watched small pickup trucks hauling large plastic crates overflowing with grapes stop in front of nearby wine shops. Machines set up to crush the grapes into pulp and juice were busy outside several of the shops. The weather and the wine inspired tourists and locals in abundance to walk up and down the gentle hills exploring one wine cave after another. Our timing was off in only one respect; we had arrived too early to hear music. By five or six o'clock many gypsy trios and quartets would be playing in the caves. However, we decided to leave before that to rest up for Monday, our last day to research our ancestors.

Late Monday morning we visited the Kapolna village hall to see if Pat could find something more about her grandmother's family, the Groffingers. One tombstone in the Kapolna cemetery had marked the remains of two brothers--one a Groffinger and the other a Kroffinger--and she hoped to discover which was the original spelling, and if the brothers might be related to her grandmother. The Kapolna village offices were much smaller and less impressive than the Kompolt Falu Ház, but a clerk there was helpful. She told Pat to return after lunch, when she would have some information for her. After lunch, Dave dropped me off at the Kal cemetery. Before they returned to the Kapolna village hall, they found a gift shop and selected some flowers for Pat's great-grandparents' grave. I explored the Kal cemetery on my own for over an hour before Pat and Dave returned.

This cemetery seemed to be three times the size of Kompolt's or Kapolna's plots, and it was impossible to walk a straight path down most of the rows because they were interrupted by random graves and steep drop-offs. I knew my search here could not be as thorough as it was in the other two cemeteries. I did find one Vizer buried there, but no Bechs. Also there seemed to be considerably fewer Germanic names overall. However, there were some Granite City names in abundance here that I not seen in the other two cemeteries: notably Balszai, Pap, Cseplye, Krecz, and Berki. After Pat and Dave joined me, we wandered about taking more photos for another hour. Our mission more or less completed, we returned to Eger for one last meal together. In the morning we left Heves, heading for the Budapest airport.

This visit to the home of our ancestors was over, but our search was not, even though we were not sure what direction to take next. Some doors had closed. We had learned from Erzsébet that Mária Vizer's son, László Paradis, had recently passed away. We hoped that some other doors would open.

And one did open five months later! When I was struggling toward a conclusion for this narrative, I took a Facebook break to look for an important personal message that I learned had been sent to me months before concerning the death of a friend. In addition I found my first message from Emöke Abasári. She had seen a copy of a letter I had sent to Elemér and Erzsébet in August, and she was inviting me to join the Facebook groups she had started: Kompolti Csaladok Története (Kompolt's genealogies); Kompolti Mozaik (images of present-day Kompolt); Kompolti Barati Kor (friends of Kompolt; and the Jakkel Forum (devoted to research on the widely dispersed Jakkel family--Jakkel is Emöke's maiden name). I encourage my readers who are on Facebook to inspect these sites. Emöke adds new information and photos almost every day.

In just a week of looking at these Facebook sites and by messaging and e-mailing this Budapest resident whose roots are deep in Kompolt, I discovered old maps of Kompolt, images of the beautiful interior of the Kompolt church, colorful photos of natural scenes in Heves, and much more. After a few more e-mails, we discovered that Emöke is related to Paulina Krisztián Vizer, my grandfather's first wife. As is more than obvious by now, Emöke provided much of the genealogical information and many of the details of Kompolt's history that have enriched this narrative.

I feel sure that more doors will open in the near future as we share information about Kompolt and Lincoln Place and Granite City, which has included a room for genealogical research and local history in the remodeling of the main library that was completed in August 2014. I have been assured by the library staff that the SIU-E interviews of Lincoln Place residents will be available there.

CHAPTER 41

A Third Visit, August 2014

WHAT WAS I DOING AT the 39th annual conference of the American Hungarian Educators Association in May 2014? I had retired from teaching three years before. My Hungarian consisted of a few phrases I remembered from my childhood plus the fragments of grammar and vocabulary I could recall from working slowly through seventeen lessons in *Halló, itt Magyarország* by myself. I was writing a book on the Hungarian side of my family, but I did not feel I had enough information or authority to give a presentation. But I had promised Arthur--someone I had only communicated with via e-mail--that I would at least attend.

Arthur Bartfay, whose mother grew up in Granite City, contacted me through his cousin Mary Ann Toth Cochran, who attended GCHS with me. Mary Ann not only has the same name as one of my cousins, but her parents' names were the same: Mary and Julius Toth. This Toth family's roots were in Miskolc, not far from Kompolt; her cousin Arthur's roots were in Nagyszecs, Heves, even closer to the Vizer's ancestral village. Arthur is an authority on Louis Kossuth's visits to America in the mid-1800s and America's enthusiastic response to his message of democracy and independence for the Hungarian nation. Arthur informed me that towns, streets in cities and villages, and even a county in Iowa were named after Kossuth; statues were erected and plaques were installed in many of the cities where he spoke, including in New Orleans. Arthur, one of more than forty presenters at the conference in Florida, would speak about a topic he was even more of an authority on: his family in America.

So I drove the five hundred miles from New Orleans to Gainesville not knowing what to expect or how I would fit in. About eighty people turned out the first night to watch a recent Hungarian movie concerning the 1956 revolution. *The Kolorádó Kid* was a tale of betrayal and revenge, a persistent theme in Hungarian history and one that reared its head in several of the presentations and discussions I attended. The next morning at the first official opening of the conference, I learned during the introductions that presenters had come from all over the United States and Canada, from Israel and several European nations. One scholar had even traveled from Japan to deliver her paper. I was relieved to learn that more than eighty percent of the sessions would be conducted in English. Topics ranged from "The Rupture in French-Hungarian Relations" by Marguerite Allen of Northwestern University to "The Prophetic Voice in the Poetry of Miklós Radnóti and Sándor Márai," by Peter Czipott an independent scholar, and from "A Critical Analysis of the Hungarian Sport Policy, 1989-90" by Emese Ivan of St. John's University in New York to "A Turning Point in Heritage Language Teaching?" by Orsolya Maróti.

As relevant as Ms. Maróti's topic was to my interests, what first led me to her was not her topic but her last name. Over the years, my curiosity about the names of people and places has led me to fascinating discoveries and occasional embarrassments. As it turned out, Ms. Maróti was not related to the Hungarian-American wife of a friend of mine whose parents had left Hungary in 1956, but she was the head of the Hungarian language department at the Balassi Institute in Budapest. In a minute or two, she convinced me that the Balassi Institute was where I should go to fulfill my dream of studying Hungarian intensely.

Three months later I was packing my bags for Budapest and the Balassi Institute, an intitative of the Hungarian government to promote and support Hungarian language and culture around the world. There are twenty-three branches located in twenty-one countries from China to Egypt and in most of the major countries of Europe. In those three months I had completed the last three lessons in *Halló, itt Magyarország* (Book 1) and reviewed other worksheets and vocabulary lists I had come across in the previous two years. I knew proper pronunciation (though it broke down when I tried to speak at a normal rate); I knew basic pronouns, present tense endings, numbers, the days of the week, fruits, vegetables, foods and drinks; I knew a bit about past tense and possessive forms, but I was capable of brain freeze or jaw freeze when called upon to utter any of the above. I had a favorite noun (*gyerekek*, children), a favorite adjective (*chodalátos*, wonderful), and a favorite verb (*főz*, cook), but "I cook wonderful children" was not a useful sentence. Sentences were, and still are, a problem.

The Balassi Institute's international headquarters is located high in the hills of Buda. Originally, this six-story building was built as a residence hall for the "heroes of the revolution," soldiers and workers who supported the Red Army during and after World War II and the Communist Party when it seized power in Hungary in 1949. In 2002 the Balassi Institute transformed this huge dormitory into its base of operations. There is a large auditorium on the first floor, classrooms and offices on the next two floors, and a more than a hundred dormitory rooms on the top floors.

Other than myself and a Swede and Frenchman nearing middle age, most of the participants in the intensive August program were college-age. Nearly eighty students, the great majority of them young women, gathered in the auditorium that first morning from almost every corner of the world: Australia, Argentina, Mexico, Canada, Japan, Korea, Taiwan, China, Russia, Venezuela, Israel, European nations from the United Kingdom to Bulgaria, and states from Florida to California. Everyone there had at least some English, so the opening remarks and all the afternoon lectures thereafter were given in English.

The Balassi Institute's students at Lake Balaton, 2014

That first day I was placed in a Beginners' class, but I asked to take the placement test to see if I could move up. I did not excel on the test, but I did demonstrate that I was not starting from zero, so I was elevated from Beginner to Intermediate. All the students in my new class had studied Hungarian for at least a year in their native countries. They were not fluent in Hungarian, but they had been exposed to listening and speaking drills regularly and were able in their oral responses to use principles of grammar that I knew only theoretically. Since the course used the "immersion method" almost exclusively, I was often lost in the back and forth of questions and answers. I did have one advantage over most of the other students, however: my focus on reading had given me a relatively extensive vocabulary. Even this advantage had its negative side though. I was not content to give obvious answers. I often attempted to use my vocabulary to fashion colorful, or unpredictable, or humorous responses. Too often I failed miserably, and the joke was on me. A raised eyebrow from our teacher was my usual reward. Then she would add the endings I had omitted or correct the ones I had butchered. Nevertheless, three hours of instruction every day for four weeks improved my ability to speak and understand basic Hungarian. The course also extended my vocabulary as well as my grasp of idioms. Most important I was motivated to continue studying this difficult but fascinating language.

Afternoon lectures covered Hungarian political and cultural history, achievements of Hungarians in music, literature, film making, science and sports. Afternoon and evening field trips included visits to cathedrals and the Jewish Synagogue, the Opera House, art museums, and the House of Terror museum (the former headquarters of both the fascist's and communist's Secret Police). The most popular local excursion was to a "rom kocsma" or "ruin pub," a sprawling network of old houses, courtyards, and junk imaginatively transformed into a vast pub with multiple bars and music venues. I would have attended more of these excursions, but this was my third trip to Budapest. I had seen many of the popular sights, and more important, I needed my afternoon nap even more than usual. On the second Saturday of the program we were bused to Lake Balaton, the largest lake in Central Europe and one of its foremost tourist destinations. We began our visit in its warm waters and spent the remainder of that long day in a borház (wine-house) high above the lake. After we learned how to suck wine out of large casks through long tubes and squirt it into glasses (and other places), we sampled and over-sampled many local vintages. It was all good and a good time was had by all.

An added benefit of this program was a renewal of my faith in the youth of the world. Participants at the Balassi Institute were unfailingly kind and helpful to each other, even more so after our day at Lake Balaton. They made an effort to include odd fellows like myself, and at lunch they even laughed at some of my puns and jokes that flopped in class. Nikoletta, the raven-haired Slovakian beauty who sat next to me in class, made sure I knew what page we were on (multi-digit numbers in Hungarian flew right past me) and what the homework assignment was. David from Paris sat to my right. His Hungarian was gathered from doing business in Budapest, so he was very good on introductory pleasantries, but he was as much in need of Nikoletta's help as I was when it came to page numbers. Two lovely and athletic German girls, Jessica and Sarah, sat next to Nikoletta. Like me they were bright and early for breakfast. Unlike me they had already walked a couple of miles up and down the Buda hills before that. Eun Jung and Eun Hee, two quiet Korean girls, sat in the opposite corner.

Facing me on the opposite side of the classroom were two sweet-tempered young ladies that I came to think of as my wards, Natsuko and Ayano from Japan. Often when these two needed something lifted, or found, or explained, I seemed to be there. Quite by coincidence, we arrived at the same time on the first day and left at the same time on the last day. On St. Stephen's Day after spending the evening with my cousin Franciska and her fiancé's family watching fireworks on the Danube, I headed into the massive crowds on Rakocsi to find the usually efficient public transportation system bogged down; roads were blocked off and buses diverted. After reading the electronic message boards and asking a few questions, I figured out how to make it across the Danube on a bus to the Balassi dorm. At that moment I noticed Natsuko and Ayano standing at a bus stop, looking confused and a bit frightened. I came up behind them, startling them, and told them to follow me. Immediately they went back to being their sweet and amusing selves. As we trudged up the hill to the dorm, Natsuko said something in Japanese to Ayano. "She says you are like our grandfather," Ayano told me, and I took it for the compliment I guess it was.

The other males in my Intermediate class were the Russian Nikita, who spoke English very well and came in with a good grasp of Hungarian. Stefan was a brilliant German graduate student who was working on a Ph.D. in Economics at Central European University, founded by George Soros in 1991 to promote the democratization and economic development of recently liberated nations in central Europe. And then there was the Canadian John. Though he had never had a course in the language, his Hungarian was too advanced for the Beginners because he had spent a lot of time with his Hungarian-speaking grandparents. At the end of the first week he was placed with the Intermediates. "János"--as everyone called him--was one of the youngest and most popular students at Balassi. He was a psychology major who wanted to be a comedian. He never missed an outing or a pub crawl, so he seldom had time for his homework. He was late for breakfast and almost every class. But he knew what he was doing: he was having a great time. János saved me from being the caboose of the class, and I was grateful.

I avoided most of the night life. I needed that nap plus a good night's sleep to keep up with homework and the better prepared students. And night life was not exactly a novelty to me. I was not twenty-one anymore, or even sixty-one. My weeknight recreation at the Institute was playing an hour or two of table tennis with Peter, the dorm counsellor. The table was slick and the lighting was bad, but it was the only game I could find in town. I had brought my paddle and a few balls along with the hope of staying in practice.

Peter was good competition and good company. His English was outstanding, but he often had questions about odd English expressions, which I enjoyed explaining to him. It seems sad to me that such a bright and curious, not to mention educated, mind would seem content in such a job--with a small salary and, as far as I could tell, not much opportunity for advancement--but I came across several young people in Hungary who reminded me of Peter. They were not unhappy, but they did not have too much optimism about their futures or Hungary's. It seemed clear to them that Hungary was falling behind economically, and they entertained little hope that it could catch up. Hungary's declining population and birth rate was looked upon as further evidence of this malaise. For so many young Hungarians the future seemed to be elsewhere--if they could get there--though they loved Hungary as much as any generation, I think. The ideal life for many educated young people seemed to be to venture to a country where they would be paid what they were worth and then to return to Hungary in retirement.

When I did go out at night, it was to visit with relatives and friends in Budapest. Franciska Vizer, a third-year student at the Budapest University of Technology and Economics (the first institution in Europe to award degrees in engineering), was serving a summer apprenticeship on a civil engineering project, and Krisztián Nagy was working full-time for an engineering firm and had an apartment in the Centre near Petőfi Bridge. We found time to get together every week, most often at The Black Dog Pub near their university. One of our frequent conversation topics was Krisztián's participation in a nationwide competition for young entrepreneurs. Krisztián has spent the past year building a 3D printer from scratch. This printer is the foundation of his business idea, and he has formed a company called 3D Most (a nice play on words: *most* means "now" in Hungarian). I recently learned that his business plan was selected among the top two hundred, which means he will receive $10,000 from the Hungarian government to help make his dream of developing his own business a reality.

I was also able to meet twice with Emőke Abasári and her husband Ferenc. The Abasáris are retired physicists who live in Újpest, but Ferenc still works part-time on a project involving lasers. Emőke worked for a Hungarian company that was acquired by General Electric, and she spent some time working for GE in New England. Now her time is filled with grandchildren, her Facebook groups, and genealogical research. In the last year she has created genealogical charts for four families of Vizers who came to Granite City more than one hundred years ago, and she is in touch with a representative of each of them online: Joyce Vizer Jenness, Kenny Wiezer, Patricia (Wiezer) Olsen Meller, and myself. The chart she prepared for my grandfather József goes all the way back to his great-great grandfather Adam Vizer, one of the original German colonists who settled in Kompolt in 1754.

One of the chief goals of my research has been to learn how the Kompolt Vizer families in Granite City are related. When I first talked to Joyce about this, I discovered that we had both visited Beck families in New Brunswick, New Jersey, in the early 1950s and we both knew about Paul Beck, who received a patent on something he invented for Johnson and Johnson. That connection seems to be through the Kovacs sisters that Joyce's grandfather and his brother married in Kompolt and brought to the United States. Emöke explained how Vizer families in Kompolt and other families with multiple branches distinguished themselves from each other by using "stuck" names (nicknames) like "Mary Ann" or "göndör" (curly). So far I have not come across an example of a Vizer marrying a Vizer in the Kompolt records, though after four generations in Kompolt some of them would have been far enough apart in the eyes of the Catholic Church to marry with its blessing. One of the thorniest problems in pursuing this research is the narrow range of given names for male and female Vizers. Josephs, Jacobs, Peters, Johns, Elizabeths, Annas, Marias, Katalins and a few others abound, repeating themselves through the generations in all the Vizer branches. Names are even re-used in a family after an infant dies as Joseph's was in my father's family. Thanks to Louis Takacs, Emöke and I have the complete handwritten vital records of Kompolt from 1752 to 1895 at our disposal. All that is needed to complete the genealogies of the Granite City Vizers, Veizers, Wiezers, and Wiesers is a vast amount of painstaking translation of ornate and sometimes cramped handwriting in German and Hungarian.

Fortunately for me, Emöke has done a great deal of this work. In late January 2015 when I was almost finished with my last editing of this text, she sent me two pieces of information that established some clear connections among the Granite City Vizers: a ship manifest and a genealogy. As I mentioned earlier, on February 10,

1914, my seventeen-year old Aunt Katie, my grandfather Veizer's second daughter with Paulina Krisztián, arrived in the United States on the Prinz Friedrich Wilhelm, which had departed from Bremen, Germany. It is clear from the ship's manifest that Emöke's grandparents, József and Erzsébet Jakkel and her father (a child at the time), accompanied Katie. They stated on their forms that their destination was Ferenc Krisztián's home in Granite City. Ferenc was my Aunt Anna Vizer's husband, Katie's brother-in-law. Aunts Katie and Anna were first cousins of Emöke's grandmother. Also in this group were close relatives of Joyce Vizer Jenness. This trio was comprised of an older couple and their adult son: János Vizer, his wife Mária Jakkel Vizer, and the twenty-five year old Ferenc. Their stated destination was the home of Péter Vizer, Joyce's grandfather. József Vizer, another brother of Péter, made the eighth person in the group traveling from Kompolt to Lincoln Place.

A few days later Emöke sent me a genealogy which showed that Kenny Wiezer's great-grandfather Jakab Krisztián and my great-grandmother Mária Vizer, who died in the cholera epidemic of 1873, were siblings. Also, the genealogy states that Pat's great-grandfather Jakab Vizer and my grandfather József Vizer were cousins. It seems that the Krisztián and Jakkel families are the glue that most closely connects the Granite City Vizer families to each other and to Emöke Abasári. For reasons I will keep to myself, I am going to assume that the Krisztiáns and Jakkels provided the best-looking and most intelligent mates to be found in Kompolt.

Carrying my suitcase out of the Balassi Institute on the last day, I ran into Natsuko and Ayano of course. We rolled our luggage down the hill and fought our way onto a crowded bus. I was headed to the Keleti, the eastern train station, where I would catch the express for Eger. They had two more days to spend in Budapest before they left for Vienna. After they stepped off the bus, they giggled and waved at me with both hands. People around me started smiling or laughing out loud, some waving back with both hands. They looked so colorful and friendly and delicate, but I was not worried about them: I had confidence another Grandfather would come along when they needed one.

This was my third visit to enchanting Eger. It's such a beautiful small city, nestled in the vineyard-rich hills above the Nagy Alföld, the Great Plains of Hungary. The grand public squares, the winding shop-filled streets climbing to the remains of the medieval fort that towers above the city, the vast City Park, which is home to four swimming pools, a thermal bath, and many flower gardens: I feel at home there and at peace.

Eger Castle, 2014

After a relaxing Saturday evening in the cafes and taverns of Eger, I climbed to the bus station Sunday morning for a ride to Kompolt, looking forward to enjoying the hospitality of the Elemér Vizer family once again. The final day of August was a beautiful day, a little cloudy with a touch of fall in the air. In New Orleans it was still in the 90s, fiercely hot and fetidly humid, a lovely day for reptiles. With almost a full load of passengers the bus began the forty-minute trip to Kompolt. I sat right behind the driver's compartment. I had traveled on this bus only once, eleven years before, and I wanted to be close to an exit and to an authority on the location of Kompolt. As the bus curled around the station, I looked back at my fellow passengers. Almost all of them were engaged with their cell phones, mumbling or tapping away the time.

The bus was about halfway to Kompolt negotiating a section of hills and curves on a three-lane highway when it swerved sharply to the right, then collided with something two or three times. I assumed that the driver had lost control and that the bus was smashing into the low, thick protective barriers that outlined each sharp curve. Then we stopped abruptly, and I heard shouts and cries behind me. By the time I turned to the shouts most of the passengers were standing and staring down the road. There was moaning and someone sobbing, "Jaj istenem!" but no one seemed to be injured. I could not make sense of all this until I too looked back down the road. A motorcycle was in pieces on the other side of the road. Its driver lay behind it. Only his motionless arm and helmet were visible to me. Another motorcyclist had parked his bike twenty yards up the road and was walking back to the wreckage.

In my seventy-one years I had never been close to a horrific accident. In the nine minutes before emergency medical techs arrived, it was hard to take my eyes from the motorcyclist's arm. It never moved. The other cyclist knelt down to look at his friend, walked up the road toward his cycle, then returned. He did this several times. The bus driver crossed the road to the wreckage shaking his head back and forth. The police arrived a couple of minutes after the EMTs and closed off the road in both directions. Not long after that the EMTs placed a black plastic sheet over the victim while a growing number of police and officials from the bus company interrogated the driver and the other cyclist.

Then it was time for the passengers to be questioned. I was the only traveler who did not speak Hungarian fluently, so the police-man skipped me until he found a woman who could translate for us. I did not have much to say; I did not see the collision--I doubt anyone on the bus could have, but I certainly did not think the bus driver could have avoided it. We were going downhill on the outside of a curve; the motorcycles must have been speeding up the hill as they swung into the bus's path. But I was not asked for my opinion: only my name, the name of the Eger hotel I was staying in, and my destination. The policeman wrote all this down in his notebook. Then occurred one of those coincidences that have haunted and so often enriched my life.

I heard a voice behind me. "Are you related to Daniel Vizer?"

"Yes, I am," I said to a husky young man two rows back.

"My name is Péter Várkany. I went to school with him, grade school and high school. Is he waiting for you at the bus stop?"

"I think so," I said. "Either Daniel or his sister Franciska."

"I'll have my mother phone them and tell them you're going to be late and not to worry. Do you know where they live?"

"I know the street name. It's close to the elementary school."

"You must be going to their grandparents' house," he said. "I can walk you there."

This is only the first part of the coincidence, though. The second came to light after we exited the replacement bus in Kompolt. Peter asked me where I was from.

"I live in New Orleans," I said. "But I was born in Illinois, across the river from St. Louis, which is where a lot of Kompolt people emigrated to in the early 1900s. I'm in the process of writing a book about my family and Kompolt and Granite City."

"Granite City!" Peter exclaimed, reminding me once again of Erzsébet Krisztián Vizer's reaction to the same information eleven years before. "I'm writing my graduate thesis on the history of Kompolt. I came across some documents in the village records about Granite City. And I have some other information I think you would be interested in. If you have e-mail, I could send all this to you online."

By the time we reached Elemér and Erzsébet's house, I had told him everything I knew about the Kompolt-Granite City connection, and Peter had told me more about his research and his new position as a history teacher at Esterházy Károly College in Eger. On Monday I met with Péter in Eger, and he gave me paper copies of a list of Granite City contributors to a 1915 fund for the widows and orphans of Kompolt (which included my grandfather's name, my uncle Frank Krisztián's name, and the names of seven other Granite City Vizers); a list of property holders and tax payers in Kompolt in 1887 (which mentions seventeen Vizers); and records of a late 19th century controversy resulting from an Archbishop's unsuccessful attempt to install a Hungarian-speaking priest in Kompolt's Catholic church. The villagers demanded another German-speaking priest and ultimately prevailed.

On Sunday after Péter led me to Elemér and Erzsébet's house, I walked to the Kompolt cemetery with Franciska, Daniel, and his fiancé, Erzsie, who is working on her Master's degree in electrical engineering. My cousin Pat wanted me to check the dates on her great-grandparents' grave, which we had cleared of vines a year before. Village records showed that Jakab Vizer died in 1961, but Pat thought the gravestone said "1963." After tearing away vines and leaves that had already grown back, I discovered that Pat was right about the date on the stone. I was left with a question: Who was more likely to make a mistake, a clerk shortly after Jakab's death or a stone cutter a few months or years later?

After we walked back to Elemér and Erzsébet's house, we took a tour of their garden. I had consumed the fruits of it twice before, but I had never had the opportunity to walk off the spacious back porch, a garden in its own right, and see the whole. First Elemér pointed out the cherry tree and the two apple trees, which flourished with not only apples but pears. Elemér demonstrated how he spliced the pear limbs to the apple tree. Then we walked down rows of beans, peas, cucumbers. lettuce, eggplant, cabbage, and the last remnants of the tomato harvest. (By the way the word for "tomato" in Hungarian is *paradicsom*, the same word that is used for "paradise." Such is the regard of Hungarians for this South American plant introduced to Europe by the Spanish.) Above us and around us were Elemér's grapes, red and white. We plucked a few off the clusters above and popped them into our mouths. They were as crisp and tasty as any I have ever eaten. Those that survived our browsing would be transformed into wine by Elemér. His deep-red and fruity Merlot was his favorite and mine. It had a tinge of sweetness that I searched for unsuccessfully in other Hungarian Merlots in Eger and Budapest. Elemér made sure I left Kompolt with a quart of it poured into a well-rinsed Jagermeister bottle.

Elemér Vizer in his garden with grandson Daniel and his fiancée, Erzsébet Ruzicska

Krisztián arrived on the train from Budapest in time for the feast that Erzsébet had prepared. He had been attending another of the three-day seminars required for the young entrepreneurs competition. As usual Erzsébet was in and out of the kitchen bringing in more food and encouraging us to eat, eat. At the head of the table Elemér did his part, pouring wine and making recommendations. Later I asked Erzsébet why she did not sit down and eat with the rest of us. "My knee hurts," she said in Hungarian and laughed while I translated that slowly in my head.

After hours of conversation and photograph albums, Daniel insisted on driving me back to my hotel in Eger. I was not afraid to return on the bus, but I was glad to have the distraction of good company when we retraced its route.

The next night Franciska, Krisztián, and I joined Daniel and several of his high school friends at a local pizza house and microbrewery. Some were still in school like Daniel; others were working in Eger or Budapest; one of them was doing well as an arborist, or tree doctor, in London. They all loved Hungary but seemed to be frustrated by the lack of opportunities there. Germans and others from northern Europe owned the companies where several of them worked, and the northerners dominated upper management. Hungary, they felt, was too small to make much of an impact on the world surrounding it. They dreamed of better jobs elsewhere and of returning to Hungary after they made their fortunes. Nor were they hopeful about the direction of their own government, not an unusual stance in many a country these days. I was surprised to learn that in spite of Hungary's great history in soccer, fencing, swimming, and other sports, they were much more interested in such outdoor activities as hiking, biking, running, and camping. Daniel and Erzsie had, in fact, just completed a month-long, seven-hundred-mile trek around Hungary. Thanks to my father I seemed to have more interest in Hungary's great history in sports than most of them did. In spite of this regrettable lapse I felt they were among the finest and brightest young people I had ever spent time with.

The next day was my last full day in Hungary. I spent it touring Eger Castle, buying a few souvenirs in the shops around it, and seeking in vain for a Merlot as fine as Elemér's. I smuggled some of the wine into a borház for my favorite waiter Attila. He was working his last day before returning to his university in Miskolc. He genially agreed with me: it was better than any he had tasted. Later in the afternoon I visited the grand and stately 300-year-old building which housed the college where Péter Várkany now teaches. He had told me of the American Studies Department there. I found their headquarters but was only able to talk to the department head's wife on the phone because he was ill. I promised to visit him at the college on my next trip to Eger. I hope that will be soon.

Appendix I

Short Stories I've Written That Are Connected to
Granite City, Lincoln Place, and the Veizers

MOST OF THE STORIES following were initially published in magazines and journals as follows:

"Suckers" in *Gray's Sporting Journal*, in Spring 1983.

"The Dad's Big Toe" in *St. Patrick's Day Short Story Contest Entries, 2010-2012*, published by Finn McCool's Irish Pub, New Orleans.

"Championship Wrestling" in *The Bookstore Reader*, University of New Orleans, 1983.

"Reginald Brewster" in *Pulpsmith*, Winter, 1986.

"Woo Woo" in *North American Review*, September 1982.

"Jijos" in *Sou'wester*, Fall, 1981.

"Fast Forward" in *Intro 14*, 1984.

"Beyond the Pier," unpublished.

Suckers

JOE WAS TRYING TO FIGURE fishing out. Maybe he wasn't old enough. Like he wasn't supposed to be old enough for a lot of other things. He was ten-and-a-half.

Joe was as close as he could get. Flat on his belly, head hanging over the ledge, glasses about to tumble off his nose into the pool. Now then. Those were sucker fish down there in that deep stream pool, still as could be at first glance, fluttering and pointing the same way, like banners and pennants at Busch Stadium. Quarter-inching along the bottom, sifting the eatables out of the silt and sand and sucking them up. Eating frog purp, Dad said.

That was why (he had this part down good) he and Dad and Zeke weren't fishing for these nice fat fish you could see. They weren't worth eating because of what they ate and how they ate, so Dad didn't try to catch them. Even for the fun of it? That was because they wouldn't bite on anything you could fish with legally in a state-stocked, state park trout stream.

So Joe was lying next to his fly rod watching their cool fish-ways. He was just enjoying, instead of trying to learn like with the trout. There couldn't anything to learn, could there, from fish that you could see? It was the fish you couldn't see, even in this clear-as-bottled water, that everyone wanted. His dad didn't even want to look at these fish once he saw they were suckers. So, he had moved on down the stream looking for rainbow trout.

Now. The trout you couldn't see unless you caught them, but then that wasn't really seeing them. They'd be flopping or squirming in your hands. Even live and hooked to a stringer hanging in the water, that wasn't like seeing real fish doing real fish things, even if they weren't only but suckers sucking. Trout on a stringer were like snakes at the zoo, not very exciting.

There was another little thing he couldn't figure. His dad and his fishing buddies said "suckers." They never put "s" at the end of any other fish's name. It was always, "We got the limit, boys, six trout!" Or "We only got fifteen crappie and four bass today." It sounded like one of those things his dad would get mad as hell trying to explain, so he guessed he'd not bring it up if he could help it.

Of course, the biggest thing he had been trying to figure out up to this time (and was about to give up on) was what he had to do to catch a trout. Eleven long trips they had made to this trout stream, eleven nights he had spent reading signs or sleeping in the cold backseat of a car so he could be at attention (or acting like he was) alongside his dad, a fishing buddy, and a stream two hundred miles away from his house, waiting for the dawn whistle to come blasting the birds out of the trees. And there had been eleven long empty-handed trips back home with nothing to tell his mother except, "We ate barbecue," or "We saw a car wreck," or best, "Dad fell in again." And nothing to say back when Dad told Mom that Joe had no patience, scared the fish away, got hungry too soon, that there were kids half his age (five-and-a-quarter?) catching the limit by noon, "If he'd just listen to me..."

But he did listen. It was harder not to listen, but there so much to remember: relax your wrist; let the current take the lure; make it move natural; watch behind you; don't let so much slack build up; take up some line; don't stand where you will make shadows on the water, stupid! And those were just the ones he had to remember before he got a strike, which had only happened once (maybe, how could he be sure?). It might have been a snag, a down-current, a turtle, or some deep grass. But Dad was sure Joe would know when it happened, something about a tingle running right up your arm. Well, Joe tingled all over when he saw or heard somebody else's strike.

Yet he still wanted to go on the long Friday night trips--loved to go. One time he snuck off and caught three different kinds of turtles. Dad wasn't impressed. He had caught a forty-pound snapper when he was ten. He had a scar to prove it, too. He always had scars to prove things. As if the last word wasn't a word, but a scar. Another time Joe climbed up a hill and found a little creek he could jump across and followed it down and around a hill until he came to a swamp it made. There were piles and piles of watercress there. Dad packed the trout he caught in all that watercress Joe brought back. Well, that was all right, but Joe knew Mom wouldn't use it in a salad then. And then (his dad didn't know about this one) one time had had fallen into the State's trout breeding pool, leaning over it just like he was this stream. He never saw any trout breeding there though, no trout doing anything different from what these suckers were doing.

Of course, Joe did fish on these trips, too. He thought he fished pretty hard for someone who'd never caught a trout. Fishing had gotten to be pretty much like praying. But he fished a lot harder than he prayed.

He had fished plenty for trout and got plenty cold and wet (and lonely, too) doing it. He thought he looked pretty good whipping a wet fly--on a calm day anyway. He could often put it where he wanted it, but where did the fish want it? That was certainly more important and no one had told him much about that, except his dad always figured they were hiding under some low shady shrub he couldn't cast to when he wasn't catching any.

If Joe ever did happen to put his bug close to a trout, he was as sure as could be that the trout would either spit it out, or spit on it. Joe didn't have much confidence left.

So, watching suckers was what he had come to. He loved fish, the idea of hem, not just the taste, He liked that they were tricky, graceful, streamlined ("stream lined," he had never thought of it that way before), dark and sparkling. They lived in another world, and died from a little of our world, just like we would die of theirs. We stood up, pointing to the sky. They pointed just the opposite, always flat with the flow of the stream.

Joe watched the suckers sifting the bottom. And he quit trying to figure it all out for a while. The pattern made by their paralleled bodies shifted, slow as clockwork, slow as pieces in a serious chess match. There were seventeen of them. Each one was different. The light scars on their backs, the nicks in their tails, the slight differences in their sizes gave each one an identity of its own.

The little school of suckers delighted Joe for a long time, or a whole lot of water. (That was fish time, and it was "stream lined," too.) Joe watched a slow-motion ballet, a conference of deep thinkers, a harm of slow, slow-dragging dancers. And they still grazed in the stream hole, never once looking up.

The Dad's Big Toe

WHEN THE DAD'S BIG TOE hurts, it is everyone's problem. The Mom has his horny-nailed and calloused right foot in her lap. laying on hot compress, then ice bag, in five-minute shifts. The Son flies off on his bicycle to the drugstore for painkillers and hopes there will be change he can pocket and bank for a new baseball glove. Big Sister checks on the warming compresses in the kitchen, then fills a jelly glass with home-made wine, which she holds in trembling hands. Little Sister sits behind the Dad's big chair listening. She sobs and sniffles. The Dad endures, but not quietly. Tomorrow he will hobble to the factory again, where the floors will seem harder, colder, and rougher.

What is this mystery of the Dad's right big toe? His left big toe and all his other toes are flexible, vital, in the prime of life. His right big toe is eighty-five years old, writhing and throbbing on its death-bed. Nine toes are late-model sedans; his right big toe is a torched jalopy. Heat, cold, pills, wine--there's no relief. Only the sobs and sniffles find their way through the pain.

"Come sit on Daddy's lap, Poochootz," he says and holds Little Sister until she falls asleep. Then he hands her off to the Mom and limps off to bed.

Before the Dad decided between hacksawing his toe off or blasting it off with his shotgun, he promised the Mom he would see a chiropractor after work the next day, though he thought that was all tomfoolery. When the Dad's pulls into the driveway that next day, the family is framed in the front window where the Christmas tree stood a week before. His left leg comes slowly out of the car and rests on the ground. Then he tugs his right leg out of the car. He stands, then straightens slowly. He limps around the car to the front walk and looks up at the family. Then the Dad does a jig step and skips up the walk. The crowd in the window goes wild.

The Mom is flabbergasted. The Dad is more talkative than ever. All night he re-enacts the treatments. "The electrodes go here, here, and here." He marks the spots with the Son's ink pen. "The shock goes bing...bing...bing." He beats out that rhythm on Little Sister's knee. "Then comes the needle. Right there." He makes an "X" on the toe, then pinches Little Sister on the leg. She screams and rubs the inked spots. Big Sister says, "I could be a chiropractor someday." Brother makes his favorite disgusting sound, effluent sucked down a drain.

Every third Friday, the Dad visits the chiropractor. When he comes home, he dances carrying Little Sister; plays Slap the Hand with Brother; puts the Mom on his lap and then pulls Big Sister into her lap.

In early spring, the toe starts to throb before the third Friday. By late spring, the toe throbs before the second Friday. By summer, the Dad's big toe starts bothering him two days after he visits the chiropractor and gets worse each day. The Dad's big toe hurts, and it is everyone's problem.

It's the Dad's birthday. He limps off to the factory for another long, painful day. He comes home, limps up the walk and takes the mail out of the box: a birthday card from the chiropractor! The Dad tosses it to the floor.

"What a quack!" he shouts. "And he's bled me for six months. I'll birthday card him." He slumps in his chair. "Never again." Little sister crawls into his lap carefully.

"Hacksaw? Shotgun? No, a bolt clipper will do," he mutters.

Big sister has been to the public library, studying bones and feet and toes--and shoes. "It's the shoes, Dad," she says. "It says so right here. Your steel-toed shoes."

The Dad sits up straight, takes the book from Big Sister, and reads a couple of pages.

"It's those shoes!" he says. "I'll just bet it's those damned shoes! I'll start with the soft-toed shoes tomorrow. To Hell with the Safety Supervisor. I was working at the plant before he spit up mush." He pats the book tenderly and grabs Big Sister's hand. "Now that's a birthday present."

Brother can think of no funny sound to make that would be appropriate, so he just says, "Happy birthday, Pop."

In less than a week, the Dad's toe is better. In three weeks there's no pain at all.

Big Sister wants to be a chiropractor.

"No!" the Dad says. "You're going to be a doctor. I don't want no chiropractors in this family. They got no integrity."

Brother is going to work on integrity, after he gets his new base-ball glove. And he is going to stop making disgusting sounds at Big Sister. He could be a doctor, too. Little Sister is as adorable as ever. The Mom is the Mom; strong and wise and good in the quietest of ways.

When the Dad feels good, it's home, sweet home, every night.

Championship Wrestling

HOWDY DOODY WAS THE FIRST new kid in the neighborhood in years. Since my dad bought the first television on our block, I got to introduce all my friends to him and Clarabelle and Phineas T. Bluster and that wacky Flub-a-Dub, who was such a concoction of creature-parts he was constantly confused about just what he was. But my favorite television show by far was "Championship Wrestling," mostly because of my former hero, Lou Midgett.

I did not expect to see Lou win all the time. As average-sized and unferocious as he was, it was a wonder he ever won a single match. But he didn't lose very often either. He had mastered the art of defensive wrestling. I was, I can see now, mesmerized by the utter simplicity and improbability of his style.

"Championship Wrestling" was aired about an hour before my bedtime, and at least once a week I went to bed chuckling at Louis Midgett's strategies and his ultimate defense: the Armadillo. His frustrated opponents kicked him; they slung him and they flung him. When they tired, they lifted him and they dropped him. Finally, the exhausted foe sank to the mat alongside Lou, wedging arm, or leg or head into whatever fleshy crevices presented themselves, trying to find a vulnerable spot in the Armadillo of Lou Midgett.

Lying in my bed after "Championship Wrestling," I ran through every pinning combination, every possibility of outrageous attack against Lou on the large-screen deluxe TV of my imagination. But

Lou always exhausted his foes, then conquered them. For example, Yukon Eric would direct a running kick to Lou's ribs and bust his big toe, or he would lose his balance trying to raise Lou over his head and Lou would fall on top of him, or he would try to gather one last ounce of momentum for a "flying mare" designed to propel little round Lou into the second row of spectators and knock himself out on the ever dangerous turnbuckle. But even when these sudden opportunities for victory were thrust upon him, Lou's expression never changed; it might have been painted on a balloon, which is, in fact, what his bald head much resembled. Lou tugged at his gray, stripeless trunks, sidled over to the ruined colossus and went through the ho-hum of pinning him. As an image of the referee reaching down and snapping Lou's tube of an arm into the air dissolved, my mind busied itself setting the opening scene of the next match: Killer Kowalski vs. Tireless Lou Midgett. At last I would fall to sleep, tucked in by my mother, snug and secure as Lou Midgett in his Armadillo.

Later in that year, in the first summer of television, a young Yukon Eric became the second new kid on the block, or so I was informed by one of the old kids on the block. I was told, in awed tones, that the new kid lifted weights. And certainly I could hear the clang and chime of iron on iron and the low whistles of forced breath that came from his garage every afternoon when I passed his house to go to the corner confectionary, but I didn't see him clearly until one evening.

I was hurrying to the confectionary to buy a nickel pack of base-ball cards when I saw a boy and a man (Eric and his father, I guessed) on their roof, raising the tallest television antenna I had ever seen. Eric stood, steadying the antenna, looking like a fair, young god about to draw back a thunderbolt; his father sat, bent to his screwdriver like Vulcan putting the finishing touch on a weapon he had forged. As Vulcan tightened the last screw, the first crooked finger of lightning ignited the sky. Eric pulled his father up with one hand, and they stood together for a moment, admiring their work. Then a second flash divided the sky, and I started running: to beat the evening storm and to catch the beginning of "Championship Wrestling."

That night I watched my favorite program more intently than ever. After Lou had absorbed a few painful forearm chops from Yukon Eric, which the referee had somehow not noticed, he dropped into his Armadillo. His fingers laced together behind his neck, his forearms guarded his ribs, and his head shifted slightly from side to side to allow his eyes to follow the pacing of this Arctic predator. When Yukon Eric aimed a kick at his head, Lou quickly altered his grip and pulled his head even farther into his fortress. This was proof against the worst kicks, slaps, gouges, and knee drops that Yukon Eric had to offer. Then Yukon Eric circled him slowly for a minute or more, but Lou Midgett did not move, did not suggest that there was even a weakness left to hide. It wasn't until Yukon Eric grabbed Lou's trunks and yanked on them that Lou made his move--a mule kick that sent Yukon Eric out of the ring to sit stupefied among the paying customers until long after the referee had counted him out. This was, indeed, a finale beyond the power of my dreams. And that evening the referee really did snap Lou's tube of an arm into the air. And that night, no matter how snugly my mother tucked me in, the sheet offered small resistance to my mule kicks.

After the raising of the gigantic antenna, Eric superseded me as the most popular kid on the block. According to some of his new friends (my old friends), his TV had not only the sharpest and steadiest picture on the block, it pulled in big league baseball games on Saturday afternoon from stations that none of them had even heard of before.

I had never been addicted to popularity. I took the exodus of my friends with the silent grace of Lou Midgett. I was content to spend the rest of my summer with my baseball cards and my dad's fuzzy, buzzy television.

But one Thursday evening a terrible thing happened: "Championship Wrestling" did not come on. In its stead Channel 7, our only channel, offered "Championship Roller Derby," which I realized (in much less than an hour) was crude and chaotic. More importantly, it did not present clear moral choices. Every skater cheated if he or she got the chance. Every one of them rabbit-punched and tripped and gouged and cold-cocked. There was not only no "good guy," the women skaters were, if anything, more ruthless and more inclined to violence than the men.

My old friends got word to me early the next morning: Eric's antenna had pulled in "Championship Wrestling" from a station in a city more than fifty miles away! The ballyhooed rematch between Yukon Eric and Lou Midgett had been wrestled, they told me, but Eric would not even tell them who had won. However, they said, knowing what a Lou Midgett fan I was, Eric wanted to "show me" in the vacant lot down the alley what had happened in the match.

"That sounds like a challenge," I said to them, and they nodded (very eagerly, I thought) and headed to the alley.

And to myself I said something like this: "If a big, overgrown goon insists on messing with a tough, smart little guy, he had best be ready to accept the consequences." Then I pulled on my black high-tops, pulled off my T-shirt, and strolled down the alley. Soon I was back in the tromped-down center of the lot, inside a tight circle of familiar faces.

I had never seen Eric off a rooftop, so he didn't seem quite so big as he had in my imagination. Still, he was the biggest kid I had ever seen. He is almost as big as my old man, I thought. My last comparison was more comforting: he is as much bigger than me as Yukon Eric is bigger than Lou Midgett.

He bellowed, "Hey, kid, I'm going to show you what happened to Lou Midgett on 'Championship Wrestling' last night!"

I said, "You may try."

"I don't need your permission for nothing, punk!" he said and smiled to all my old friends. "This is my block now."

I let him lunge at me a few times just to get us both warmed up. He barely touched me. His mediocre sense of balance had given me an opening or two, but I knew my game. He was breathing hard and becoming more cautious, taking shorter steps and lurching forward less often. He was tired, almost staggering. The time had come to finish him off.

My Armadillo was fish-tight. Arm, leg, neck muscles strained. My fingers locked behind the back of my neck. A weed speared the inside of my nose, but I just smiled to myself and gently snuffled. My ribs were steeled, protected by my forearms. My elbows guarded the sensitive and mysterious solar plexus. But the wild, self-defeating assault I expected was never launched.

Instead, I heard Eric's voice: "And then this no-muscle Midgett made a turtle out of hisself like that one there." I almost lifted my head to correct him, but instantly suspected that this was his deep purpose.) "And then Yukon Eric gave him a few little kicks..." (I ignored them) "...and a few knee drops..." (I absorbed them) "...and then Yukon Eric--can you hear me, turtle?--he grabbed Lou Midgett by his ankles, like this..." (too late for the mule kick, I remember thinking) "...and jerked him up, like this...and then there was nowhere for the turtle to go but..."

The emergency room.

That's where I woke up, flanked by Dad and Mom. The X-rays were negative. My eyes did the right thing when a little light was shined directly into them. By my chin was jabbed into my left shoulder, and my neck could not pull it back.

For the next month I had to sit sideways to watch television. Worse, I could no longer sleep on my back; therefore (as I discovered) I could not dream. With one pillow under my shoulder and two under my head, I had to lie on my left side. My knees, quite naturally it seemed, drew up tight to my chest. And no matter how tight my mother tucked me in, it didn't feel right, ever again.

Reginald Brewster

YOU WERE ALWAYS DIFFERENT. TUTHILL was your middle name. ("Tut-tle" you always proudly corrected.) Your father was folded over a tank hatch six months before you were tugged into WWII. You cried for a reputable haberdasher in three languages and suffered the string of ailments and Texas relatives that came instead. By the time we looked at each other through thick glasses in the fourth grade, your legs were strong and fast but bowed, not from Texas but from polio. You arrogated the the rumbling mumbles and precise flutings of an English lord, not from polio but from Texas. You were always cockeyed.

In three years we had published a weekly, concocted indelible dyes and explosives, bored a hole through your roof for your telescope, made and lost a fortune in guppies, collected call-signal cards from eighty-seven commercial stations and two-hundred-seventeen ham operators, discovered Frankie Lyman, Booth Tarkington, and Nervous Norvous, learned Morse code, chess, and twenty-five ways to reduce authority to apoplexy.

All good things must end. Your crazy-wicked stepfather was unpastured. And you spent your early adolescence checking your food for crude poisons and nastiness and jumping out of your bedroom window after midnight. You kept your mind sharper than he kept his hunting knife.

Came high school they safety-pinned your stepfather's slippers to his long underwear again and you were free to clomp anywhere in the heaviest black boots you could find. Your hair duck-tailed, like your toes. You spent high school talking to the dean of boys on the phone, impersonating a string of non-existent male relatives. By dark you had grease up to your armpits and a still balky antique Ford-V8. You could rebuild carburetors from memory. You swept childhood into a deep box with your greasy arms and slid it under your bed to make room for your one teenage memento: a trophy honoring you as the author of the Most Spectacular Crash, Summer 1960, Riverside Speedway.

You continue your education up the river a few miles. You live in your car. You wreck it and lose driving privileges in states east and west of the Mississippi. (You were in the middle of a bridge, remember? You don't remember.) You live with an older woman, a librarian and an anarchist waiter. They let you down in turn. You live in the library. You talk to your professors in three languages. You graduate Phi Beta Omniscient. Doors are opening. Philology at Harvard? Modern languages at Yale? One blackball and it's down the trickstairs to Arkansas to analyze he diphthongs in "Sooooooooooeeeee Piiiig!"

It gets better for a while. It gets worse. Arrogance in St. Louis. Opium in Indiana. Strange politics in San Francisco. Where are you now, last seen waving your cravat at a spurting radiator? Where are you now, old buddy?

Woo Woo

Woo Woo Wes has a pickup truck. The first with a cover on it in the Greater St. Louis area, he told me. He drove down to West Memphis, Arkansas, to buy one as soon as he saw it written up in *Motor Trend*. Wes amazed himself again. He could never have imagined driving to Arkansas for anything, even lunker bass. But he went and did it anyway. He was down there before he knew it. Wes does things like this all the time. They always amaze him. And sometimes me. I'm the new guard, Green.

Woo Woo Wes has a pickup truck with a top on it. He is, I imagine, in it now. Everyone else on the second shift has gone home, or left anyway. If there weren't so many working graveyard shift lately, I could see that truck real good; maybe even hear it. Woo Woo Wes isn't working overtime. But some might say Wes and Nellie the Welder are. Others might say they aren't working at all. I don't say much of anything. I'm Green, the Guard. I got tired of being Greasy Green, the Oiling Machine.

Woo Woo Wes has a pickup truck with a top on it, and a lady welder in it. But if Wes's wife calls, I don't believe I can see it at all from here, ma'am. And I can't leave my post for a minute because I'm by myself and I can't leave the gate with all the vandalism lately. You wouldn't want to see anyone's vehicle damaged, would you? I can't be sure, but I think I saw him leaving with Steve and Johnny in the rush at midnight and he's probably going to have a drink or two. It **is** Friday night.

I didn't need to be coached, but Woo Woo Wes coached me anyway. Then he said, "You're the guard, and you're Green. Get it?"

Woo Woo Wes has a pickup truck with a top on it, a lady welder in it, and a guard who can't quite see it. And that guard is so green that Wes's wife didn't make sounds like she believed him. 'Cause she'd been there before, and she knew the policies, and she hadn't heard about no vandalism lately, and she could certainly find out quick if he left with Steve and/or Johnny because she had a phone just like their wives did and just like every other bar in town did. And did I want to come clean with her?

"Can't be too clean. I'm Green," I chuckled.

"And didn't you use to be Greasy, Mr. Green?"

Woo Woo Wes has a pickup truck with a top on it, a lady welder in it, a guard who can't quite see it, and a wife coming up fast on it who can.

"The woman in question drove past the guardhouse in a late model green Ford at a very fast rate. However, I was able to confirm as she passed that her car did have an official parking sticker on it, so I was not extra alarmed. She proceeded to the lot at the same pace, and I followed on foot. Then I heard a crashing sound, and when I arrived at the scene of the accident I saw that the green Ford had encountered a late model blue Ford pickup truck, license number BS 1141, Illinois. The woman in question was already out of her car when I arrived at the accident scene. She was yelling at the truck she had evidently crashed into, something like, 'Wes, I know you're making woo woo in there! You better come out fast!' The woman went to a side vent of the pickup truck. (It had a kind of sheet metal cover over the back of it.) And then she seemed to pouring something through that vent. Shortly after that, the rear of the pickup truck started leaking what appeared to be smoke. And shortly after that a man and woman jumped out of the little rear door in the cover over this truck carrying what appeared to be some of their clothing and ran toward a nearby vehicle, a red late model Chevy Impala, and jumped into it. The woman who had driven in was still yelling and couldn't be reasoned with. So I proceeded almost to the guard shack to call in my superior to ask about the advisability of calling in outside authorities. I had proceeded almost to the guard shack when I heard an explosion and rushed back to the scene of the accident. The late model pickup truck was in flames and the man who had jumped out of the truck jumped out of the late model red Chevy Impala (which then proceeded to drive away) and was running to the scene of the fire. The woman shouted at him, something like, 'I guess you won't making any more woo woo in that pickup truck.' It looked as if the man was preparing to attack the woman so I proceeded to refrain him forcibly, sustaining some minor cuts and bruises and tearing my new uniform, for which I would appreciate being reimbursed for since I was just doing my job.

Signed, M. Green

Woo Woo Wes had a pickup truck with a top on it, a lady welder inside it, and a wife outside it. I'm still Green; but I learned a lot.

Jijos

A NOISY CROWD, MOSTLY MEN and boys, moved down an alley. They were a little dressed up for an alley, but they were correcting this as quickly as they could. Ties were sliding off, buttons were pinched from their holes, sport coats were folded over forearms or thrown over shoulders. All were talking, gesturing with beer cans, cigars, thick hairy hands--or laughing. The banter was American, but the shouted words that soared like skyrockets every few seconds and burst above the crowd were Bulgarian, Armenian, Hungarian, Macedonian, Spanish--all the languages of Backlot, the little world behind the mills and foundries.

Twenty-five years before these men had dug, hauled, nailed and painted (or gotten in the way of those who had) until they erected a community clubhouse for Backlot that was still standing, still serving their community. Today was the 25th anniversary of that accomplishment, a reunion of men, women, and energy.

Seedy won the trophy for coming the longest way. He was finishing his long Army hitch in Hawaii. Shammy and Theresa won the trophy for most kids. Tsigan had the youngest kid, two months, and the youngest wife (but there wasn't an award for that). Tsigan announced that at the fiftieth reunion he was going after Shammy's award, and he was going to win for youngest again, too, and he raised his trophy with one hand and his baby with the other. Augie got a special award for still living in the same house in Backlot he was born in.

"Now that took imagination and ambition!" Tsigan shouted.

"It did," said Augie, a little off the mark as usual. "I made up the awards." His older sister, sitting beside him big as a Buddha, smacked her forehead with both her meaty palms. "Well, I mean to say, me and my sister Gerda made them up, except for the special one I thought up night before last."

"Hey, Augie," someone shouted from a banquet table, "ain't Gerda living in the same house she was born in, too?"

When Augie tried to come up with an answer that would neither infuriate the woman who cooked "pigs in the blanket" for him just as good as his mother's, nor deprive himself of his trophy, Gerda was nodding vigorously and circling her ear with her right index finger, "winding up" Augie in front of his hundred oldest friends.

"We'll split it then," Augie announced.

"The wisdom of Solomon resides in that big head," Tsigan shouted, and Gerda kept nodding.

Augie cleared his throat. "I hope that meets with everybody's general approval."

"That's fine, Augie. You're in deep enough," Gerda said.

"Yeah, deep as usual," Tsigan added.

JoeMeesh had come from Detroit; Cheenchy from Florida; Zorro from Seattle (he thought he had the long-distance award sewed up until Seedy appeared). Popoff had just moved from Backlot, across the river to St. Louis County. Today they were reunited and moving down the alley joyfully.

Augie, in front of the pack, yelled, "This is it!" and started scratching a line across the alley with a broom handle.

"You think we don't remember your back alley, Augie? Isn't Mr. Getchoff gonna try to chase us out?" Tsigan asked.

"Not unless you believe in ghosts," Popoff said.

Tsigan, who didn't believe in them anymore, said, "He's gone, too? He wasn't so old."

"OK, everybody, listen up!" Augie yelled. "In front of the line is a hit." He gestured with his free hand. "Behind is a out--catcher has to catch it clean on a miss, though. No three strikes." He raised his voice, directing it toward the knot of potential players who were paying more attention to getting rid of their beer and their coats than to Augie.

"Outfielders! Caught in the air is a out. No rebounds, ricochets, or skips."

Somebody was listening. "What no pitching rules?"

"Pitching is strategy. No rules needed. If the batter don't like what he sees, he don't have to swing."

"No catching rules?"

"Oh, yeah. One-handed catching only. No trapping, no pockets and no cuffs. How did I forget that?"

Because you're catching, Augie?"

"And the geedus? What's the geedus, Augie?"

"That's up to somebody else."

"A hundred dollars a man, or I'm wasting my time," JoeMeesh shouted.

"You used to say the same thing when we played for dimes," Tsigan said.

"Only now it's true, Tsigan. Who's in for a hundred? Four on a team."

Eight were in. The ones who had raised their bushy eyebrows comically, or who looked around to see who had that kind of money to piss away, or jammed their fists in their pockets and kicked at cinders, were now a part of the growing crowd of spectators. Little boys were sent off to fetch mothers, uncles, sisters, brothers, and beer.

"We'll play nine innings, OK?" Augie asked. "Now who's choosing sides?"

"Let's flip if off," Joe Meesh said. "I feel lucky. Winners keep the quarters."

"Big Time JoeMeesh," someone called from the crowd. "You want to take it all back to Meeshigan."

They flipped and matched until two were left, Cheenchy and Tsigan.

"Match me for first choose," Tsigan said. They flipped together. Tsigan laughed and snatched Cheenchy's quarter, shouting, "I win seventy-five cents already; now let's start on the hundred dollars."

Tsigan looked the six players over slowly, trying to remember what skills they had once possessed and what, if any, they might have left. "I take JoeMeesh. He's hungry."

"But he hasn't seen the sun twenty years, much less played jijos," Cheenchy countered. "I'll take the pride of Backlot, Augie!"

"Don't you know Augie come out of the Navy unfirm? I'll take Seedy. I'll bet he can still catch 'em in his teeth like he used to those sunflower seeds.," Tsigan announced, impressed by his superior judgment. "Seedy, you still eat those seeds till your lips get cracked and puffy?"

As little Seedy shook his head no, Cheenchy said, "Nah, he ain't nervous no more you're going to try to take his sister out."

Cheenchy looked carefully at each of the three players remaining, trying to come up with some good reason for taking one over the others. Then he tapped one finger to his head and widened his eyes. "I'll take Shammy. He always wore glasses."

Tsigan looked at Zorro and Popoff and came up with his idea, tapping his head with his own crooked finger. "I'm taking Zorro, the good sport. Popoff will be so mad about getting chose last, he won't get a hit or catch nothing the whole game."

Cheenchy called to Popoff, "Come on over here for the pregame. If you let that gypsy get your goat, he's going to steal your chicken next." Cheenchy continued in grand manner to his team: "We got what it takes. Pure minds, pure hearts, and pure bodies.

Don't let me down and lose my hundred. I'm going to pitch just to make sure we win."

"Not with my money!" Popoff yelled.

"Mr. Papadoneff, please. remember I chose you. And also remember that I am a master pitcher. And finally remember that there's a couple guys out there in the crowd who want to play." Cheenchy turned to the crowd. "Who wants some action?"

Popoff headed to the outfield. "You never could take a joke, Cheench. Always want to be the boss."

Cheenchy watched Popoff retreating to the outfield with satisfaction. "Play up in front of the trash cans, Popoff, so you can get the low ones. There's no home runs today. Right, Augie?"

"Right, Cheench. Don't worry if it goes over your head, Popoff. It's just a single. How'd I forget to say that?" Augie shrugged.

"How'd your mama forget who your daddy was?" someone shouted from the back of the crowd.

"What kind of hoosier trash talks like that?" Cheench yelled. "What kind they got living in Backlot now?"

"It's all right, Cheench," Augie said. "They're just stupid is all. And saying that in my backyard is going to curse them."

"That's one of Tsigan's gypsy friends trying to get your goat again. Lock your chickens in the freezer when they're around. You know how they play. Nothing's changed."

Cheechy rattled his hand around in a paper sack and came out with a fist full of bottle caps. He examined each cap, dropping them one by one into his cupped right hand. "What's with these caps?"

"You hadn't noticed, eh?" Augie said. "No more cork to gouge out, Cheench. You'll break your thumb nail ripping at that plastic."

"You mean they're all the same weight? And how you supposed to throw a flutter ball without a loose cork, Augie?"

Augie shrugged. "In twenty years they won't even have bottle caps no more. Be thankful for these, Cheench." Then he nodded his lion's head.

Cheenchy zinged a few bottle caps toward his catcher. The first two started at Augie's belt, then jumped like frisbees in an updraft. Augie snatched them at eye level. The next started in the same plane but changed from a bullet to a diving gull in mid-flight and bounced off Augie's shoe.

"Sorry, I don't get down like I used to, but keep firing, Cheench."

"You better loosen up then. I want to see cinders all in your knuckles after this game, Augie."

"And I want to see blood all over your thumb, Cheench. Can you mash 'em?"

"Yeah, but my thumb's not what it used to be."

Tsigan, who had just finished talking to his players, asked the world, "Play ball?"

"Yeah, or play with yourselves," Cheenchy shouted back.

"Good. They think they're ready," Tsigan said. "And who's throwing out the first bottle cap of the season? Your sister, Augie?"

"How about giving the honor to your dancing bear, you chicken thief!" Cheenchy yelled.

Popoff shouted from the trash cans, "Let's leave family out of this, Cheench. You don't want Tsigan's grandma mumbling over you."

"Is she still selling advice?" Cheench asked.

"Does wolfmen growl?" was Popoff's answer.

Tsigan had the broom stick in his hand, looking a little sorry he had started the family stuff. He shook his bat like he couldn't wait to hit.

"OK, bat up, shut up, and sit down," Cheench chanted as he started his first slow windup. He came from down under. The pitch bellied away from Tsigan, who leaned toward it. Then the cap seemed to find a slit in the air and whirred like a tiny saw toward his fists. Tsigan tried to get his stick out of the way, but a ridge or two of the bottle cap ticked it and the cap fell behind the line.

"And you're out!" Augie shouted.

Tsigan winced, glanced at the bottle cap at his feet and spun his stick into the air. JoeMeesh caught it and took a few practice swings.

"They don't play this in Detroit, JoeMeesh?" Cheenchy interrupted his concentration. "What do they do there for exercise? Chase Macedonians? I mean something kept you in shape for twenty years."

Joe was still concentrating, trying to remember as many tricks of the game as he thought Cheenchy had.

Cheenchy slipped in a fat one, belt high, but JoeMeesh wasn't ready. "Taking one, huh, Joe? That's smart."

Cheenchy held a cap behind his back and pinched a rim down as he reminisced. "JoeMeesh. Old JoeMeesh. Misspent his youth shooting pool, playing jijos, and dealing cards. Always talking about leaving Backlot. Now he don't want to say nothing."

"Pitch it, Shlonko!" JoeMeesh invoked part of Cheenchy's last name to show him he was serious now.

The mashed cap spun toward JoeMeesh's shoulder, then broke down and away. He took a big swing, too big, and missed, as Augie hopped in his crouch and snatched the cap just before it hit the cinders.

"Back to Michigan," Cheenchy directed, snapping his fingers as if he'd just bowled a strike. "Who's next?"

Seedy had caught the bat, but he was looking for Zorro.

"Can't make up your mind, Seedy? Look, I'll give you an easy one to hit." He held up a bright green cap that sported flashy gold lettering. "The prettiest one in the bag, Seedy. Come on and dent if for me. My thumb is tired."

Seedy shrugged his slight shoulders, went up to the line, and shifted to an exaggerated crouch, his little black eyes gleaming over his bony arm.

"One little wiggle and it's the Army's answer to Stan the Man Musical," Cheenchy called to the crowd as he rolled the spiny edge of the green cap between his thumb and pointer. Then he wound up and sailed the cap in a slow whispering arc.

Seedy looked twice, reached for it, and sent it skittering up the alley where it came to a stop at Popoff's feet.

Cheenchy gestured with his pitching hand. "Just like I told you, Seedy. A hit. A hit." Then Cheenchy turned around and retrieved the green cap. "And what kinda outfielder are you, Popoff? You don't even make a relay throw."

Popoff dropped his eyelids halfway and yawned, slumping against the splintery shed.

"That shed is older than you, Popoff. Be careful you don't wind up in Mrs. Zaharian's garden."

Popoff's mind was racing behind half-closed eyes, but he couldn't think of a comeback that wasn't too filthy for the growing crowd.

Cheenchy stuck the green cap back in his left hand. Zorro stepped up to the line, slashing Z's in the air with the broomstick; he stretched his neck so that the scar which had given him his name was clearly visible to Cheenchy.

"Has this one got old!" Cheenchy said. "The neck used to say just 'Z.' Now it's so wrinkled it spells out ZODIAC, and by God, I think he's got all those signs folded in there, too."

Zorro, a man of action not talk, called to Cheenchy, "You looked in the mirror lately, Grandma?"

Cheenchy smiled sweetly, pursed his lips and delivered. It spun low and outside. Zorro reached and missed, but Augie had no chance of catching it.

"That's a free one, Zodiac."

"For you too," Zorro answered.

The next pitch started in at Zorro but didn't break. It came in steadily rising and struck Zorro in the forehead. Zorro made with his hands as if flies surrounded his head.

"OK, I'm going to let you see this one," Cheenchy warned him.

Hands behind his back, Cheenchy felt for the dented green cap in his left hand and slipped it into his right hand. Cheenchy started the cap in at Zorro's head again, but this time it dropped hard and spun away.

Zorro chopped at an inside pitch that never came. Augie inched forward on his haunches, snatched it cleanly at shoelace level, and Tsigon's team was retired in the first inning.

JoeMeesh took the bag of bottle caps from Cheenchy and started warming up. His tosses lacked the speed and variety of Cheenchy's, but he had remembered two things for twenty years--all through the Navy years and the Cadillac years in Michigan--when to change speeds and what each hitter's weakness was.

JoeMeesh retired Cheenchy's team in order on two foul ticks and a lollipop of a pitch, cap upside down. to Augie, who bitched, "Nobody threw me one like that in twenty-five years."

JoeMeesh added, "I'll bet that ain't all you forgot."

Inning after inning, pitching dominated. The bottle caps got more dented and more tricky; the batters more frustrated and more drunk. Cheenchy's team got the bases loaded in the fifth with two outs and Augie at bat. But JoeMeesh put him down quick with a dark one, an old rusty mud-packed cap he'd dug out of the alley with a popsicle stick. Augie tried to declare the pitch illegal after he had waved at it. JoeMeesh asked him one question: "Who made the rules, Augie?"

After nine innings, forty-five minutes, and very few hits, the jijo game was still scoreless.

Augie suggested, "Anybody keep track of the hits? We used to break ties that way."

"Not for a hundred dollars," said JoeMeesh hard and fast.

Cheenchy said, "How about three more innings, and we'll count hits in case nobody can score a run."

Seedy jumped to the next obvious point. "And what if it's still tied then?"

The crowd in the yard, which had tripled in size since the first inning, was parting. A smallish priest, dwarfed by a husky, middle-aged woman, Augie's sister Gerda, walked through the crowd toward the alley.

The priest waggled his palm and shook his head. "Boys. Boys. Don't let us interrupt the game. We just wondered where everyone had gone. We don't get to see most of you often enough anymore."

The players were mumbling, "Yes, Father," as they had thirty or more years before when guiltily confronted by the priest, feeling they had done something wrong but weren't sure what it was.

"It's a wonderful and a blessing to see you boys gathered here from all over the world. You rose from poor little Backlot and made something of yourselves. And you've made your parents, God rest their souls," (his eyes sought out those who had lost their parents) "and all your friends proud of you. Go on with your game, boys. I must get back to the rectory. Come by and see us there before you leave town, if you have time."

The players mumbled again and glanced around self-consciously as the old priest tottered away, touching many arms as he made his way back through the crowd. Gerda stayed.

JoeMeesh and Cheenchy looked at each other and raised their shoulders and eyebrows quickly, anxious to get on with the game.

Gerda, employing her own rather slight inclination to indirection, raised her hands and opened them in front of her as if to catch her meaty breasts should they drop in mid-speech. "Whatever could be wrong? You nice altar boys having a little fun?" Her tone shifted. "Taking half the people away from the booths at the reunion to stomp on my flowers and watch you gamble and curse away the afternoon." She paused, looking the crowd away from her flower beds. "Don't you know those children you are sending for beer could get arrested!" She paused again to let that sink in. "Here you come from all over the country to show some respect to your old neighborhood, and you wind up playing bottle caps in the alley. None of you has changed a bit! Big shots! Big wheels! And still just like little kids! Don't you know we got plenty of little kids in Backlot today, not much better off than you were. And what are you doing for them? I'll tell you. Nothing!"

Now they understood what they had done wrong, though they didn't like hearing it from Gerda. As usual, someone had to come along behind nice old Father Frank and spell things out.

Augie started, "Well, Sis, somebody asked me if anybody still played jijos, and so we got the old gang back together, and we didn't want to be swinging bats and throwing things around all those people at the reunion--"

The others were audibly agreeing with this version until Gerda provided her own conclusion. "And everybody else followed to see some old fools play with bottle caps for a hundred dollars a man."

No one disagreed with her. Unexpectedly Gerda returned to indirection like a windmilling softball pitcher (which Gerda had been) to gather momentum to speed home the final strike: "Just so you're having fun, boys. Isn't that what the clubhouse was built for anyway? To help all you boys grow up into big strong men, so you could leave Backlot and make America a better place?"

The players weren't shaking their heads with her anymore. Though they thought they agreed with her. Like the experienced batsmen they were, they held back and waited for the next hitch in her delivery.

"And now the clubhouse is falling down. Or were you too full of bygone days and beer to notice?" She turned to the crowd, "So why don't everybody go back to the reunion and have a good time and spend a lot of money? Be very careful of my flowers. They're all over the place."

Gerda's hands came to rest on her ample hips as she slipped in the last strike. "Fellas, the clubhouse usually takes fifty percent on gambling concessions." She turned to follow the crowd, then looked back. "But I'll leave that between you, your checkbooks, and your consciences, if you have any."

The players gathered again in the tight circle they had made when choosing sides. Twice Augie started to say something, but never got past throat-clearing. He wasn't sure who to apologize to. Or what to apologize for.

Finally JoeMeesh laughed. "And we used to play this game because it didn't cost nothing." Then he laughed harder. "Let's go see Father Frank and tell him the score."

Tsigan said, "There's only one way to show up Gerda, fellas."

"How's that?" Augie asked, for he'd gone years without doing that even once.

"We give a hundred percent!" shouted Tsigan.

"Yeah, a hundred dollars a man or I'm wasting my time," JoeMeesh shouted, setting off the spark.

Quickly, the beer and good spirit that had accumulated in each of them that afternoon moved past the tension of competition and reunion. And they lurched down the alley toward the rectory, smacking and grabbing each other, laughing to rattle the trash cans.

Fast Forward

MEMOREX 37, SIDE I (JULY 5, 197_)

I am tired of answering questions about my mother, Tatosian. I didn't come here for that. I am sick of seeing my shiny fat face on the evening, news, the morning news, the noonday news. But I can't stop watching. Is that me howling and tearing my hair in front of millions: "Mother, I'm sorry! I'm sorry! Mother come home"? My life was passing before my eyes, Tatosian.

You were supposed to be my friend, Tatosian, as well as my boss. We grew up together, didn't we? You couldn't have telephoned me in Trinidad? You couldn't have put together more words than "Emergency. Fly soonest. Chicken Bizarre," like it was a business message to deduct?

You sat right there, Tatosian, three months ago, on your fat ass. You scooched your finger across the franchise map from Key West all the way to Trinidad. You told me I was the only person you trusted to train the managers there. But any other person you would have called back to St. Louis when you found out those Trinidaddy gangsters were stalling for a higher percentage. What kind of message did you send then? "Travel. Eat. Enjoy. Deal stewing. Chicken Bizarre." And what message did I send you? "OK. Tell Mother not to worry. Vas."

I know this much from the newspaper, Tatosian, not to mention the neighbors: My mother was already in New Guinea! And you're still claiming you didn't know?

This is as good a time as any to bring up Chick-Sha-Bob, which you insist on calling "Chicken Shish" at board meetings, Tatosian, even though it's our number three best- seller and holding. My mother, God protect her, created it to avoid cooking lamb for my father. "A small sacrifice for marrying outside the tribe," he used to say. You yourself heard him say it fifty times. And I might as well bring up Chicken Blitz and Chickenini, too, totally my creations, which are steadily increasing their shares nationally and internationally. Who else in the franchise has come up with three best-sellers? Not you, Tatosian. Since you left Squat and Gobble and came up with this fancy chicken idea, what have you created but Chicken Ararat, which doesn't even sound right?

My mother was in New Guinea! And what was I doing in my ignorance: I traveled; I ate; I enjoyed. Don't you think I know why you wanted my educated palate in South America, Tatosian?

You don't have to ask how many new creations I've come back with. I'll tell you: Enough to start my own franchise! Do you hear that? And if you do not give me rights to my three original ideas, I'll meet you in court, even though you like that kind of publicity. You're liking this kind of publicity, aren't you, Tatosian? But your mother's safe and sound on her falling down porch on Tulip Street, isn't she? She's not kidnapped and maybe dead, is she?

Memorex 37: Side I (July 6, 197__)

It always does me good to hear my mother's voice, Miss Ryan, but especially now. Even on this worn cassette, I think you can hear her kindness and warmth coming through. I can detect disappointment there, too; she was sincerely trying to help me re-create my father's family history, but as you could probably tell, she is not a storyteller and could not make herself into one, even for her only child's sake.

I carried this tape with me to the West Indies and South America on my endless journeys to increase Chicken Bizarre's share of the world gourmet fast food market. (Strike that last reference if you would, Miss Ryan. My former employer does not descrve to get any free publicity out of this interview.)

I want to give you the whole story, Miss Ryan--all I know, anyway. I hope you understand why I'm being so careful with the news media since that interview at the airport day before yesterday. I was still trying to figure out who was the celebrity all the cameras were there for, when that Rod Rossiter came out of nowhere and started assaulting me with his microphone. Honestly, do you think he really believed my mother's kidnappers were cannibals? We used to play that game on kids who fell asleep in class. We'd put a match to some smelly rag and yell: "Wake up, jerk! The school's on fire!"

I was overwhelmed, though, that so many people in the world have been touched by the anguish I expressed in that interview. I've already received more telegrams of condolence than I can count. And only eleven insulting ones. And eight psychics insist that she is alive and well, also Mrs. Horvaty down the block, an old widow my mother used to take soup to. "You going to chew Mrs. Horvaty's food for her again today, Mom?" I'd say. "Chewed Chicken: I like the sound of that. Think it'll sell, Mom?"

Perhaps I shouldn't have been surprised. Mother has always been deeply involved with the church and its missions. Primarily though with the one down the street. The old movie house with the shattered marquis?

How could I forget this? I went to shave this morning and look what I found under the sink. "Dear Vasil, I've gone to New Guinea. Don't worry, Mom." It's like a voice from beyond, Miss Ryan. So I've been trying not to worry.

MEMOREX 37: SIDE II (JULY 9, 197_)

The last report I was given by the Missionary Board says her abductors allowed her to take five hundred fertilized eggs and a kerosene incubator with her, but no change of clothes. I am encouraged, Mr. Brunet. I am trying to believe she was simply returning a favor or doing a good deed. Mother's like that. I'm not sure what the government's interest in my mother's disappearance would be, Mr. Brunet--and you say you can't share that with me--so I'll just keep telling you about Mother until you stop me.

Well, it's always been easy to achieve a reputation for generosity with Mom. She's had so precious little from life, it always seemed to me, and yet received so much satisfaction from her small portion. Why, even unintentional or automatic offers of aid received her warm thanks. She would remember the name of the grinning lady who handed her a cheese cube on a toothpick and startle her with it six months later at a crowded bus stop downtown. She would always say, "You're welcome, son, and thank you," to that witless, sullen bag boy at Shirpansky's who mumbles, "Thanks for shopping Shirpansky's."

The mailman, Makloski! Over the years he's delivered free soaps, pet food, diet cookies, toothpastes, granolas, instant eggs, unmentionables, and coupons by the shoebox-full. To my mother, he's a saint, a Santa Claus. Her appreciation of him is not dampened when I inform her (as I often do) that delivering these samples is his job and nothing more--and that he has taken a federal oath to do so faithfully and in all weather. Nevertheless, it's cookies and milk for him twice a week, and at the kitchen table, no matter what the neighbors might think.

My mother has always been patient with what she calls my dubiousness (or "jubrousness" when she takes on her down home accent). "Vasil you're jubrous as a possum on the trot. How did I ever raise such a mistrustful boy?" she told me the last day I saw her. Makloski had delivered a two-ounce box of dry cat food, and I had just told her that he would deliver five hundred more before he finished walking his route. She patted my hand and said, "Mr. Makloski does not have to tote all those packages, dear. He could save them for his family or...Why, only last month I read in the newspaper about a mailman in Philadelphia who threw hundreds of little soap bars in the sewer. Of course, he had a bad back, poor man, like your Uncle Elrod." I had read this news item, too, but I was in no haste to admit it. Besides, I was more worried about who she'd give the cat food to. I let Mom sum up: "I don't think goodness should be taken for granted any more than the other, Vasil."

"What other, Mom? What other?" I asked her. She couldn't think of any she'd care to mention, she said, but there was plenty enough in the newspaper.

"Remember, Mom, evil is all around you, so keep the doors locked at all times while I'm in Trinidad."

"Yes, I will, Vas," she said. "But goodness knows, there's evil enough in every one of us."

This was the right moment to bring up Dolgaroff, he of the seven hungry cats. "Do not give that box of cat food to Dolgaroff!" I said.

He is an older man, a recent widower, a Bulgarian gone mad. My mother is the widow of a Bulgarian three years now: Vasil Podoloff, a good man, a little crazy too in his way. But this ugly devil Dolgaroff is so crazy he thinks he has some claim on my mother. And he's not the first. Dolgaroff was following her to Shirpansky's three times a week like a puppy dog, holding his bandaged hands in front of him like little white paws. Mother insisted that I was not to hang him from his own naked trellis by his leather suspenders, as I had volunteered to do.

"Mother," I appealed to her, "this man is lecherous and capable of violence. A month ago, not two weeks after his wife passed away, he chopped down his rose bush and tore the branches out of his trellis with his bare hands. Tomorrow I'm going to leave you for a month, and I won't have any peace of mind if I'm worrying about Dolgaroff misunderstanding your kindness."

She did not look convinced, so I said, "Travel, Mother. Travel. There are so many places I have not had time to take you to see. New England in the fall: think of the colors! Mother, you haven't even been to Washington, D.C. I'm going to leave $2000: travel. In a month Dolgaroff will either be completely crazy and put away, or he'll have come to his senses and won't bother you."

She didn't make me any promises, Mr. Brunet. And I didn't make her promise. If she had said, "I promise, Vasil. I'll go to New England," that's what she would have done. Mother can be stubborn sometimes, but she always keeps her promises. Why was I in such a hurry that day? Why couldn't I detect that something was troubling her?

Now do you understand how a man can tear his hair in front of millions and cry, "Mother, I'm sorry! I'm sorry! Mother, come home"?

What a country, Mr. Brunet, to make a son like me (I'm using the newspaper's words) "a national symbol for the rift between generations and the love it will take to heal it." Believe me, being famous for a few days is no consolation for my suffering.

MEMOREX 40: SIDE I (JULY 12, 197_)

Yes, I am overjoyed my mother is safe with Chief Entiku, Mrs. Fernoli. She has sent me a telegram. It says he is a very nice man and not to worry. Also to send another micro-cassette recorder.

According to the information I've received from an Australian newsman, the tribe has moved onto the mission grounds and is already taking instructions in the faith from my mother and a Dr. Paul, recently dispatched from Australia. Four-hundred-ninety-eight of the eggs hatched, which seems to have been a record, or a miracle.

I wish the media here would stop referring to my mother as "the latest wife of Chief Entiku." The Chief evidently does have several wives, but I assure you my mother is not one of them. The Australian said the Chief could not afford to let that much magic go unincorporated, and my mother had struck a pretty good deal for her religion. New Guinea is that man's beat! He ought to know if my mother is married or not!

I'd like my feelings considered in this article, too, Mrs. Fernoli. I chose your magazine first precisely because you do **not** sensationalize. Let's keep the focus on my mother, all right? I am trying to gather financial backing for a small, a modest and tasteful franchise operation, and, though the money your magazine has offered is important to me in that venture, I do not want this article to give the impression that I am in any way directly responsible for my mother's actions or her state of mind, whatever it is. Ascribe my famous screams, my hysteria, to the obvious--shock, surprise. For Christ's sake I thought my mother was at home in her kitchen rotating her African violets.

I do want you to feel free to use some of the materials I have gathered on my family over the past few years. Let me start off with some facts.

Flora Inez is my mother's name, not Flora Belle or Floral Lee as you see in most of the newspapers. Who in the world are they talking to!

The neighbor ladies always looked so much older, dressed older than Mother. She wore bright colors as unselfconsciously as a bird. All they had ever known was the dust and smoke of the city and the dust and smoke of the Orthodox Church. My mother had known wildflowers and golden harvests and the clean white spire of a Baptist church on a grassy hillside.

My mother is not old. You can see that even in the wire service photo. And she is lovely, though a late, a very late bloomer, I think.

My theory, Mrs. Fernoli, is that each face is destined to be beautiful through at least one of life's stages. I think I can demonstrate this to you with help from the family photograph box which Mother left in the closet over there.

Let me arrange these pictures in order: here's Mother as a hollow-eyed and long-headed baby; a stunned and horse-toothed adolescent here; a downright skinny-looking honeymooner with shadows where her cheeks should be, and here as a haggard mother with the corners of her mouth pulled down as if by the chubby two-year-old clutching her legs. (That curly-headed youngster could serve to illustrate my brief fling with Good Looks if he didn't have his head buried in his mother's house dress.)

But now in this last photograph--this is the one you may print--I think you will agree with me that Beauty has come to my mother. Her cheeks have finally filled out, her cheekbones are more striking by being less prominent, and her eyes are clear and dark, and at last, you will notice, she's looking into the camera without apology. It is a copy of this picture that I carried with me to Trinidad.

I would like to play this tape for you, but just enough for you to hear my mother's voice. I can sum up what's on it and add a lot more besides—"Land o' Goshen, what is that little doodad?" That's Mother, Mrs. Fernoli.

I had been warming her up with some questions I already knew the answers to: who chose my name? what were the first words I said clearly? did I like to play by myself or with other children? I had just pulled out of my shirt pocket something I was sure she had never seen before.

I could have told her it was an electronic pencil sharpener or a grease thermometer, and she would have believed me. But I didn't. I felt it was important that she understood what I was doing.

"It's a micro-cassette recorder," I said, and she nodded her head, but I knew she still didn't know what it was. "It's a machine that records voices onto tapes so you can save them. Like photographs."

"Oh, I know about that!" she said. She wanted t assure me she'd been paying attention for the past thirty years.

Then I say to her, "This is for the family history I've been trying to assemble, Mother. I want to record Uncle Dmitri's voice and Aunt Dramina's. And when I come back from Trinidad, we could go to the country and record Uncle Elrod and Grandma Crockit."

"Won't you need a larger one for that, Vasil?" she asks me. And I laugh and tell her no.

"Could you record hymns on one of those?" she asks. I assure her that she can record a whole church service if she wants. Perhaps, I'm thinking now, she was already planning to go to New Guinea then. There's a tone in her voice I almost don't recognize. On the other hand she often hums and sings hymns when the noises from the steel mill drift this way at night and she can't sleep, though I think she must have been even more restless when my father was working there on the night shift.

Anyway, when I attached the tiny mike and set it in front of her on a sliver of styrofoam, she picked it up as lovingly as if I had given her a rosebud. "Thank you, Vasil," she says.

I was overjoyed that she seemed so relaxed. Much as she trusts me, I knew she would strive to follow that old country saying of hers: "If you can't tell nothing good on nobody, don't tell nothing at all."

"Mom," I say to her, "what was it like when you first got off the train here with Dad?"

I had heard Dad's version many times: surrounded by her bundled-up new relatives who were spilling out excitement in Bulgarian, she had grabbed my Dad's hand as if they were lost in a blizzard; she'd never heard a foreign tongue before, and when Dad started talking in Bulgarian too, she looked as if she didn't know him and started weeping.

But how does she answer me? "Your father has so many kind relatives, dear. And they were all so glad to see him back from his travels. He'd been going from job to job for four years during the Depression, you know, seeing the world."

"Mother," I say, "I already have quite a few pages of notes I took from Dad on that last fishing trip we made. What I mean is, Mom, I'm interested in your reactions, your point of view on those early years here."

She nodded and smiled, but she doesn't say anything. "Is she thinking?" I asked myself. "Or is she waiting for me to ask her something else?" At the time I remember I was a little irritated she was wasting tape.

Finally I ask her something else: "Wasn't it lonely for you, Mom, in those early years? You didn't know anyone within three hundred miles. I know Dad was working lots of overtime and wasn't around much to keep you company. And there were all those other things he was involved in--selling burial insurance in St. Louis at night and refereeing soccer games on the weekend.

"Well, I was busy raising you, Vasil. And of course there were the children at the Mission. I always tried to do what I could there."

"Do you still go?" I ask her. I couldn't resist teasing her like this. I sleep extremely late on Sundays when I make it home at all.

"Of course I do," she answers me real quick, a little sharp for Mom.

That must have made me want to get a little more of a rise out of her. "Did you ever save any Bulgarians over there, Mom?"

"Just you, Vasil," she says. That'll be me whooping at the end of the tape, of course. I appreciate it when Mom can get one in on me. I'll take some of the credit, though; Mom doesn't provoke easy.

That's all that's on the tape, Mrs. Fernoli. You're welcome to take it with you tonight if you like, but I'd appreciate if you'd return it before you leave for New Guinea. Please give my best regards to Mother, and I'd appreciate it if you would deliver this cassette recorder to her. Tell her I'm getting by just fine (though I miss her fried chicken) and that I'm trying to start my own little business, which I hope to have in operation by the time she comes home. Tell her I'm trying not to worry, but I'd worry less if I knew just when she was returning.

Memorex 44: Side II (Aug. 15, 197_)

Don't think I would have come back here, Tatosian, if you had not asked me. Even though (as you no doubt know and I strongly suspect had something to do with) I have failed in my attempt to raise money for my own franchise.

On that other matter, I will not be convinced, until I hear it from her own lips, that she made you promise **not** to tell me she had gone to New Guinea and even encouraged you to extend my stay in Trinidad.

I'm assuming we're here to make a deal, Tatosian. And I'm prepared to offer to drop my suit against Chicken Bizarre if you agree to reinstate me to my former position and compensate me for my lost income over the past month (not subtracting from that the price of the round-trip ticket to New Guinea you sent me yesterday with no explanation beyond the insulting implication that I needed a rest and ought to go visit my mother). I suspect your motives have more to with transporting my discriminating nose and educated palate to New Guinea for your ultimate benefit and profit. So be it, Tatosian. Lucky for you, your motives coincide with my mission in life. However, I assure you that I will quit on the spot if you ever again refer to any of my creations as Chicken Shish, or if you ever again refer to that pygmy bigamist (whom I intend to treat with no more respect than I do Anton Dolgarov) as my stepfather.

Beyond The Pier

A LIGHT RAIN FALLS ON Decatur Street. It is coming softly and straight down. It is darkening a pearl-gray hat, the kind Harry Truman used to wear. Many other surfaces are changing shades. Suddenly I recognize the gray hat and its plain dark band and the short stocky man with the graying shingle of hair and deeply creased neck. He turns toward me to jam a some coins into the orange newspaper machine. It's not my father.

My father was barbecuing in his garage on a dreary Sunday morning--coughing, cursing--watching the rain make his tomatoes bigger and better. "He should take as much time with his kids, especially his son," his son thought, his son who could only start a fire under almost perfect conditions and was almost an Eagle Scout, his only son who at thirteen was already taller than him and finding it hard to hide his surprise and delight at that.

Yes, his son was practically a genius, his son thought, but it was almost a year after his father died when he realized that spending a whole morning in a smokey garage slowly, slowly cooking pork steaks and ribs to perfection could be an act of love.

My four-wood shot is dropping quickly. It catches a sand trap on the way to the green. My cart and bag bump along behind me as my partner Ben lags behind. Beside the shimmering green, two men in drab overalls stand gesturing. The shorter man's movements are more forceful; there is endurance and righteousness in his extended arms, the arm-basket of his supplication. The other man throws his arms to the side weakly, and the two of them disappear behind the high back side of the green. I assure myself they can't agree on a which water outlet to use. Soon I am close enough to hear a familiar raspy voice from behind the green. Suddenly Ben yells, "Come back! Your ball's here, in the trap!" Then I realize the raspy growls are Spanish. I grab my wedge, feign surprise, and walk back into the trap. It takes me more than a minute to squirm my feet to a solid footing.

When I was nine and played baseball every day for ten hours, Mr. Ecks stole my ball. He was the manager of a team of older kids from another part of town that practiced on a field near my house. He thought he could get away with my ball until I introduced him to my old man just as he loading his car trunk with gear.

Ecks stood a head taller. "I don't know what this boy is talking about," he said.

"There's some things I don't think my boy would lie about," said my old man.

"I know how many balls I had when I came out here," Ecks said and swept a long arm toward the ball field and his players, who were stopped in their tracks.

"It's got a red scuff by the label," I said. "And one loose stitch."

My old man glared at Mr. Ecks. "Let's put it this way. One of you is getting a whipping."

"Well, let me check those balls again," he said.

I ran to the trunk of Ecks' car, pulled out the ball bag, and snatched my ball, pointing at the red scuff and the loose stitch.

"That's that," said my old man. And we walked home side by side.

The fishing is slow but steady. There's no point in moving when you're getting a strike every fifteen minutes or so. This is just the kind of fishing that separates the men from the boys. A moment of haste or indecision is a lost opportunity. And I have lost more than one opportunity because I have been watching an old fellow down the bayou not miss any of his.

It is some time before I recognize that crooked left-armed roll cast. And that calm, sure landing net technique.

I weigh anchor, unannounced.

"Hey, I just caught one here," Richard says.

"Yeah, but it's always better down there. We'll just let that wind drift us."

My boat sighs through the hyacinths.

I am fighting the light breeze with my paddle, trying to keep a decent distance from the old man. He turns from the bank and wastes a cast to the middle of the bayou. "Y'all doin' any good?" he asks.

"Some good," I answer.

He doesn't recognize me. I don't recognize him.

Federal Steel Castings gave my father silicosis, a lung condition which killed many of his friends before getting to him. FSC crushed his brother-in-law with a twenty-ton locomotive underframe. That factory and others polluted the air and water for the rest of his large family. It worked worked him so hard that at the age of 56 the TB which had been lurking in him for thirty years took over.

Two years later, after 6000 pills and 200 days in the sanatorium, I took him to the National Institute of Science and Industry in Washington, D.C. I saved the best for last: a black brontosaurus of a ten-wheel locomotive that came to life every fifteen minutes through the miracle of stereophonic sound.

He measured the engine slowly with his eyes and said, "I made it." He peered between the wheels on both sides. He moved some parts that looked immovable on the front and rear of the engine. Then he said, "I forgot. Before 1930 we put the trademark on the inside of the end plate." He crawled halfway into the underframe and pointed. I crouched beside him, and there it was: a shield the size of a half dollar contained the raised letters, FSC.

The timing was perfect. As we backed up to admire the whole of what my old man had made, the sound show began. The puffs, the chuffs, the grinds, the clatters were all coming from the right places. And even more amazing, my father was clapping his hands.

A little boy is walking through a shopping mall. His back tilts slightly to the right and forward, and his arms swing wide as he takes long bent-legged strides. "He looks as if he is trying to imitate and keep up with his grandfather at the same time," I say to myself. In the dense crowd ahead someone has turned quickly and is parting the crowd with his arms and body. It is a short old man who bursts from the crowd, jerks up the boy with one arm, and throws him over his shoulder like a sack of potatoes. It is a short old man who walks with a hobble just like my father's, but it is not my father.

Thanksgiving dinner was on the table, steaming like a geyser. Melanie was too young to eat anything there, but she was strapped in and propped up so Grandma and Grandpa feast on her chance smiles. But her lips just writhed slowly as she grunted softly. Her eyes glazed as she reached beyond herself for strength. And everyone but her grandfather and me, her teen-aged uncle, deliberately ignored her. They were waiting for "Grace" to be said. I could almost hear the cranberry quiver. At Melanie's first little sigh, my old man smiled proudly. "That's it honey," he said. "Make a big pile for Grandpa." Melanie raised her fists and smiled radiantly.

I am going nowhere. It's late at night, and I don't feel like another beer, and I don't want to sleep. Maybe, I think, the morning paper is out. I walk six blocks up to Canal Street. A tall skinny old man leans against his counter. His fists are jammed into a ragged brown trench coat. His head is so loose in the hood of a navy blue sweat shirt that the back of the hood points out straight as a wind sock when he turns his thin face to mine. He slides a hunk of cast iron off the stack of papers. Tips have taken my change, and all I have is a twenty. I'm embarrassed.

"That's all right, Mac," he says. "Catch me tomorrow."

"You want some coffee?" I ask. "I can break this bill around the corner."

"Naw, Mac. It's all right. I trust you."

He folds the newspaper, and I wedge it under my arm. I get all the way home and unfold it before thinking, "Wasn't that just like my old man!"

Uncle Carl, Mother's brother, the Jeff to my father's Mutt, the country sage to my father's city slicker, had been buried an hour before. The gloom was thick in his crowded home. The days of death and months of waiting for it were in everyone's eyes, in everyone's hunched shoulders. My father swiped at the gloom with a few words to Uncle Gilbert about Carl's comic impatience and his lunch bucket full of pills and ointments. Soon the surrounding folks were laughing at my dad's version of how Carl had gotten him turned around and lost in his own hometown. And then Aunt Martha, Carl's widow, who always laughed as soon as my father started a story, was laughing louder than anyone, gasping, "John, tell about you and Carl jumping the curb to beat Carney Walsh to Bessie's wedding and scaring Grandma Byrd out of her wits." Grandma Byrd, mostly deaf but laughing with everyone else, croaked, "What-ee?"

A fight erupts in the hallway, flows into my classroom. Suddenly I am sitting on the floor. My legs scissor a girl I don't know. I have Belinda by the wrists. She finally drops the pencil she was jabbing with. Students ten-deep surround us. It seems like an hour before the assistant principal and another teacher wearily push through the crowd. I hand over the girls. No one is hurt, and no one is screaming anymore. The crowd dissolves, looking for keener action before their next class. I am standing alone in my room, tucking my shirt back into my pants and laughing. "Maybe Mom's right," I say to myself. "Maybe I am just like the old man."

Silicosis is a very special disease. You will only "catch it" if you work too many years in clouds of dust or fine sand--or both. The silica irritates the lungs. The lungs form lesions, then lifeless fibrous tissue. They fossilize.

More and more nights my father had to sit up in his easy chair in order to sleep. One morning his heart failed. Somehow he lasted almost two weeks, surviving the fussy tubes and noises of Intensive Care to die in a quiet single room.

Two days later many came to see him. Not too many of the older mourners--relatives and fellow foundry workers--looked as healthy as he did. None of them thought it was at all strange that a dime-sized gold shield containing the raised letters "FSC" above a tiny diamond should be gleaming (and twinkling) on his left lapel.

The pier is crowded, but no one has caught a fish in hours. Suddenly the water is boiling. The blues are all around us. Reels are singing and folks are whooping. But I don't have mine yet. Beyond the pier, dolphin are playing, herding them in, feasting. In good time the butt of my rod digs into my belly and forces a grunt, which I turn into a short, joyful cry.

Appendix II

HEADS OF FAMILY WHO ARRIVED IN KOMPOLT IN 1754
FROM ALSACE

Note: Family names are written first in Hungary, then given names. In 1754 these German names would have been reversed and many would have been spelled differently. As time passed, these names changed to reflect Hungarian spelling, but they tended to retain their pronunciation; for example, Wieser in German is pronounced almost like Vizer in Hungarian and Veizer in English. Names that had meanings in both languages were often translated into Hungarian; for example, Schmidt to Kovacs (blacksmith) and Wolf to Farkas. I reprint on the page following the list given to me by Daniel Vizer.

Adam Jozsef	Gerndorf Ferenc	Kirsch Miklos	Schneider Janos
Adam Marton	Grebner Janos	Klein Gerard	Schneider Tamas
Ambrosius Matyas	Grosz Ferdinand	Knitl Peter	Schroder Janos
Ambrosius Henrik	Grosz Henrik	Kromback Andal	Stahl Jakab
Arndt Henrik	Gyorgy Gerard	Kromback Janos	Stahl Peter
Ballusz Keresztely	Haiderick Peter	Kutser Lajos	Stahl Vilmos
Berger Andras	Halbreisz Fridrik	Linhart Vilmos	Szeifer Albert
Blau Karoly	Haman Peter	Luchlasz Adam	Szobel Henrik
Burkhart Venantinus	Hoffman Janos	Maar Andras	Szolbach Peter
Christian Jakab	Hon Marton	Niklasz Peter	Tornbach Tamas
Christian Janos	Hornhauser Herman	Plozer Peter	Torner Jakab
Dilligy Peter	Hueber Jozsef	Prenner Gerard	Trencz Jozsef
Dorner Peter	Jaeger Henrik	Procher Henrik	Wagner Janos
Eberling Godefridus	Jaeger Vilmos	Rausch Konrad	Wagner Keresztely
Engel Janos	Jaeger Vilmos, Jr.	Sandor Joszef	widow of J.Weber
Engel Lorincz	Jekl Joszef	Schmidt Herman	Wieser Adam
Fejer Pál	Jekl Marton	Schmidt Jozsef	Wieser Adam Jr.
Folger Janos	Kalthan Adam	Schneider Henrik	Wieser Jakab
Francz Janos	Keksz Janos	Schneider Henrik Jr.	Winter Keresztely

DONORS TO A COLLECTION FOR THE WIDOWS
AND ORPHANS OF KOMPOLT IN 1915 FROM FORMER
RESIDENTS LIVING IN GRANITE CITY.
THEY RAISED A TOTAL OF $108.50. THE ORIGINAL
DOCUMENT WAS FOUND IN THE CITY COUNCIL
RECORDS OF KOMPOLT BY PÉTER VÁRKONYI.

Engel Támas	$10.00	Krisztián Ferenc	2.00
Wizer András	5.00	Juhász István	3.00
Wizer József d.	2.50	Vágner János	2.00
Wizer Jakab d.	5.00	Wizer Katalin	1.00
Wizer Péter d.	5.00	Szeifer Péter	5.00
Hornhauser János	.20	Pinter János	2.00
Gyamati Béla	.25	Mayer József	5.00
Wizer Jakab gecsi	2.00	Udvari János	1.00
Jéger Péter	5.00	Bodnar Pál	4.00
Horvath András	2.00	Wizer József begró	.50
Hornháuser Laszló	.50	Scűcs István	2.00
Jéger János, siter	1.00	Klement János	1.00
Dorogházi Jozsef	1.00	Szabó Orbán	2.00
Wizer Mátyás	5.00	Lovász Andrásné	1.00
Krisztián János	.50		
Udvari Mária	1.00		

The original document is handwritten. Hungarian accents were used but most people from Kompolt spoke both Hungarian and German; several of these family names, including "Wizer," were in transition to their American spellings.

BIBLIOGRAPHY

Primary sources:

Anyakönyvek, 1819-1895/Római Katólikus Egyház, Kompolt (Church records of Births, Deaths, and Marriages).

Documents from National Archives in St. Louis on John Veizer's service in the Civil Conservation Corps, 1933.

Genealogies of four Granite City Vizer families from Kompolt, compiled by Emöke Abasári.

Genealogies of Bech families in Kompolt, compiled by István Tarnavölgy.

Naturalization records of Madison County, Illinois.

Passenger records from the American Family Immigration History Center, Ellis Island.

Records of the Kompolt City Council provided by Péter Várkonyi.

Southern Illinois University-Edwardsville interviews of Lincoln Place residents, conducted by students in an oral history class taught by Dr. Annie Valk in 2000 and 2001.

United States Census data, 1920 and 1940.

Secondary sources:

Applebaum, Anne. *Iron Curtain: The Crushing of Eastern Europe, 1944-1956*. New York: Doubleday, 2012.

DeChennes, David. "Hungary Hollow: Bulgarian Immigrant Life in Granite City, Illinois, 1904-1921," *Gateway Heritage*, Summer 1990: 52-61.

Dawidowicz, Lucy S. *The War Against the Jews, 1933-1945*. New York: Holt, Reinhart and Winston, 1975.

Engelke, Georgia, et al. *Granite City, A Pictorial History*. St. Louis: G. Bradley Publishing, Inc., 1995.

Fermor, Patrick Leigh. *On Foot to Constantinople: From the Middle Danube to the Iron Gates*. New York: New York Review Books, 2005.

Gaddis, John Lewis. *The Cold War: A New History*. New York: The Penguin Press, 2005.

Granite City, IL, Chronicle: A Historical Journey. (A Facebook group containing photos and information.)

Granite City *Press-Record* articles from the 1930s and 1940s.

Baudot, Marcel, et al. eds. Trans. Jesse Dilson. *The Historical Encyclopedia of World War II*. New York: Facts on File, 1977.

Kompolti baráti kör (Kompolt's friends), Kompolti családok története (Kompolt's genealogy), Kompolti képek (Pictures of Kompolt), and Kompolti mosaic: Facebook groups maintained by Emöke Abasári.

Lowe, Keith. *Savage Continent: Europe in the Aftermath of World War II*. New York: St. Martin's Press, 2012.

Magris, Claudio. *Danube: A Sentimental Journey from the Source to the Black Sea*. Trans. Patrick Creagh. New York: Farrar, Strauss & Giroux, 1989.

Manoyan, Dan. *Men of Granite*. Bloomington, Indiana: AuthorHouse, 2007.

Meller, Patricia. *History of the Jakab Vizer Family*. (Unpublished.)

Moreno, Barry. *The Illustrated Encyclopedia of Ellis Island*. New York: Fall River Press, 2010.

New York *Times* archives concerning Kompolt and Heves from 1880-1910.

Petras, Ronald. *Lincoln Place: In Honor of a President* (an unpublished history of Lincoln Place.)

Puskas, Júlianna. *Ties that Bind, Ties that Divide: 100 Years of Hungarian Experience in the United States*. Trans. Zora Ludwig. Teaneck, New Jersey: Holmes and Meier Publishing, 2000.

Short Chronology of Kompolt. Trans. Daniel Vizer. (Unpublished)

Taylor, Graham Romeyn. *Satellite Cities: A Study of Industrial Suburbs*. New York: D. Appleton and Co., 1915.

Wikipedia articles on the CCC, Granite City history, General Steel Industries, NESCO, Silicosis, Forced labor of Hungarians and Germans after WWII, et cetera.

Acknowledgements

THIS BOOK WOULD MUCH HAVE been much more detailed and authoritative, not to mention more accurate, if I had started my research when my father and his brothers and sisters were still alive. However, I would like to think they were speaking through my cousin Barbara a few years ago when, after I told some family stories at the breakfast table, she asked me, "When are you going to write all this down?" Thank you, Barbara, for assuming that I would. I wish your father Ronnie had been around to help me see farther into the past.

Before Barbara focused my attention and set me on my task, my cousin Pat Olsen Meller had started collecting and organizing photos and letters her mother Matilda Wiezer Olsen had left her. Pat showed me what enthusiasm and persistence can do. Our visit to Kompolt with her husband Dave was informative, thought-provoking, and great fun.

The genealogical and historical contributions of Emöke Abasári, not to mention her deep love for Kompolt, added a dimension to this undertaking that would have been impossible to create without her energy and expertise. Recently, a nephew of Margie Magyar Veizer, Louis Takacs, who is now a librarian in Amsterdam, has provided historical records concerning Kompolt to me and Emöke that will, I think, lead to further revelations.

I would also like to thank Ronald Petras, whose years of research on Lincoln Place, especially its Hungarian community, have been helpful and instructive. Other who have shared their knowledge of Lincoln Place, Granite City, Kompolt, and/or the Veizer family include my cousins Jim Giese, Mary Ann Toth Schweppe, Ronnie Veizer (through his wife Wilma), George Veizer, Jr., Joyce Vizer Jenness, and Kenny Wiezer; and present or former Granite City residents Helen Kuenstler, Vicki Andria Siers, Joey Ybarra, Alyce Sigite, Mary Ann Toth Cochran, Warren Taylor, Virgil and Betty Kirksey, and Steve Horvath.

I cannot thank Elémer and Erzsébet Vizer of Kompolt enough for their repeated gestures of hospitality over the years. Their grandson Daniel provided me with an English-speaking connection to Kompolt as well as a list of the eighty German families who settled Kompolt in 1754. This, my first document on its history, gave me an inkling of how much could be known. Their granddaughter Franciska and her fiancé Krisztián Nagy provided me with guidance and good company in Budapest and with translation and good company in Kompolt. I would be remiss indeed to omit the open-handed and openhearted aid of Kompolt Mayor Zoltán Balász and his staff, Zuzana Finta's translation, Péter Várkonyi's research, and István Tarnavölgy's genealogies.

I must thank Norma Asadorian, the President of the Lincoln Place Heritage Association and the force behind their annual mid-September festival, for making me aware of the 2000-2001 interviews of Lincoln Place residents. These interviews were conducted by Norma and other SIU-E students in Dr. Annie Valk's Oral History class. Those Lincoln Place voices made their world come to life for me. I thank the interviewed and interviewers, as well as Jeanette Kampen of the Six Mile Regional Library District, who allowed me repeated access to the typescripts of the interviews, which now reside in the Local History and Genealogy room at the renovated downtown library.

Finally I want to give Patricia Olsen Meller, Helen Kuenstler, and my sister Shirley Veizer Goin credit for having the patience to read earlier versions of this narrative and offer corrections and encouragement. Errors factual, grammatical or orthographical are my own, as are any embarrassing omissions.

P. 14 - Adriatic port Fiume, Austria-Hungary

37-38 - Armenian genocide

18 - 1907 3,000 deaths in Am. mines

67 - food, music & dance   68 polka

69 - first fast food - Burger Chef

78 - G.I. racist talk & attitudes

80 - Rigged game black peo. were forced to play

31 - KKK - America for Americans / anti immigration

93-94   StL Browns

97   thankies ride on monkeys

99   Buster Wortman network

115   Kirkpatrick Homes

116   Talk would inebriate them ... alcohol unnecessary

116   Names listed in book title

117   bottle cap ball & cork ball

121   Name ok. Aunts

132   Bacon over fresh lettuce (Toth)

154   Leith's dad - TB sanatorium

215   Beginning Short Stories

Made in the USA
Lexington, KY
14 April 2015